To Jerry and Yvonne, and L

Debates
in British politics
today

MANCHESTER
UNIVERSITY PRESS

Politics Today

Series editor: Bill Jones

Contents

IV: Debates on issues

List of tables

List of contributors

Arthur Aughey is Senior Lecturer in Politics at the University of Ulster

Barrie Axford is Principal Lecturer in Politics at Oxford Brookes University

Rob Baggott is Professor of Public Policy at De Montfort University

Moyra Grant writes books and articles on British Politics and teaches at Mander, Portman and Woodward sixth form colleges

Clive Gray is Principal Lecturer in Politics at De Montfort University

John Greenwood is Professor of Public Policy at De Montfort University

Bill Jones is Research Fellow in the Department of Government at the University of Manchester

Geoff Lee is a senior consultant with ADC Limited and an Associate Lecturer with the Open University Business School

Philip Norton (Professor the Lord Norton of Louth) is Professor of Government and Director of the Centre for Legislative Studies, Department of Politics, University of Hull

Colin Pilkington is Former Lecturer in Political Sociology at the Liverpool Institute of Higher Education and is currently Chief Examiner in GCSE Politics for AQA–NEAB

Lynton Robins is Principal Lecturer in Politics at De Montfort University

Vivien Robins is Senior Lecturer in Education at De Montfort University

Tony Stott is Senior Lecturer in Public Administration at De Montfort University

Graham P. Thomas teaches Politics at Reading College of Technology and at Reading University

Jonathan Tonge is Lecturer in Politics and Contemporary History at the University of Salford

Duncan Watts is Editor at PARC, the Politics Association Resource Centre, Manchester

David Wilson is Professor of Public Policy at De Montfort University

Introduction

Nothing ever gets settled in this town (Washington). It's not like running a company or even a university. It's a seething debating society, in which the debate never stops; in which people never give up . . . and that's the atmosphere in which you administer. (George Schulz, former US Secretary of State)

Politics arises from conflict within or between societies and is resolved in the main by argument, reasoning and persuasion rather than by brute force. If politics is essentially concerned with the peaceful resolution of disputes, then debate is the main method it employs. Socrates asserted that 'the partisan, when engaged in a dispute, cares nothing about the rights of the question, but is anxious only to convince his hearers of his own assertions'. However, in a fully functioning democracy mature political debate is conducted not through assertions alone but on the basis of facts and evidence as well as the relative strengths of arguments. Socrates also advocated the benefits of argument as the surest route to truth. He taught through the careful, forensic questioning of statements; if they survived his interrogation, they were held to be sound. If they were found wanting, they were discarded.

Partly as a result of the ancient Greeks' method of sorting out the true from the false, the debate came to occupy a central place in Western intellectual life. In a modest way this book is concerned with the tradition of debate, with each chapter providing a model for deploying the skills of setting out rival propositions along with their associated defence, rebuttal or, if appropriate, demolition, before drawing conclusions. We hope to show that sometimes 'conclusive' evidence turns out to be dubious in one way or another – it may be out of date, misinterpreted or misapplied – and so a critical attitude has to be developed enabling sound evaluation of each point of an argument. On other occasions it may be the development of a specific argument which may lack logic and so the skills of analysis are called upon to reach an overall evaluation.

At the level of national debate the cases for and against are rarely disputed in an atmosphere of political calm. Values intervene constantly; for example, the debate about Britain and the euro is not concerned purely with economic well-being for those who noisily join the discussion, but includes questions about national identity and sovereignty. The student of politics, not to mention the concerned citizen, has to listen to the debate, understand its complexities, unravel associated ideology, identify any hidden agendas, identify the weaknesses and weigh the balance of argument before making up his or her own mind. This book will provide the uninitiated with an introductory guide to making sense of turbulent political debate.

From the outset we recognise both the strengths and the limitations of the approach adopted. This book will make a contribution towards making good the problems routinely reported by examiners who lament the inability of many Politics students to progress beyond the descriptive in their essays and examinations. *Debates in British Politics Today* addresses this deficiency through showing the basic mechanics of how argument is constructed and pursued. Along with the detailed debate, each of the twenty chapters includes a boxed summary showing the principal contested arguments. In this way students are provided with the basic framework of each debate, enabling them to tackle the text with a higher level of prior understanding and confidence.

Of course, the skills of political debate are not only a requirement of further and higher education courses in Politics but also of wider citizenship. This is because a sound grounding in the skills of argument is a prerequisite for effective participation in such debates. A second strength of this book will hopefully be the contribution that its contents make to citizenship education. The skills of political reasoning, the use of valid evidence to support arguments and the ability to evaluate fairly rival viewpoints are also important for the competent citizen as well as the student of Politics. In many ways, debate is central to our social and intellectual life. And it need not always be a sombre or humourless activity. As Alexander Pope observed, it may also involve good fun since 'True disputants are like sportsmen; their whole delight is in the pursuit.'

Finally, we acknowledge that *Debates in British Politics Today* represents only the first step towards greater levels of competence, both in the academic study of Politics and in the political literacy of effective citizenship. This is because the authors have consciously oversimplified their subject material in the interests of greater clarity. They are not providing a *discourse* on each topic comprising a number of arguments, one shading into the next, but rather they have followed the tradition of *debate*. They each have explored the case for and the case against – the pros and cons – before drawing their conclusions. For those wanting to follow each debate to a more sophisticated level, the authors have provided guidance on further reading. We are, then, acknowledging but not apologising for this book being concerned with the more confined process of debate, since many real conflicts are based around two basic viewpoints and much politics is conducted along simply contested two-party lines. In flight political reality is frequently oversimplified or distorted into simple dichotomies. While reflecting this reality in its structure, we nevertheless hope the book will also enable its readers to become suspicious when presented with arguments which have been condensed into simple choices.

Lynton Robins
Bill Jones

I

Debates on the constitution

1

Do we still need the Monarchy?

Bill Jones

Introduction

Until quite recently many commentators believed that the Victorian essayist and journalist Walter Bagehot had said the most perceptive things about the institution of Monarchy: 'The best reason why monarchy is a strong government is, that it is an intelligible government. The mass of mankind understand it, and they hardly anywhere in the world understand any other' as well as 'So long as the human heart is strong and human reason weak, Royalty will be strong because it appeals to diffused feeling, and Republics weak because they appeal to understanding' (1867).

However, despite the continuing relevance of many of his observations, it is doubtful if he would judge the modern institution in Britain as 'strong'. Indeed, the death of Princess Diana in August 1997 – following in the wake of a decade's poor publicity – focused further unflattering light upon the Royal Family. In consequence, a number of commentators pronounced its time was up. Writing in the *Guardian* on 17 September 1997, Jonathon Freedland saw the Monarchy confirming 'ours as a semi-feudal society'. The Monarchy, he concluded, 'cannot be reformed. It must go.' Andrew Rawnsley writing in the *Observer* on 14 September 1997 called for a republic. At the very least, the low esteem in which the Monarchy is now held has enabled republican arguments to re-enter the mainstream of political discussion for the first time in a hundred years.

Background

Alfred the Great (849–99) was the first English king to achieve nationwide authority; the Danish King Canute (944–1035) added to this political unity for the kingdom. Kings in those days were tribal chiefs with, in theory, 'absolute' power to make, implement and interpret laws of the realm. In practice they also needed to keep on the right side of the powerful elements in the

kingdom and held regular meetings of the *witangemot* to seek advice and support from the landowning elite.

Eventually this meeting became formalised and was used when the Monarch wished to raise funds for war, building or other purposes. King John was
judged to have exceeded his powers and was brought into line by his nobles
via the Magna Carta in 1215. The power to advise was soon linked formally
to the provision of finance and the emergent 'Parliament' soon became engaged in a tension which became a struggle with the Crown over the best way
to run the kingdom, especially which religion it should officially endorse. Eventually the Civil War (1642–49) struck down the Monarchy in the name of a
'sovereign popular will' but the Cromwellian interlude was not deemed either
popular or successful. In 1660 Charles II was restored. William of Orange's
invited takeover in 1688 was conditional that Parliament would be supreme.
This constitutional settlement's implications were worked out in the eighteenth century with Robert Walpole as the conduit between George I – a poor
linguist and not interested in public affairs – and his senior ministers: effectively becoming 'Prime Minister'. From then on Parliament took over the reins
of government and popular sovereignty its legitimacy as the Great Reform
Act of 1832 wrested away from the Crown and the aristocracy the ability to
determine the colour of the government of the day. The Monarchy under
Victoria (1819–1901) set the pattern for the future of an institution hugely
respected for most of the time and laden with ceremonial duties, but with no
effective political power. Bagehot distinguished famously between the 'dignified'
parts of the British constitution and the parts which actually worked. Few
have disputed that the British Monarchy remains squarely in the former
category but the question now being asked more insistently is whether – with
all its dignity – it has finally outlived any practical usefulness. The case for the
Monarchy will be considered first, followed by the case against and then a
conclusion which also looks at the question of future reforms.

The case for the Monarchy

Tradition

Enoch Powell argued that the Lords should continue because 'it has always
been there, it is there because it has come to be there.' Others would apply the
same logic to the Monarchy. Tradition is important to the British, who take
pride in their history and value their stately homes and ancient Monarchy.

Democracy

- Adonis argues that the Monarch helps to integrate the wide class differences
  in Britain, especially between the middle classes and the aristocracy during
  the nineteenth century and the working classes in the present one.

- The Royals have always felt an empathy with the working classes: witness George VI's statement on 1930s unemployment that 'something has to be done'; the Royals' warm regard for Ernest Bevin, Harold Wilson and Jim Callaghan; and the expansion of the annual garden parties to include a wider cross-section of society.
- The Queen's tendency is for an inclusive consensual politics, not the ideologically divisive varieties of Left or Right.
- The Monarchy's continuing popularity with the voters; even after the death of Diana, 74 per cent wished the Monarchy to continue in 'modernised' form and only 5 per cent wished for a republic to replace it (see table 1.1).

Politics

- *Choosing the Prime Minister.* In law the Monarch invites the leader of the winning party after an election to form a government and if there is no clear majority has discretion as to whom to invite. Peter Hennessy argues that even if these powers are not used they could be 'active' and their potential use consequently influences political conduct. Moreover, if proportional representation becomes a reality the Monarch could become crucial in choosing the leader of coalition administrations. Ben Pimlott argues that this power – after all, the most important one surviving – is exaggerated; if the Monarch ever exercised it, it would be removed.
- *Advising the Premier.* The Queen sees the Prime Minister every Tuesday for an hour and exercises her right to 'warn, consult and advise'. So far she has 'advised' ten Prime Ministers and it would seem her relationships with them have varied. Churchill was warmly avuncular and talked about horses; Eden found it a chore; Douglas Home thrived as a fellow aristocrat; Wilson treated her warmly as an equal and became a favourite; Heath was distant and cold; Callaghan bluff and friendly and a devoted monarchist. Thatcher was a problem as she too was cold and not easy; she used to return from her audiences allegedly dying for a drink. On one occasion, over the Falklands, according to the late Lord Wyatt, the Queen openly contradicted her and made her blush. There were no problems with Major, however, nor so far as we know with Blair; indeed he seems to have taken over the decision making after Diana's death and proved invaluable to the institution.

Head of armed forces

It was rumoured that in the 1970s there were some members of the armed forces and the security services who contemplated a coup and it is argued that the loyalty of the armed forces to the Queen would stop anything like that happening; as in the case of King Juan Carlos of Spain in 1981 when he foiled a right-wing coup attempt.

Table 1.1   *The popularity of the Monarchy*

1	How many marks out of 10 would you give the Queen as Britain's head of state and Prince Charles as Prince of Wales for the way they carry out their roles?		

% giving 10 out of 10	*1981*	*1997*
Queen	71%	10%
Charles	58%	5%

2	Which of these options would you prefer:

a	The Monarchy should continue in its present form	12%
b	The Monarchy should continue but be modernised	74%
c	The Monarchy should be replaced with a republic when the Queen dies	5%
d	The Monarchy should be replaced with a republic as soon as possible	7%

3	Assuming that the Monarchy continues, do you agree or disagree with each of these statements?

		Agree	*Disagree*
a	The Royal Family should become much more informal, and less concerned with preserving their traditional ways	81%	15%
b	The Royal Family is out of touch with ordinary people in Britain	79%	17%
c	The Royal Family should not take part in field sports such as fox-hunting and grouse shooting	62%	23%
d	The Queen should start to give interviews like other public figures	49%	39%
e	The Queen should give up functions such as signing new laws, opening Parliament and formally appointing a Prime Minister and stick to purely ceremonial duties	37%	57%

4	If the Monarchy does continue, when the Queen dies, do you think the crown should pass to Prince Charles or straight to Prince William?

Charles	38%
William	53%

Source: Observer, 21 September 1997.

Cost

- It costs the taxpayer over £50 million annually to keep the Monarchy. Some say this is too much but the argument against this is that the nation wants a 'splendid Monarchy', as do the tourists, and that this sum is derisory compared with the overall cost of the public sector and a tiny fraction of overall public expenditure.
- Some argue that the splendid nature of the Monarchy attracts thousands of tourists to these shores and more than off-sets any cost incurred.

Symbolism

- Bagehot argued that the people needed a symbol to appeal to the people, whose reason is 'weak . . . women care fifty times more for a marriage than a ministry'; in other words, Monarchy is part of the necessary obfuscation whereby wise men rule foolish subjects.
- Pimlott sees the Monarch as symbolising the nation and providing some unity above party, a mirror in which the nation sees itself and sees what it wants to see; hence the role of ceremony and its popularity. The coronation was watched by 27 million people, many of them on television for the first time. Millions of sets were hired for the duration of the ceremony and then maintained afterwards, helping to establish television viewing as the nation's foremost leisure activity and ensuring its importance in informing the nation politically.
- All nations need some 'legitimising' process whereby laws are passed. The Monarchy, with the State Opening of Parliament and the Royal Assent, fits this role perfectly.
- The early Press Secretary Sir John Colville was known for telling the press to go away but his successor, Sir William Heseltine, was more open and approved the documentary by Richard Cawston, *The Royal Family*, in 1969. More publicity followed and the Investiture of the Prince of Wales was another huge national event just like the subsequent royal weddings of the 1980s.
- The Queen makes an excellent ambassador, representing the country abroad and attracting huge crowds wherever she goes.
- Hugo Young wrote in the *Guardian* (5 November 1997), 'For those with souls open to such sentiment, she does personify the dignified aspect of the nation: its feelings, and its need for a single, slightly mysterious figure to represent them.'

Moral authority

Queen Victoria probably set the template of the allegedly 'perfect family' which was to be a model for the nation. The Archbishop of Canterbury in 1964, when Prince Edward was born, invoked the idea of the Christian 'united, happy' family setting an example to the nation. While there are problems with this, some argue that the Queen still sets an example of duty and patriotism which is inspiring; others see similar traits in Prince Charles.

The case against the Monarchy

Tradition

This, it can be argued, is a very limited argument as it ultimately justifies no change at all. It would have us hang on to all the powers that the Monarchy and the House of Lords have relinquished, for example, and consequently cannot be taken seriously, despite the romantic notions of high Tories.

Democracy

- The hereditary nature of the Monarchy makes it inimical to democracy, the tenets of which would justify abolition or, at a minimum, radical reform rather than maintenance.
- The Monarchy is the lynchpin of an inegalitarian social class system which gives advantages to the better off and sustains the disadvantage of the less well off.
- The Queen hands out meaningless baubles such as honours to already successful people which merely succeed in placing them above their fellow citizens.

Politics

- In a true democracy Prime Ministers do not need to be chosen by an elderly woman who happens to have been born into royalty. In a true democracy it should be the people who make such choices.
- Nor do Prime Ministers need advice from such a person when so many expert advisers are at hand.

Head of armed forces

The headship of the armed forces is only symbolic and the dangers of a coup in such a stable democracy are in any case negligible.

Cost

- It is true that the percentage of total spending is tiny but if this argument were applied generally it would justify exponential public spending.

- Ordinary people do not think in such terms; they see such sums in terms of new schools or hospitals which could be built or the fact that the Royal Family is already fabulously rich and does not need any assistance from the taxpayer to lead their lifestyle.

Symbolism

- Other countries manage to have democratically elected symbolic heads of state, for example Ireland, the USA or Germany.
- The ceremony associated with the royal involvement in politics is seen as a bore by most people.
- The average citizen – especially women, whom he patronised shamefully – is more intelligent than Bagehot realised, or has become better informed as a result of education.
- Bagehot may have been right, however, to assert that the secret of the Monarchy's success was its mystery and one should not 'shine light upon magic'. By inviting publicity into their lives the Monarchy cheapened itself and set in train a process it could not control. In the earlier years of the twentieth century the media respected the need for privacy of the Royal Family and willingly colluded in hushing up scandals concerning affairs and so forth. In the 1970s and 80s, however, the competition between newspapers, as readerships fell, contributed to a 'gloves off' mentality by Fleet Street, regarding not just the Royals but any public figure. But it was the Royals who attracted the most attention.

Moral authority

- The scandals associated with the marriages of the Waleses and the Yorks brought the institution into great disrepute.
- The death of Diana focused the spotlight upon the previously immune person of the Queen and her family, who were accused of being cold and dysfunctional. In an attempt to still such criticism the Queen made an unprecedented personal live broadcast to the nation expressing her sorrow at Diana's death.
- The nation does not need a single family as its moral touchstone.

Conclusion

So, do we need the Monarchy? Having looked at the points for and against, which case is superior? This must be a personal judgement but the balance would appear to be on maintaining a popular institution but reforming it quite drastically. The institution has gone through crises before, as in the last century and the Abdication crisis in the 1930s. Each time it has retrenched and come back strongly. In 1994, 70 per cent of respondents said that the nation did not need the Royal Family but by 1998 the figure was down to 52 per cent. The popularity of the Monarchy is bound to fluctuate according to mood and events. For example, Prince Charles seemed to make a comeback in popularity in 1998 after making a visit to South Africa with his sons where the royal widower was seen expressing genuine care for his sons. The ICM poll in the *Guardian* (15 August 1998) revealed that 52 per cent thought he would make a 'good king' compared with only 40 per cent a year earlier. However, a majority agreed that the Royals were still out of touch with the public and another majority felt that the Prince should not marry his mistress, Camilla Parker-Bowles.

The Royals have established the Way Ahead Group to address the future needs of the institution. In March 1998 it announced: a reduction of the twenty-two people allowed to use the title HRH down to possibly the sovereign and the heir; and curtseying rules to be relaxed. Small steps, maybe, but all in the right direction.

It was rumoured that Charles would like the Queen to abdicate and let him take over. If she survives as long as her mother has to date, he will be seventy-five when it is time for him to assume the throne. She is unlikely to abdicate as she enjoys the work and believes she is the one to do it. What else could she do? Wouldn't an abdication for the 'convenience' of her son betray the duty to which she has dedicated her life? The thing which Charles most seems to want – marriage to Camilla Parker-Bowles – he is also some way from getting. As long as there is a majority in the country – which includes his mother, it should be said – marriage is likely to be a formality their already intimate life will be denied.

In August 1998 Mark Leonard and Nick Hames of the think-tank Demos produced a report on the Monarchy which recommended: the abolition of the automatic right of succession with a public right to veto an unacceptable royal candidate in a referendum; the education of young Royals at state schools and treatment in NHS hospitals; loss of headship of the Church of England; the Speaker to take over the responsibility of selecting the Prime Minister and dissolving Parliament; and abolition of the Royal Assent and the establishment of an Office of the Monarchy run by the Civil Service. Demos is close to New Labour but Tony Blair distanced himself from the report even though some of its recommendations are likely to become fact in the new millennium. It seems, however, that while the British public thinks its Monarchy is worth retaining, it prefers one which is less remote and less 'splendid', or wasteful, in its way of life: the ghost of Scandinavian monarchs seem to bicycle through the recommended alternatives to present arrangements.

Retaining the Monarchy

The case for

- Tradition: it is part of the national identity.
- Democracy: it helps to reduce differences between classes.
- Politics: the Queen helps to choose Prime Ministers when there is no clear majority.
- Head of the armed forces: the Queen commands loyalty of armed forces thus precluding a coup.
- Cost: tiny percentage of public expenditure.
- Symbolism: emotional symbol appeals to citizens; above party and symbol of national unity; serves to legitimise legal process; the Queen is an excellent ambassador overseas; Royal Family provides ready source of symbolism through its accessibility to the media; the Queen is a perfect fulfilment of these symbolic requirements.
- Moral authority: Royal Family provides touchstone of how family life should be led.

The case against

- Tradition: the 'no change' argument invalidates all democratic reform.
- Democracy: absurd for the Queen to be head of supposed democracy; provides a foundation of an inegalitarian social system; the Queen is the source of a divisive honours system.
- Politics: no need for the Queen to choose the Prime Minister; nor to give advice to the Prime Minister.
- Armed forces: chances of a coup remote in a stable democracy.
- Cost: wasteful exhibition of luxury.
- Symbolism: other countries survive well with elected head of state; citizens do not need irrational symbol to lead them; publicity has cheapened Monarchy's life.
- Moral authority: royal behaviour has removed any possibility of Royal Family being a moral touchstone.

Reading

Adonis, A. and Pollard, S. (1997) *A Class Act*, Hamish Hamilton.
Bagehot, W. (1867) *The English Constitution*, Fontana (1963 edition).
Lord Hailsham (1992) *On the Constitution*, Harper Collins.
Hennessy, P. (1995) *The Hidden Wiring*, Gollancz.

Hennessy, P. (1996) *Muddling Through*, Gollancz.
Marr, A. (1995) *Ruling Britannia*, Michael Joseph.
Norton, P. (2000) in Bill Jones, (ed.), *Politics UK*, Pearson, 4th edition, chapter 17.
Pimlott, B. (1996) *Harold Wilson*, Harper Collins.
Pimlott, B. (1992) *The Queen: A Biography of Queen Elizabeth*, Harper Collins.
Powell, E. (1982) 'Reforming Parliament', *Teaching Politics*, May, pp. 167–77.
Sampson, A. (1992) *The Essential Anatomy of Britain*, Hodder and Stoughton.
Thatcher, M. (1995) *The Downing Street Years*, Harper Collins.
Young, H. (1990) *One of Us*, Pan.

2

Has Prime Minister Major been replaced by President Blair?

Graham P. Thomas

Introduction: the 'presidentialising' of British politics

Arguments about the role of the Prime Minister and the extent to which he or she dominates the British system of government are perennial controversies among observers. While it is clear that the Prime Minister is the key figure in the British political system, there is no consensus on the precise nature of his or her powers. Many commentators have suggested that Britain has *prime ministerial government*, that he or she totally dominates British government and Parliament alike. Thus Britain has developed a virtually presidential style of government. Others take a more traditional view, arguing that there remain effective constraints on the Premier's power and that *Cabinet government*, the essence of which is collective decision making, survives.

However, both theories are deficient. The premiership is a highly dynamic office; the personality of the Prime Minister is a crucial factor, and time and circumstances will alter the extent to which the incumbent can and will use his or her powers. As Asquith stated: 'The office of Prime Minister is what the holder chooses and is able to make of it' (Asquith, 1926, p. 185). Policy making is highly complex and rival claims about the virtually presidential powers of the Prime Minister and of the collegiate nature of the Cabinet system are superficial and misleading.

The debate about prime ministerial power

The prime ministerial or presidential model

The view that Cabinet government has been replaced by prime ministerial domination amounting to the virtual presidentialising of the system was set out by the Labour politician Richard Crossman. He wrote that the powers of the Prime Minister have steadily increased and that the 'post-war epoch has seen the final transformation of Cabinet Government into Prime Ministerial Government' (Crossman, 1963, p. 51). To describe the Prime Minister as *primus inter pares* (first among equals) or as Chairman of the Cabinet was totally misleading. His or her dominance over the government was based on the right to select the Cabinet and to dismiss members at will; to decide the Cabinet agenda and to control its business; to announce decisions without taking a vote; the power to select, shuffle and dismiss ministers, to appoint key civil servants and to control the machinery of the ruling party; all reinforced by media concentration on personality at the expense of policy or issues. The Cabinet no longer acts and takes decisions as a body. Instead, decisions are taken by departmental ministers and by Cabinet committees with the Prime Minister exercising a dominant role in all major areas of policy. This development has so far advanced as to make the British Cabinet resemble the American Cabinet, where collective responsibility does not exist: each Cabinet member is solely and directly responsible to the President.

Collective responsibility has become 'collective obedience by the whole administration . . . to the will of the man at the apex of power' (Crossman, 1963, p. 53). Allied to the declining power of Parliament to check the executive, a consequence of the rise of disciplined parties, the power of the Prime Minister is awesome in the extreme. He or she has a unique role in integrating the whole government and controls the three areas of central authority: the Cabinet, the Civil Service and the party machine. Because the Prime Minister is the only person who can exert central authority in *all* these fields, the system can correctly be described as prime ministerial.

The 'chairmanship' model

Crossman's thesis has been attacked as an oversimplification and a distortion of a complex reality. While it is clear that the Prime Minister has a formidable range of powers, he or she is subjected to limitations sufficient to ensure that the Prime Minister is not a figure set apart but remains the leader of a group whose support is vital. Thus the Prime Minister is only as strong as Cabinet colleagues and the party allow him or her to be.

The Prime Minister's control over the government can be exaggerated. There are continuing constraints from the Cabinet as a collective body, from powerful colleagues such as the Chancellor and the Foreign Secretary, and from the party. If the Chancellor and the Foreign Secretary take up a position in opposition to that of the Prime Minister it is likely that the latter would have to give way, perhaps unless supported by the rest of the Cabinet. Margaret Thatcher was forced to accept entry to the Exchange Rate Mechanism (ERM) when Sir Geoffrey Howe and Nigel Lawson both threatened to resign. It may even be that contemporary Prime Ministers are *more* vulnerable to leadership challenges than in the past; Thatcher was brought down by a challenge in 1990 and Major was forced to put his leadership on the line in 1995.

Although the Prime Minister may be able temporarily to keep items off the agenda he or she is unable in the long run to prevent senior colleagues from bringing to the Cabinet a matter they think significant. Nor is the agenda merely a matter for the Prime Minister's own whim or inclination. The absence of evidence of Cabinet revolts against the Prime Minister does not indicate subservience to his or her will but most likely that final decisions are agreed ones, reached after a process of adjustment and compromise.

In choosing a Cabinet the Prime Minister does not have a free hand, and often has to choose those for whom he or she has little personal or political sympathy. Prime Ministers have to choose the leading figures in the party; otherwise they risk possible leadership rivals sulking on the backbenches with little to do except seek opportunities to create embarrassment and discontent. Sacking powerful figures can be dangerous. Major's dismissal of Norman Lamont created a bitter and determined foe who constantly attacked his former friend and who acted as a focus for right-wing discontent from the back benches. Prime Ministers often prefer to move those seen as threats rather than dismissing them. Because the Prime Minister has no department of his or her own he or she will be at a serious disadvantage compared with colleagues. Despite the changes in recent years to the organisation of No. 10 Downing Street, the Premier lacks the kind of organisational support available to the President of the United States. The Cabinet Office serves the Cabinet as a whole and not just the Prime Minister, and civil servants are loyal to their departments rather than to one person, however eminent. What has been referred to as 'ministerial government' is a check on the power of the Premier. Departmental ministers have their own position to defend and their own agenda to pursue, and will seek to resist prime ministerial interference. Thus it is possible to over-emphasise the Prime Minister's influence over policy. No one, not even a Prime Minister with a policy agenda as comprehensive as that of Margaret Thatcher, can survey the whole of an increasingly complex field. However much the Prime Minister may attempt to dominate the policies of his or her government, the pressure of time and of events limits what can be achieved.

The personality/circumstances view

Both the 'presidential' and the 'chairmanship' schools have been criticised for failing to take adequate account of the differing personalities of post-war Prime Ministers, of ignoring political circumstances and what Harold Macmillan referred to as 'events'. 'The truth is that the powers of the Prime Minister have varied with the personality of the Prime Minister, or with the particular political circumstances of his tenure' (Blake, 1975, p. 51). Prime Ministers have differed widely in terms of personality and how they have perceived the job. Some have tended to dominate in Cabinet; examples include Churchill, Heath and Thatcher. Others, such as Alec Douglas Home, took a more limited view of their role. Major's weakened position after 'Black Wednesday' meant that his ability to impose his will on his ministers was limited, hence his exasperated reference to Eurosceptic colleagues as 'bastards'. Several commentators have pointed out the unhistoric nature of much of Crossman's analysis. In the nineteenth century some Prime Ministers (e.g. Gladstone and Disraeli) were dominant in their Cabinets, while others were not. In many respects Lloyd George displayed those 'presidential' characteristics which Crossman portrayed as a mainly post-1945 development.

Similarly, the situations faced by Prime Ministers differ. Temperament is a vital factor. While possession of the right temperament is no guarantee of success, its absence is a sign of certain failure. Prime Ministers are judged partly on what personal resources they bring to the post and on how well they use those resources. Political ability is an immense source of strength. Margaret Thatcher's main claim to the support of her party was her ability to win general elections; her supporters often pointed to the contrast with her predecessor, who lost three of his four elections. Factors such as the ability to work hard, to identify clear aims, to take quick decisions, and so on are all involved. Successful Prime Ministers need three basic characteristics: strong ambition, unusual luck and, above all, remarkable physical stamina. Time is another important element. Prime ministerial power is not a static thing; it can vary markedly during a period in office. At times the Prime Minister will appear to have almost presidential powers, while at other times the constraints will dominate. The careers of both Margaret Thatcher and John Major demonstrate this essential truth. There is no reason to think that things will be different for Tony Blair.

The Major premiership assessed

It is difficult to understand John Major's time in office without appreciating the extent to which his style of government was a reaction against that of his predecessor. This was a constant source of irritation to Major, who was notoriously thin-skinned, 'as his predecessor celebrated what he dismissed as a golden age that never was' (Kavanagh, 1997, p. 194). Proponents of both the 'presidential' and the 'personality/circumstances' theories find much to support their theses when considering Margaret Thatcher's time in office. The 'presidential' school, which saw a trend towards a more personal style of government, regardless of the actual incumbent, emphasised the increasingly centralised decision making, while the 'personality' school stressed what it saw as the factors peculiar to Margaret Thatcher, such as her dominant and distinctive character and the way she imposed her will on all around her.

Although the long-term trend had been to increase the power of the Prime Minister at the expense of the Cabinet, Thatcher took the process a considerable step further. At least for a time she ensured that the Cabinet was packed with her own supporters (particularly in posts connected with the management of the economy). She interfered in departmental matters to a marked degree; she clearly had a very broad personal agenda, far more so than that of most post-war Premiers. In Cabinet meetings she usually announced her views at the start of a discussion, in effect challenging her opponents to make their position clear at the outset; previous Prime Ministers tended to allow discussion first and then put forward their views in the summing up. Ministers who became critical of her style or policies were softened up for dismissal by a campaign of leaks and innuendoes orchestrated by her Press Secretary, Bernard Ingham.

Commentators stressed the reduction in the number of Cabinet and Cabinet committee meetings and Margaret Thatcher's fondness for often informal consultation with close colleagues and advisers as a way of downgrading or bypassing the full Cabinet. Ministers quickly learned that what mattered was getting the approval of the Prime Minister for their projects. Once that had been achieved, approval by the Cabinet was a virtual formality. It could be argued that such arrangements were not new. What was new was the extent to which Margaret Thatcher behaved in this quasi-presidential fashion and the degree to which she refused to disguise or dissemble about the use of power.

Yet the ease with which she was eventually ousted from the leadership of the Conservative Party (and thus of the premiership) shows the sterility of the 'prime ministerial' versus 'Cabinet government' argument. The downfall of Thatcher and her replacement by Major brought about significant changes in the conduct of the Cabinet. Major was more of a conciliator and a seeker of agreement, and the circumstances of his coming to power made such a change inevitable. However, it would be rash to ascribe *too* much to personalities. Many of the developments of the Thatcher years represent long-term changes, and the premiership of Blair is already demonstrating the tendency to gather power in the hands of the head of the government.

John Major entered the Commons in 1979. He was successively a government whip, Under-Secretary for Social Security, and Minister of State at the Department of Health and Social Security, before entering the Cabinet as Chief Secretary to the Treasury in 1987. He was Foreign Secretary for a few months in 1989 and then succeeded Nigel Lawson as Chancellor, a post he held from 1989 until he became Prime Minister and leader of the Conservative Party following the resignation of Margaret Thatcher in November 1990.

Major's use of his powers was less authoritarian than that of his predecessor. The handover from Thatcher to Major saw a change in the use made of the Cabinet, which had a more prominent role in policy making. At least until 'Black Wednesday', Major's ministers felt that they were a Cabinet of 'chums' and that Cabinet meetings were 'fun', in contrast to the increasingly strained atmosphere which had prevailed at the end of the Thatcher era. More matters were dealt with in Cabinet committees. There were fewer bilateral meetings and *ad hoc* groups. The advantage of this was that Major was able to take controversial policy decisions, such as the abandonment of the poll tax and the ratification of the Maastricht Treaty, without any Cabinet resignations. The disadvantage was slowness of decision making and the appearance of drift, indecisiveness and weakness, something which Major conceded once he left office, although he claimed it was his way of keeping a divided Cabinet together.

On the other hand, it would be a mistake to overstress the differences between the two leaders. Both sought to prevent conflict in Cabinet by avoiding discussion of controversial issues, although neither was entirely successful. They both ensured that the most sensitive decisions were endorsed by the full Cabinet and both spent considerable time when necessary preparing the ground. Cabinet under Thatcher and Major had fewer formal papers presented to it and took fewer decisions than before 1979. Cabinets followed the same format and were of similar average length. There was much leaking from both Cabinets and this reached torrent proportions after 'Black Wednesday', when relationships broke down, the Cabinet fell into factions and trust was irrevocably lost. This inhibited freedom of discussion in Cabinet and probably contributed to failures in decision making.

John Major was conscious of the criticisms of Margaret Thatcher's style of government. This, plus his more collegiate approach to the premiership, inevitably meant a less strident leadership. His desire to be a team leader and to get Cabinet behind a decision was the principal difference between his and Thatcher's style. He used free-ranging discussion as a way of maintaining collective agreement. Major claimed that he went to a lot of trouble to listen and to respond to what people said, and that he tried to soothe wounds. He strongly disliked tension and unpleasantness and sought agreement wherever possible.

Even after Major's unexpected victory in the 1992 general election he was in a weaker position than his predecessor. There remained a widespread public impression of Major as a Prime Minister 'on trial', that he was somehow temporary. It was in part due to the image of Major conveyed by programmes such as *Spitting Image* as a grey, boring nonentity and to the unprecedented press campaign in newspapers such as *The Times*, the *Sunday Times* and the *Sun*, normally loyal to the Conservative Party and almost fanatically devoted to Margaret Thatcher when she was Premier.

Major began his premiership with two principal disadvantages. The first, which Major acknowledged, was that he reached the top of the 'greasy pole' too early, with insufficient experience of life and of politics. More importantly, he had had no time to prepare his programme for office. 'The most telling criticism of his premiership is that it lacked coherence. Major himself was neither a conceptual nor a strategic thinker; rather he was a tactical operator. He was uncomfortable making pronouncements on ideology and broad policy direction' (Kavanagh, 1997, p. 133).

There were several criticisms of John Major:

- He was accused of not being a good butcher, of being unable to sack ministers when necessary. This was the case when Norman Lamont stayed on after the fiasco of Britain's forced withdrawal from the ERM. Equally, when eventually Lamont *was* sacked, Major was attacked for having made a scapegoat of someone who was, after all, merely carrying out the Prime Minister's own policy. Major was accused of letting personal friendship get in the way of doing the correct thing when he tried to hang on to David Mellor.

- It was suggested that Major's nerve went in a crisis, especially on 'Black Wednesday', when he was said to have had a virtual nervous breakdown although those close to Major emphatically deny this happened. On the other hand, he showed great poise and real qualities of leadership during the Gulf War. In general, he was said to be too sensitive to criticism. He read the press obsessively, in contrast with his predecessor, whose Press Secretary made a carefully filleted summary for her.

- Mainly from the Thatcherite Right came the jibe that Major lacked vision. It was clear that he was not a 'vision' person, and his calls for a 'classless society' and an appeal to 'back to basics' fell flat. He was a poor speaker, although better with small groups of supporters than with a large and perhaps sceptical audience.

- A significant criticism was that he dithered and could not make up his mind, resulting in drift, uncertainty and indecision, especially over Europe. His unwillingness to assert himself and bang the table infuriated some, and led to charges of letting circumstances and other people determine issues rather than forcing a resolution himself. Supporters pointed out that he swiftly disposed of the poll tax, which was converted into a 'council tax' and disappeared from view as a political issue.

In the days following 'Black Wednesday' Major contemplated resignation. The government began to fall into factions and ministers such as Redwood, Howard, Lilley and increasingly Portillo, became less and less guarded in their expression of dissent from Major's policies, especially on Europe. The balance of power in the Cabinet began to drift away from Major. The Tory press turned against Major to a degree never before experienced by a Conservative leader, the party's reputation for managerial and economic competence (itself a myth of gigantic proportions) disappeared, and Major seemed to the electorate to have lost his grip and to be divorced from reality.

For most of the 1992–97 Parliament the government appeared to be drifting helplessly, battered by a series of policy reverses and a torrent of sleaze. Critics from a variety of perspectives were united in finding John Major's government the least competent and most corrupt for many years. The Prime Minister's popularity slumped. Increasingly, friends of Lady Thatcher attacked Major's leadership of the government and the party. The dismissal of Norman Lamont in May 1993 was seen as another example of Major's weakness in the face of public anger at the handling of the economy and party anxiety about electoral prospects. Lamont's resignation speech in the Commons added to Major's woes; the sacked Chancellor said, 'We give the impression of being in office, but not in power.'

Criticism of Major's leadership grew. In an unguarded off-camera talk to a television journalist he referred to three right-wing Eurosceptic Cabinet ministers (thought to have been Peter Lilley, Michael Portillo and John Redwood) as 'bastards'. Later another leak had Major referring to some of the rebel backbenchers as 'barmy' and as 'several apples short of a picnic'. In the autumn of 1994 a group of eight Eurosceptic MPs were deprived of the Tory whip, which, however, was swiftly restored without any promises of good behaviour. As criticism grew Major surprised most political commentators, and most of his own party, in June 1995 by resigning the leadership of the Conservative Party (though not the premiership) and offering himself for re-election. His decision was triggered by continuing press and party unrest about his leadership. Major was challenged for the leadership by the Eurosceptic Welsh Secretary John Redwood, who resigned from the government. The rest of the Cabinet rallied to Major, though with varying degrees of zeal, and at least one, Michael Portillo, set up a campaign machine to be ready in case of an inconclusive first ballot. Most of the 1922 Committee signed Major's nomination papers and he received the lukewarm support of Lady Thatcher. Major was re-elected leader by 218 votes to 89 to Redwood, with the surprisingly low number of 20 abstentions.

On 1 May 1997 Major led his party to its most severe defeat this century and he announced his resignation as Prime Minister and leader of the Conservative Party.

Tony Blair as Prime Minister

Tony Blair became the fifth Labour Prime Minister at the age of forty-three, the youngest Premier since 1812. It is clear that he is running his government on a tight rein from the centre. The aim is to ensure that New Labour is more successful as a party of power than was Old Labour, that Labour becomes the 'natural party of government', a label claimed by the Tories for much of the twentieth century. It is also clear that Blair and his circle are determined that government should not descend into a directionless shambles, as is alleged to have happened under John Major. In coming into government Labour felt that the country had not been governed in any coherent sense but had drifted aimlessly under an administration wracked by ideological divisions and personal animosities, leaving the Civil Service to do the best it could to avoid total disaster.

Blair has expanded the role of the No. 10 Policy Unit and the Cabinet Office in an attempt to drive policy forward. John Prescott was appointed Deputy Prime Minister and put in charge of a range of responsibilities, such as the environment, local government, regional policy and transport. Gordon Brown at the Treasury was another important appointment, although rumours surfaced concerning tension between the Prime Minister and Chancellor, dating back to the succession to John Smith. Blair brought many of the figures who had worked in his office in Opposition to serve in the Private Office, the Political Office, the Press Office and the No. 10 Policy Unit. Jonathan Powell was made Chief of Staff and Alistair Campbell Press Secretary. A large number of political advisers were appointed, both to assist the Prime Minister and also to help departmental ministers. This was a deliberate attempt to ensure that ministers do not become too dependent on their civil servants, as is alleged to have happened under previous administrations. Some critics see it as a step along the road to an American-style system, in which the top echelon of advisers is appointed along party lines and disappears when governments change. Although Blair has strengthened central control over the government, he has been willing to delegate considerable discretion over policy to those ministers he trusts, such as Mo Mowlam at the Northern Ireland Office.

It is clear that Blair is determined that Whitehall departments should not be able to work independently of Downing Street and that ministers should not be allowed to build up their own empires at the expense of the unity of the government as a whole. The emphasis will be on carrying out the manifesto in line with the core strategy and philosophy of the government. Although the kind of control of policy attempted by Margaret Thatcher will not be part of the Blair style, the lesson of the Major administration, that of the danger of virtual civil war at the heart of government, has been learned. In particular, there have been efforts to ensure that the announcement and presentation of policy initiatives have been co-ordinated through No. 10. Attempts have been made to continue Labour's successes in presentational matters which contributed to the victory in May 1997.

In July 1998 the Prime Minister announced organisational changes, based on a report by the Secretary to the Cabinet, Sir Richard Wilson. He had pointed to several weaknesses in the way government business was organised. The linkage between policy formulation and implementation needed further improvement and cross-departmental issues of policy and service delivery often were not handled well. Wilson concluded that there was scope to improve the performance of the centre of government in promulgating best practice and innovation. Blair announced significant reforms to the Cabinet Office, into which was absorbed the Office of Public Services. He also set up a new Performance and Innovation Unit in the Cabinet Office to focus on issues which cross departmental boundaries and which will challenge the Treasury's power to interfere in the work of other government departments.

As part of the changes, Jack Cunningham (said to be highly regarded by Blair as a 'joined up' politician) was moved from the Ministry of Agriculture to become Minister for the Cabinet Office and Chancellor of the Duchy of Lancaster. Immediately dubbed by the media 'the enforcer' of Blair's policies (a title rejected by No. 10 and by Cunningham himself), he became the

Minister in charge of presenting government policy on radio and television. The Prime Minister's official spokesman (Alastair Campbell) said that his job was to ensure that the Prime Minister's objectives and the government's programme would be pursued throughout Whitehall. Cunningham said that his priority would be to curb the activities of spin doctors and gossipy ministerial aides, a clear reference to criticisms that the government was in danger of falling into factionalism, based on personal rivalries and animosities, largely originating in the supposed feud between Blair and Brown. Press comment stressed that his task would be to bring a greater element of formality and organisation to the working of government, to oversee policy and to sort out disputes between ministers. In particular, he would be expected to spot trouble in advance and to foster closer relations between the Cabinet Office secretariat, the No. 10 Policy Unit and the Treasury. Cunningham attended Blair's weekly planning meetings at No. 10 with the Chief of Staff, the head of the Policy Unit, Sir Richard Wilson and the heads of the Cabinet Office secretariats. There was a consensus that these changes, plus the government reshuffle of July 1998, would strengthen Blair's hold on the government. Although they did not amount to the creation of a Prime Minister's department they did mean a significant extension of the power of No. 10.[1]

This fanned the debate about what some have called the 'Blair presidency'. It is clear that in Opposition Blair had concluded that Cabinet government in the traditional sense had been a dead letter for thirty years and was now incapable of dealing with what Peter Mandelson called the 'wicked issues' which cut across departmental boundaries. Hence the strengthening of No. 10 and the Cabinet Office and ensuring that the Treasury had a more strategic role in pushing forward the government's aims. It is clear that Blair has little interest in lengthy Cabinet discussions of policy. On a number of key issues, such as the transfer of exchange rates to the Bank of England and the use of proportional representation for European Parliament elections, the Cabinet was informed rather than consulted. Cabinet meetings are much shorter than in the past and, according to some observers, there is little in the way of a formal agenda. Even Cabinet committees have been downgraded in significance.

The Blair style has been criticised by the veteran Whitehall observer, Peter Hennessy (1998a, b). He reported that Blair's closest aides had announced a change from 'a feudal system of barons' to a more Napoleonic system, by which they meant that under Major central direction of the government had disintegrated and senior ministers had behaved in a semi-independent manner. Under Blair there would be close control from the centre, with all significant issues cleared with No. 10 in advance of being announced. Hennessy saw this as the danger of the imposition of a highly personalised command premiership and a threat to any kind of collective leadership of the government. For Hennessy 'there are reasons for concern. The importance of being collective is not fully and properly appreciated in Blair's No. 10' (Hennessy, 1998a, p. 16). He was particularly concerned about new rules for contact with the media, although other commentators felt that this was a continuance of existing trends rather than anything new. Pointing out that the British system is based on a *collective* rather than a *single* executive, Hennessy asked: 'Surely as a political nation we did not struggle to replace the single executive represented by the seventeenth-century sovereign by a more collective form of cabinet governance only for it to mutate once more into an elected monarch?' (Hennessy, 1998a, p. 19). Hennessy concluded that although the Prime Minister may *think* he is running a Cabinet government the reality is the reverse. 'The forms of cabinet government may still be apparent, the substance is not. And the sooner his cabinet ministers, the Downing Street collective as a whole, put that right the better it will be for the government and the country' (Hennessy, 1998a, p. 20).

Not all observers take this rather caustic view of the 'Blair Project'. Hugo Young reviewed the first six months in office and pronounced the verdict 'Amazingly good so far' (*Guardian*, 30 December 1997). Vernon Bogdanor (*Guardian*, 4 June 1997) argued that the system suffered from a lack of support for the Prime Minister and that Blair's effort to rectify this 'hole in the heart of government' should not be seen as a move towards a presidential style of government but an attempt to remedy the chronic weakness which was the legacy of the Major government. Gray and Jenkins asked whether a variant of traditional Cabinet government was in place, one 'in which Downing Street is at the centre of a tightly controlled presentational machine but the departments hold the initiative for policy' (*Guardian*, 4 June 1997). Jack Straw (BBC Radio 4, 8 October 1998), one of the most significant figures in the creation of the 'Project', drew a comparison with both Thatcher and Major. He pointed to the similarities between Blair and Thatcher, both very dominant in their parties, popular in the country and with very clear ideas of the direction of government policy. In consequence, they are more dominant in Cabinet than more quiescent leaders such as Major. However, Straw also drew attention to the limits of prime ministerial power by pointing out that it is Secretaries of State who bring proposals to Parliament and, although the Prime Minister appoints them and can dismiss them, he can not keep dismissing them, something even Thatcher was eventually forced to realise. In many ways the triumphs of the government have been Blair's triumphs. He continues to be highly popular with the electors, taking his party along with him. He has a high profile in international affairs and enjoys what appears to be a close relationship with President Clinton. Although European statesmen and women regret British unwillingness to embrace the single currency, Blair is on friendly terms with the leaders of France and Germany, especially after the triumph of the centre left in both countries. Bill Jones' judgement is that if Blair 'has a defining characteristic as a premier it is that he is so intensely personal in his style. Rather like Clinton, perhaps, he seeks to reach out to people and make them feel he understands and cares about them – and succeeds in doing so' (Jones, 1999, p. 22).

Has Prime Minister Major been replaced by President Blair?

The case for

- He is a centraliser intent on expanding his own power.
- He operates a 'Napoleonic' system of control from the centre.
- He maintains an iron grip over the parliamentary party and the Labour Party in general.
- No. 10 exerts control over ministers by insisting that all contacts with the media are cleared in advance.
- Blair has little contact with Parliament; the twice-weekly Prime Minister's Question Time has been reduced to a once-weekly event.
- He has surrounded himself with a group of cronies who are his creatures and who have little in common with Labour Party members at large.
- Changes to the organisation of the Cabinet Office have expanded Blair's control to the extent that a Prime Minister's Department exists in all but name.
- He has diminished the importance of Cabinet by downgrading meetings, taking decisions in bilateral meetings with ministers, and so on.

The case against

- The change to a more centralised system of government pre-dates Blair and is a feature common to most Western democracies.
- Blair's changes to the machinery of government have been an attempt to remedy perceived weaknesses of the Major government.
- Moves to strengthen the centre have been urged by a variety of commentators as a way of combating the tendency to 'departmentalitis'.
- The attempt to co-ordinate media contacts was a response to the prevalence of leaks experienced by previous governments and a way of preventing ministers from pursuing their own agendas.
- The change to the format of Prime Minister's Question Time had been foreshadowed in Opposition and was an attempt to get away from the 'yah-boo' style of confrontational politics and to provide information to MPs.
- All Prime Ministers have needed to work with a small group of trusted allies; there is nothing new or disturbing in Blair's reliance on people such as Powell and Campbell.
- The reduction in the role of the Cabinet is not new and there is little evidence that ministers are alarmed at the trend.
- Blair has not surrounded himself with 'yes men': Brown, Cook, Straw and Prescott are powerful figures who have their own policy ideas and do not simply do the bidding of the Prime Minister.

Conclusion

It can be argued that there is nothing new in the way Tony Blair runs his government. The description of the role of Prime Minister as *primus inter pares* has long ceased to have any validity and the Cabinet is no longer the central decision taker. From this perspective Blair is simply responding to long-term developments enhancing the position of head of government which can be seen in most Western democracies and which were given fresh impetus by the Thatcher phenomenon.

> A lasting effect of [Thatcher's] long premiership may have been to colour popular perceptions of political leadership in Britain and the criteria which one applies to effective leaders. The media and the voters have come to expect a premier who is visionary, decisive, authoritative and able to personify the party. Mrs Thatcher was as much a product of these pressures as a cause of them. (Kavanagh, 1997, p. 200)

So far, this analysis describes the Blair 'presidency', but as the sheen is wiped off the government Blair will need his colleagues to help shoulder the blame. The nature of government will become clearer as time passes. What is certain is that this essentially flexible and adaptable system accommodates both circumstances and personalities. No single model applies over time. 'Events, dear boy, events' may produce something nearer to a collective system. Time will tell.

Note

1 The appointment of Cunningham was subsequently not regarded as a success and he left the government in the 1999 reshuffle.

Reading

Burch, M. (1994) 'The Prime Minister and Cabinet from Thatcher to Major', *Talking Politics*, 7:1, Autumn.

Crossman, R. (1963) 'Introduction to Walter Bagehot', *The English Constitution*, Fontana.

The Earl of Oxford and Asquith (1926) *Fifty Years of Parliament*, Cassell, vol. II.

Foley, M. (1994) 'Presidential politics in Britain', *Talking Politics*, 6:3, Summer.

Gray, A. and Jenkins, B. (1998) 'New Labour, new government? Change and continuity in public administration and government 1997', *Parliamentary Affairs*, 51:2, April.

Hennessy, P. (1998a) 'The Blair style of government: an historical perspective and an interim audit', *Government and Opposition*, 33:1, Winter.

Hennessy, P. (1998b) 'Re-engineering the state in flight: a year in the life of the British constitution', *Lloyds TSB*.

Hogg, S. and Hill, J. (1996) *Too Close to Call. Power and Politics – John Major in No. 10*, Warner.

James, S. (1996) 'The changing Cabinet system', *Politics Review*, 6:2, November.

Jones, B. (1999) 'Tony Blair's style of government', in B. Jones (ed.), *Political Issues in Britain Today*, Manchester University Press, 5th edn.

Kavanagh, D. (1997) *The Reordering of British Politics: Politics after Thatcher*, Oxford University Press.

Kavanagh, D. and Seldon, A. (eds) (1994) *The Major Effect*, Macmillan, 1994.

Lord Blake (1975) *The Office of Prime Minister*, Oxford University Press.

Shell, D. and Hodder-Williams, R. (eds) (1995) *Churchill to Major. The British Prime Ministership since 1945*, Hurst.

Thomas, G. P. (1998) *Prime Minister and Cabinet Today*, Manchester University Press.

Thomas, G. P. (1998/9) 'The Prime Minister and Cabinet Today', *Talking Politics*, 11:2, Winter.

Young, H. (1994) 'The Prime Minister', in Dennis Kavanagh and Anthony Seldon (eds) *The Major Effect*, Macmillan.

3

A constitutional question: the United Kingdom or federal Britain?

Colin Pilkington

Federal or unitary?

It would be convenient if all the political entities that we generically call countries, states or nations were homogeneous in having populations that are religiously, ethnically, linguistically and culturally united within clearly defined geographical boundaries. Unfortunately, this is not the case. Most countries, whether by conquest, amalgamation, annexation or mutual interest, are made up of divergent and sometimes conflicting groups: Catholics and Protestants in Ireland, Serbs and Croats in the former Yugoslavia, Flemings and Walloons in Belgium, Jews and Arabs in Israel, and so on. Virtually every state in the modern world has significant minorities within its borders that are so different ethnically or culturally that they could well form a separate national entity themselves.

One of the principal functions of a constitution is to reconcile the different social, ethnic and political groupings living within the state or other sovereign body. There are largely two ways of creating a political union out of a regional cultural diversity, these two ways being known as unitary and federal systems:

- In a *unitary system* there is one sovereign authority with the sole ability to legislate, administer and adjudicate for the whole of the state or society. If power is devolved to the regional components of that society it is with the consent of the central authority, which supervises such devolution and can revoke it. Various areas or districts of the country can pass and administer their own local laws but those laws can only be passed because the national legislature has delegated the right to make secondary law to the local authority.
- In a *federal system* the component provinces or regions within the national state each possess their own supreme authorities which have legislative and executive jurisdiction within their areas of competence; the central

authority or federal government merely retains the most important functions such as economic planning and defence. To maintain relationships
within the conflicting interests of federal component states means that a
federal system must be regulated by a written constitution and controlled
by a Supreme Court. It is these regulating bodies which decide the dividing
lines between federal and subsidiary authorities, which apportion responsibilities and which determine the extent to which the component states of
a federal body have the right to pass their own primary laws.

There are those politicians, such as Margaret Thatcher, who think of
themselves as Unionists, who campaign vigorously against what they see
as the break-up of the Union in movements towards nationalism or devolution and to whom any hint of federalism is anathema. To such politicians
the United Kingdom is the perfect example of a unitary state, with one
sovereign Parliament controlling all aspects of the governance of Great
Britain and Northern Ireland. And it is the defining feature of a unitary
system that it should have one sovereign body made up of just one executive, one legislature and one judiciary. In 1997, when framing the Scotland
Bill which would create a devolved Parliament in Edinburgh, the clause
concerning the Civil Service in Scotland stated, 'This ensures that all the
staff of the Scottish Administration should be civil servants in the Home
Civil Service. Maintaining a unified Home Civil Service is considered to be
essential for the preservation of the Union'.[1]

However, despite fulfilling the criteria of that strict definition of unity, the
United Kingdom is not, strictly speaking, a unitary state, being neither unitary
nor federal but rather is what is known more simply as a *union state*:

- Like a unitary state it has a single sovereign Parliament but that Parliament did not originate as a single body but grew from the merger of previously separate assemblies, formed through the Union of the English
  Parliament with the councils, assemblies or parliaments of Wales (1536),
  Scotland (1707) and Ireland (1801). Compared with a federal structure,
  therefore, the component Parliaments have surrendered their jurisdiction
  and sovereignty and, even where some devolution of power occurred, as
  was the case with the Stormont government of Northern Ireland, the
  devolved assembly nevertheless remained subordinate to the national
  Parliament and could be suppressed, as indeed was Stormont when direct
  rule was imposed in 1972.
- Unlike a unitary state, on the other hand, the component nations of the UK
  continue to possess pre-Union rights and institutions peculiar to themselves
  which maintain some degree of administrative autonomy. This is even
  reflected in the constitutional terms given to the component parts of the
  Union: England and Scotland are kingdoms, Wales a principality and Northern Ireland a province. The most obvious example of differing political

institutions is the Scottish legal system, which is distinct from the English system in enacted law, judicial procedure and the structure of the courts. There are also other factors, as with the issue of Scottish banknotes or an education system so different that someone with an English teaching qualification cannot automatically work in Scottish schools. In Wales there is legislation ensuring that the Welsh language has equal status with English in the courts, schools and local administrations. Northern Ireland is the one part of the United Kingdom which up to now has been allowed to use proportional representation regularly in elections and which has its own distinct Civil Service. And these three national entities within the UK have had their own government departments for some time in the Scottish, Welsh and Northern Ireland Offices, providing administrative devolution in a number of discrete areas. Even England has semi-autonomous regions in the palatinates of Chester, Durham and Lancaster; each of which has had its own legal institutions and courts in the past, and the last of which has its own Cabinet minister in the Chancellor of the Duchy of Lancaster. For all these reasons and more, the UK cannot be regarded as ever having been a single monolithic structure.

Devolution or subsidiarity?

Devolution is the process by which political power is transferred from the centre to local or regional bodies, which carry out governmental functions while leaving sovereignty in the hands of central government. It appeals to the British public outside London, who resent the domination of south-eastern England and feel alienated as a result, and is particularly true of Scotland, a separate country until 1707, and for Wales, with its own language and culture: although it is a reaction not unknown in parts of England such as Cornwall and Tyneside, which feel just as equally distant and alienated from a political culture based in the south-east.

Devolution is not new in the UK:

- When Ireland achieved Home Rule in the 1920s, six predominately Protestant counties in the north-east formed a separate province still subordinate to the British Crown and with MPs in the Westminster Parliament, but where most executive, legislative and administrative matters were devolved to a Northern Ireland Parliament at Stormont which lasted until 1972. This devolved government was restored in 1998 as a result of the Good Friday settlement for Northern Ireland.
- In Scotland a movement for Home Rule began in the nineteenth century; alongside that for Ireland, ten Home Rule Bills were presented to Parliament between 1886 and 1914. The Scottish National Party (SNP) was founded in 1927 but made little headway until the 1960s, when alienation

from the unionist parties and the discovery of North Sea oil led to an up-surge in nationalism. The minority Labour government tried to gain the support of the SNP after 1976, a proposal for a devolved Scottish Parliament being put to the Scottish people in a referendum in 1979. Of those who turned out to vote 51.6 per cent said 'Yes', but that was only 20 per cent of the electorate and a winning threshold of 40 per cent of the total electorate had been imposed.

• Home Rule Bills were proposed for Wales at the end of the nineteenth century, but these were even less successful than those for Scotland. Since Welsh nationalism is a cultural thing linked to the Welsh language, and only about 20 per cent of the people of Wales speak Welsh, the nationalist movement has tended to become concentrated in the north-west and west where Welsh is most widely spoken. Many cultural aspirations were achieved when Welsh-language activists forced the government into recognising the legal existence of Welsh, enacting a requirement for there to be bi-lingual official forms and road signs, although these limited successes did seem to do little more than whet the nationalists' enthusiasm for more political recognition. In the 1960s and 1970s Plaid Cymru began to win by-elections and Wales was also offered devolution in 1979. This was rejected in a referendum, only 20 per cent voting 'Yes' to 80 per cent voting 'No'.

By 1980, devolution was declared a dead issue in both Scotland and Wales and was ignored by the Thatcher government. However, the sidelining of local government during the 1980s led to an increased awareness of the gulf between decision makers in London and the general public in the rest of the UK. This led to renewed calls for devolution, not only for Scotland and Wales but as a possibility for the regions of England; not to mention its relevance for the possible settlement of the Northern Ireland situation.

While the Tory governments of the early 1990s were very much opposed to political devolution, they were nevertheless quite happy with administrative devolution as represented by the Scottish and Welsh Offices. In November 1995 plans were announced which would have increased the powers and scope of the Scottish Grand Committee and created a new standing committee for Scottish legislation, hopefully giving Scotland a new voice at Westminster without weakening the Union in any way at all. The Major government had lost the 1997 election before these plans could be put into effect but the plans were indicative of how the Conservatives were thinking.

In England, in 1994, as part of the same programme of administrative devolution that hopefully would defuse demands for political devolution, the government created ten Government Offices for the Regions, merging the regional offices of the Departments of the Environment, Employment, Transport, and Trade and Industry. These integrated offices served the same administrative functions for the English regions as the Northern Irish, Scottish and Welsh Offices have done for the national regions. In 1998 the Labour government followed the lead set by the Conservatives and these ten regional offices were reinforced by eight Regional Development Agencies, which John Prescott as Minister for the Regions, and an enthusiast for devolution to the English regions, would like to see as embryo strategic authorities, if not actual regional governments.

A political concept often associated with devolution is *subsidiarity*, which, as a term, has been in use for some time. However, it came to have a specific application in the negotiation sessions leading to the Treaty on European Union (Maastricht), when a particular interpretation of subsidiarity was developed in order to counter British fears of what was seen as the pro-federalism of the Maastricht Agreement. In Britain, unlike the rest of Europe, federalism was equated with centralism, giving rise to fears of a powerful federal administration in Brussels imposing its will on the member states, with no regard being paid to the wishes of national Parliaments. What was developed at Maastricht, therefore, was a form of subsidiarity, defined in the Treaty as being when *decisions are taken as closely as possible to the citizen*: 'In areas which do not fall within its exclusive competence, the Community should take action, in accordance with the principle of subsidiarity, only in so far as the proposed action cannot sufficiently be achieved by the Member States and can therefore, by reason of the scale or effects of the proposed action, be better achieved by the Community.'[2]

The argument against the centralising powers of the EU is that Brussels is deemed to be too remote from the people and, for certain critical legislation, decisions need to be taken by competent authorities closer to the people – such as national governments. It is here that the proponents of subsidiarity seem to have made a rod for their own backs, since simply because a proposal is thought to be inappropriate for Community action does not necessarily mean that action by national governments is any more appropriate: it could well be that regional or local action might be more suitable. Certainly, the SNP adopted the concept of subsidiarity with enthusiasm, with its slogan of 'Scotland in Europe', meaning that, in matters of importance to Scotland, there need be no intervening English-dominated body between Brussels and a Scottish Assembly or Council. There is, however, an anomaly in the fact that, although the Conservative government advocated subsidiarity to prevent centralisation in Brussels, that government remained very ardently centralist in its management of the affairs of the United Kingdom.

Federal union or independence?

For a long time the debate over the constitution in Britain has been the debate as to whether a federal or unitary government is the best solution. Over recent years, however, there have been a number of factors that have moved the debate on into new fields, turning it into one which seeks to retain the

United Kingdom as a union state despite the virtually irresistable impetus towards fragmentation represented by the various nationalist and separatist forces at work. There was a time when an approximation of a unitary constitution was believed to be the best guarantee of union but recent years have seen a move towards devolution as offering a federal option as an alternative form of unionism, so as to prevent any possible break-up of the United Kingdom through demands for complete independence for the constituent parts.

The factors leading towards devolution have included:

- The successive recessions of the 1980s and early 1990s hit the outlying regions of the United Kingdom such as Scotland and Wales – and indeed those northern and western parts of England such as Cornwall and Cumbria – with far worse effect than they did the Home Counties of England.
- Feelings grew in Scotland and Wales that the London Parliament had neither the time nor the interest to give proper consideration to non-English problems. For example, Alex Salmond, leader of the SNP, reported that, during the whole of 1996 the House of Commons spent only one hour discussing the Scottish National Health Service, as against days of debate concerning the NHS in England and Wales.
- The British government has proved very ready to experiment with new political initiatives by imposing them on the Welsh or Scots before the English. For example, the highly unpopular poll tax, which caused riots when introduced into England and which had to be withdrawn as the first act of the post-Thatcher government, was imposed on Scotland for a whole year before it was applied to England. In Wales the reform of local government was not open to public debate as it had been in England. Instead the Principality had a system of unitary authorities imposed upon it by the *diktat* of the Secretary of State for Wales (who, ironically enough, was himself English).
- For eighteen years the United Kingdom had a series of Conservative governments, and yet over the same period both Scotland and Wales returned an ever-decreasing number of Conservative MPs in successive elections. For all those eighteen years there were large stretches of the United Kingdom which had political loyalties – to Labour, to the Liberal Democrats or to the Nationalists – that were diametrically opposed to the governing party of what was supposed to be a united country.
- Pressure groups working for changes in the political community, such as Charter 88, have encouraged the growth of what has been called the *bottom-up* process, in which the demands of the people are heard and followed by the policy makers, rather than a *top-down* process, where the wishes of the policy makers are imposed on the people. Such a process demands something like devolution in order to produce the subsidiarity which brings decision making closer to the people.

- There were those, even among those who wished to see Britain remain a united kingdom, who saw that resistance to the more moderate forms of devolution played into the hands of those nationalists who called for complete separation. It is recognised for instance that, prior to 1916, the people of Ireland would have been quite content with the form of devolution known as Home Rule which had been suggested by Gladstone and others. It was the refusal of successive British governments to grant Home Rule, coupled with the brutal repression of those who openly supported separation, which led to a hardening of attitudes, the elevation of extremist activists into the role of patriotic martyrs and thereby ultimately to the separation of the Republic of Ireland from the United Kingdom.

These various factors working together since 1980 had led to a situation by the time of the 1997 general election in which all major parties – with the single exception of the Conservative Party – were in favour of some form of devolution – for Scotland and Wales at least. As a result, negotiations on devolution began immediately after the Labour government took over in May 1997, leading inevitably to legislative action since Labour had the wholehearted support of the Liberal Democrats and the nationalist parties. Devolution for Northern Ireland, as it was developed after the 1998 Good Friday Agreement, was slightly different in being a pragmatic decision, imposed of necessity on a bitterly divided community that had already had decades of experience of devolved government. It therefore represents a special case outside the normal arguments for and against devolution.

Proposals for Scottish devolution resulted in a Scottish Parliament of 129 members in Edinburgh, 73 members being elected by 'first past the post' in the existing parliamentary constituencies but with 56 top-up additional members chosen proportionately in the country's regional Euro-constituencies. The Scottish Parliament has all the powers of the Scottish Office and is able to legislate on anything at all which concerns Scotland, with the exceptions of overall economic planning, some Home Office concerns, foreign affairs and defence. The Scottish Parliament also has tax-raising powers, able to deviate from the standard UK income tax rate by plus or minus three pence, powers which represent the ability to pass some primary legislation. Within the Parliament there is a Scottish executive, with its own Chief Minister, although there is still a Secretary of State for Scotland to represent Scottish interests at Westminster.

In Wales the plans for devolution produced a sixty-member Assembly with forty members elected by 'first past the post' and twenty additional members elected proportionately for five Euro-constituencies. Unlike Scotland, the Assembly is unable to pass primary legislation and does not have tax-raising powers. As an example of devolution within devolution there are built-in safeguards to protect the interests of north and rural Wales against domination by Cardiff. As is the case with Scotland, Wales continues to be represented at Westminster by a Secretary of State.

As regards devolution for England, the Labour manifesto in the 1997 election stated that 'demand for regional government so varies across England that it would be wrong to impose a uniform system'. The most likely form of devolution for England is an extension of the plan for elected mayors, not only in London but for other major cities, in what has been called 'a great experiment in sub-national government . . . a force for more social democracy'.

With devolution having gained official recognition, backed up by legislation, the argument has switched to the relative merits of:

- a devolved, and possibly federal, Britain which nevertheless remains a United Kingdom;
- the fragmentation of Great Britain into the independent countries of England, Scotland and Wales.

The Labour Party, with its Liberal Democratic allies, sees devolution as the means by which a union state might be maintained. Nevertheless, there are two other perspectives that, although completely opposed to each other in virtually everything else, nevertheless view devolution as the first irrevocable step that will lead inevitably towards independence for the constituent countries of the UK.

The Conservative perspective

The Conservative point of view, a view which led the party to head the 'Just Say No' campaign in the devolution referendums, carries the very strong conviction that the devolution of government means the fatal weakening of the cement binding the Union. According to those Tories such as Sir Teddy Taylor who ardently campaign against devolution:

- The Scottish Parliament and the Welsh Assembly have such limited powers that they are little more than sterile talking shops, a waste of time and money.
- Any regional parliaments or assemblies are bound to be in permanent conflict with Westminster over responsibility and resources.
- Regional parliaments and assemblies represent yet another unwanted layer of government for an already over-governed people.
- If Scotland and Wales have their own assemblies where they can deal with Scottish and Welsh affairs without English interference, but also continue to send representatives to Westminster who have a say in English affairs, then this is bound to lead to English resentment and the possibility of separatist demands not only by England, but by the English regions as well.
- These varied conflicts inherent in devolution will tend to lead to calls for the regional chambers to go their own way and separate from a Westminster that is preventing them from reaching their potential.

The nationalist perspective

Both the SNP and Plaid Cymru feel that, while devolution is better than nothing, there remain powers in the hands of Westminster which would be much better and more democratically dealt with in Edinburgh or Cardiff. As far as Scotland is concerned, for example, Alex Salmond of the SNP has mentioned:

- A defence policy that sees nuclear missiles based on Scottish soil against the wishes of the Scottish people.
- The unfairness of an economic policy which sees oil revenues generated in Scottish oil fields largely go to swell the British coffers in London.
- A policy towards the EU which ignores the need for Scotland to speak directly to Brussels.

Between these two perspectives, which would either like to see devolution scrapped in favour of returning to a unitary state or would prefer the option of going forward to full independence, there is a third way in which the Labour government and its allies see the application of devolved government as the surest safeguard of a continued Union. On 12 November 1998, an article entitled 'The SNP nightmare', by Gordon Brown, Chancellor of the Exchequer, appeared in the *Guardian*.

As his starting point, Gordon Brown took a proposition by Arthur Schlesinger which states that 'countries break up when they fail to give ethnically diverse peoples compelling reasons to see themselves as part of the same nation'. The question according to Brown was whether there was a sufficient degree of common interest to keep the different nations of Britain together and to repel the political nationalism that would tear the UK apart. The Chancellor saw the conflict between the Labour Party and the SNP as being a conflict between the politics of social justice and the politics of ethnic identity.

What Brown is calling for is a unified country within which diversity is welcomed and celebrated in what he calls 'a multi-cultural, multi-ethnic and multi-national Britain' – the triumph of a new pluralism. This recognises the fact that there are some things which have a local or regional imperative which need to be dealt with by seeking to get close to the people through the national divisions of Britain. On the other hand, there are some things, such as the NHS, the burden of public spending and national economic policy, that can only be supported by the solidarity of common citizenship across the entire United Kingdom. As Brown himself says in conclusion, 'we achieve more working together than working apart . . . solidarity, the shared endeavour of working and co-operating together, not separation, is the ideal worth celebrating, and [we need to recognise] that the future in a global economy lies in a new pluralism'.

Devolution: alternative outcomes

Devolution is now in place, with a Parliament in Scotland and an Assembly in Wales, but the result of the devolution process has yet to be seen. Already the Speaker of the House of Commons has had to forbid discussion of matters that are now the concern of Edinburgh or Cardiff, and an increasing number of voices are asking by what right Scottish and Welsh MPs can discuss and vote on purely English matters. There would seem to be two possible outcomes:

1   A devolved, federal Britain which remains a Union state

- England, or the English regions, would have to be granted devolved status.
- The House of Commons might well become the English Parliament, dealing with devolved powers.
- A reformed and elected House of Lords could become a federal Parliament, dealing with those matters not regarded as devolved issues.
- There could be further devolution by the creation of elected mayors and strategic authorities beyond London.
- Full devolution along these lines will prevent conflicts between national and regional parliaments and will prevent the devolved bodies from being mere 'talking-shops'.

2   The break-up of Great Britain with independence for England,
Scotland and Wales

- This is likely to begin with Scotland, where the SNP is already set to become the largest party in the Scottish Parliament.
- There are bound to be disagreements over an economic policy which appears to favour the London economy at the expense of the devolved regions.
- The regional policy of the EU will strengthen those in Scotland and Wales who wish to have direct relations with Brussels and ignore London.

Notes

1   Scottish Office (1998) The Scotland Bill, Clause 47.
2   Treaty for European Union, Title II, article 3b.

Reading

Lynch, P. (1996) 'Labour, devolution and the West Lothian question', *Talking Politics*, Autumn.

Lynch, P. (1997/98) 'Devolution and a new British political system', *Talking Politics*, Winter.

Mitchell, J. (1996) 'Reviving the Union State', *Politics Review*, February.

Moran, M. (1995) 'Reshaping the British State', *Talking Politics*, Spring.

Pilkington, C. (1999) *The Politics Today Companion to the British Constitution*, Manchester University Press.

4

The Belfast Agreement: as good as it gets or worst of all possible worlds?

Arthur Aughey

The Belfast Agreement comprises the following key elements:

- A 108-member Assembly to cover matters devolved to it by Westminster. The Assembly can only take decisions on a cross-community basis, meaning either majorities of both unionists and nationalists present and voting, or 60 per cent of all members including at least 40 per cent of unionists and 40 per cent of nationalists.
- An Executive of that Assembly chaired by a First Minister and Deputy First Minister responsible for policy on matters such as economic development, education and agriculture. The Executive is not to be chosen by the First and Deputy First Ministers. Parties with sufficient seats in the Assembly are automatically eligible for ministerial office (allocated according to the d'Hondt procedure).
- Westminster to retain control of matters relating, for instance, to security foreign policy, taxation and the European Union. There will be a continuing role for the Secretary of State for Northern Ireland.
- A North/South Ministerial Council to consult on cross-border policy co-operation between the Northern Irish Executive and the government of the Irish Republic. The Council will be accountable to the Assembly and to the Irish Parliament.
- A British–Irish Council comprising representatives of the British and Irish governments, and members of the newly devolved institutions in Northern Ireland, Scotland and Wales. Its purpose will be to consult on matters of mutual interest.
- Co-operation between London and Dublin to continue in a new British–Irish Intergovernmental Conference, although members of the Northern Ireland Executive will be eligible to participate in its deliberations.
- Articles 2 and 3 of the Republic's constitution (which made a claim to the territory of Northern Ireland) to be amended to embody the principle of consent in Northern Ireland for constitutional change.

- Provision for the early release of terrorist prisoners over a two-year period.
- Provision for reform of the policing system.
- Provision for the decommissioning of terrorist weapons over a two-year period.
- Provision to ensure equality of rights for all in Northern Ireland.

The case for the Belfast Agreement

This Agreement takes seriously the claims of both unionism and nationalism. But it also suggests how their assumptions might be opened up to reflection and self criticism. And it is by so opening them up that a worthwhile future can be secured. The key starting point of such reflection and self criticism is, as the Agreement yet again confirms, that it is both politically unacceptable and morally unconscionable to solve political problems by force.

In terms of the conflict it seeks to address, the Agreement is based on the following reading of the positions of nationalism and unionism.

- At the heart of nationalist politics, constitutional or republican, is an aspiration to Irish unity. The supplementary assumption of nationalists is that there does indeed exist a single Irish nation. That nation has been denied its political completion. Its right to self determination has been frustrated.
- The real problem for Irish nationalists is that the majority of people in Northern Ireland do not understand themselves to be members of the Irish nation as defined by Irish nationalists. No statements of goodwill or promises of generosity have been sufficient to dispel the unionist suspicion that the political project of Irish nationalism – as formulated and re-formulated by its ideologues – is designed ultimately to defeat and to destroy them. Unionists will not be allowed to be 'Irish' on their own terms but will be compelled to subscribe to an alien dogma. And unionists simply refuse to be defined in those terms.
- At the heart of Ulster unionism is the fact of the Union. The assumption of unionism is that continued membership of the British state is necessary for its protection and survival on the island of Ireland. Its contemporary supplementary assumption is that the acknowledgement of the authority of the British state in Northern Ireland is a sufficient condition for the accommodation of cultural and religious diversity. In sum, unionists propose that the stability of British statehood in Northern Ireland is the only guarantee of sustaining rights, liberties and public welfare.
- The real problem for unionists has been that a minority in Northern Ireland has never fully acknowledged the legitimacy of the state because the character of that state is held to be incompatible with that minority's sense of its own nationhood.

Catholics simply cannot accept the unionist position if it means giving up permanently their aspiration to Irish unity. For most Catholics, Northern Ireland as constituted hitherto is not understood to be a political form which allows for equality of respect. On the contrary, they believe that it has sustained inequality.

However, just as many northern Protestants have continued to think of themselves as Irish, or Northern Irish, by nationality and to distinguish between that and support for Irish unity, so too have many northern Catholics distinguished between emotional attachment to the symbols of British statehood and a utilitarian calculation of the material and civic advantages of membership of that state. The persistence of the traditional conflict between unionism and nationalism has never permitted any substantial connection between these calculations – affective or utilitarian – and political stability. There have been many honourable proposals in the past to change that reality. The Agreement is yet another but this time makes that connection a real possibility.

If one accepts the realistic constraints of British and Irish policy and holds to the principles of non-violence and consent, then certain logical possibilities are laid out in the Agreement which assume, but also test to the limit, the good faith of politicians. That is a risk but there comes a time when risks have to be taken. You cannot learn to swim without getting wet. If Northern Ireland politicians are ever to regain a sense of responsibility for policy making, then at some time they must be (substantially) trusted to take the necessary plunge. The Agreement does this in the following and balanced way.

- If nationalists really are sincere about persuading unionists of the value of being fully part of an Irish nation, and if they are sincere about an inclusive rather than exclusive definition of it, then it is reasonable to expect that they should be true to their own assumption – namely, that the harmony of the nation is the pre-condition for the unity of the state. That end should be worked for at commercial, cultural and environmental levels, which could realise practically the benefits, where possible, of an island community. On the other hand, unionists too should acknowledge that there may be positive benefits to be had by working co-operatively and constructively at all these levels. These communities of interest, if they were to be realised, would be defined by unionist as well as nationalist expectations. This is provided for in the work of the North–South Council. In sum, since nationalists assert the primacy of a pre-political unity (the nation), then it cannot be imagined without unionist consent.
- With a coerced or enforced political unity off the agenda the 'oneness' of the island in many mutually beneficial ways can become a practical reality. This would enable people in Northern Ireland to live their lives – business, cultural, social – if they so wished, partly or even mainly in the context of the whole island without in any way weakening the position of

Northern Ireland as part of the United Kingdom. This now becomes a real possibility under the terms of the Agreement. This is an 'agreed', not a 'united', Ireland.

- If unionists are really sincere about the positive benefits of British statehood then one would expect them too to act on the basis of their own assumption. Just as pursuit of cultural and economic co-operation on the island of Ireland pre-supposes the detachment of the idea of the nation from the idea of ethnic homogeneity, then so too would the pursuit of equality within Northern Ireland as part of the United Kingdom depend on the detachment of the state from a single community. Since 1972 this has happened anyway, driven mainly, though not exclusively, by British policy. Unionists are invited to recognise necessity and to make a virtue of it. Unionist interests can best be served within a framework acknowledging cultural diversity, a framework which would not be incompatible with the political Britishness of Northern Ireland. Provisions for the Assembly and the British–Irish Council hold out the possibility of achieving this. And it remains an obligation for nationalists, on that basis, to participate constructively in a system which would accord them equality of status and equality of rights.
- If unionist consent is required for constitutional change, unionists must recognise the need for nationalist consent to a settlement which enables them to live in dignity and security short of unity or joint authority. And as the European Union develops a common citizenship, residents of Northern Ireland could be in the happy position of being British, Irish or European as the mood takes them while remaining, constitutionally, citizens of the United Kingdom. Once again this becomes a possibility under the terms of the Agreement. This is an 'agreed', not a unionist, Northern Ireland.

In sum, respect for the principle of consent in the Agreement severely qualifies the aspirational drive of contemporary Irish nationalism. But the changes required are also far from congenial to the immobilism of traditional Ulster unionism. Nevertheless, new conditions might be built which could deprive them of their destabilising power.

Despite what was achieved on Good Friday 1998, of course, it is still not certain if the people of Northern Ireland can achieve a sustainable and workable compromise which would bear any relationship to the logic outlined here. On the other hand, the Agreement invites the acknowledgement that to seek the attainable is not to sacrifice political imagination but rather to demand it. It invites the people of Northern Ireland – indeed the peoples of these islands – to re-write their story and to substitute an epic of peace for an epic of war. It is an enterprise worth the risk. Indeed, it is an enterprise substantially endorsed by the people of Ireland, north and south, voting in the referendum of 22 May 1998.

What does the result of the referendum tell us about the Agreement? It tells us five things.

- First, the result confirmed the democratic legitimacy of the Agreement. Furthermore, it establishes the Agreement's moral authority. The 71 per cent vote in favour within Northern Ireland and the 95 per cent vote in favour in the Republic of Ireland have brought into existence a new potential for political accommodation. The Agreement can be said to provide an escape from the violent and self-destructive code which has characterised politics in Northern Ireland for the last thirty years. In particular, it allows those hung up on historical hooks to escape from ideological futility. In the light of what might now appear possible, political parties and paramilitary groups can acknowledge the self-defeating commitments formerly and dogmatically held. One might say 'that was then and this is now', and acknowledge that some possibilities are more promising than others.
- Second, the possibility provided by the Agreement is the consolidation of 'middle Ulster', those of whatever class and whatever religion who have an interest in peace, security and stability. Middle Ulster has not been engaged in the hot war of paramilitarism but it has been part of a communal cold war, the major weapon of which has been suspicion. The artist Wassily Kandinsky believed that in the course of the twentieth century we would see the triumph of 'and' over 'either/or'. Northern Ireland is potentially on course to achieve that objective. In short, instead of divisive contention it is now possible to envisage connection between unionists and nationalists. Furthermore, middle Ulster now has the opportunity to engage intelligently once again with the corresponding 'middle Ireland' in the Republic. This connection potentially puts together an island-wide constituency in favour of stability, the value of which should not be lost on both communities in Northern Ireland and is certainly not lost on the British and Irish governments.
- Third, the achievement of the Agreement is that it provides for a new and possibly decisive condition. Post referendum, that condition may be taken to represent an act of self determination within the terms of the Downing Street Declaration of December 1993, namely that 'it is for the people of the island of Ireland alone, by agreement between the two parts respectively, to exercise their right of self-determination on the basis of consent, freely and concurrently given, North and South'. This is an 'agreed' Ireland, not a united Ireland. Behind this consensus now stand not only the British and Irish governments but also the governments of the United States and of the European Union as well as international opinion.
- Fourth, it is impossible to say, of course, with absolute certainty that the Agreement has finally eliminated violence for good. However, there is reason to believe that, when the institutions provided for in the Agreement begin to deliver, there will continue to be a marginalisation of those organisations which would try to assert the priority of unfinished historical business over the compromises so arduously worked for. For example, the decisive response of the British and Irish governments to the Omagh

bomb outrage on 15 August 1998 and, moreover, the rejection of that violent act by everyone in Ireland, would appear to confirm that assumption. In this sense, and despite the apocalyptic concerns voiced by those opposed to the Agreement on the unionist side, it is difficult to envisage the sort of sustained terrorist campaigns which Northern Ireland has witnessed over the last three decades. The moral obligation now rests post Agreement with the (former) terrorists to disarm and to make the irrevocable transition to democracy.

- Fifth, the referendum result shows how to deal with the problem of 'terrorists (i.e. Sinn Fein) in government'. In the spirit of the Agreement and a new beginning in Northern Ireland there would be a fundamental distinction between having an electoral mandate and subscribing to the requirements of governmental authority. The first is a factual statement, a percentage argument. The second is an ethical requirement. The numerical claim of the first must not outweigh the ethical requirement of the second because proper acknowledgement of a mandate for government depends upon an acceptance not only of the letter laid down in the Agreement but also of its spirit. No one, in other words, can claim a mandate to do wrong. Wrong in this case means profiting by the advantages of democratic procedure but refusing to accept the obligations of democratic procedure. In practice this would mean a declaration that war is no longer an option in Northern Ireland and that terrorist weapons will be decommissioned. People in Northern Ireland now have a real chance to force terrorists, with the moral authority of everyone on the island of Ireland, to accept that: 'Your day is done. Give peace a chance. It's time for politics.'

In short, the truth of the matter is simple. In the words of the First Minister of Northern Ireland, David Trimble, the Agreement is 'as good as it gets'. This is a valid judgement not only for Ulster unionists but also for everyone in Northern Ireland and for the rest of the United Kingdom. Working the Agreement satisfactorily will change the whole international perception of Northern Ireland. From an example of bigotry and violent contention Northern Ireland will become an example of how to overcome an ancient quarrel and how politics can give hope for the future.

The case against the Belfast Agreement

The faith that it is possible to get agreement on the future of Northern Ireland rests on certain rationality assumptions about the parties involved. A simple distillation would be this. A settlement would be possible if all the parties in Northern Ireland came to accept the impracticality of winning outright but yet came to realise that it was possible to obtain objectives important for their respective communities. This view involves three interlocking assumptions:

- that a rational distinction can be made between political symbol and political substance;
- that politicians in Northern Ireland are capable of recognising the distinction between symbol and substance;
- that a deal could be made on the basis of politicians reasoning the value of substantial advantages even if they had to swallow a certain amount of distasteful symbolism.

In short, the calculation has been that unionists will ultimately swallow the symbolism of cross-border co-operation with the Republic of Ireland in order to secure the substance of Northern Ireland's place within the United Kingdom, and that nationalists will ultimately swallow the symbolism of Northern Ireland's Britishness in order to secure the substance of what John Hume has called a 'new beginning' for relationships on the island along with 'parity of esteem' for the nationalist tradition. The Belfast Agreement incorporates these very elements.

Unfortunately, Northern Ireland politics is based on very different rationality assumptions. Symbol is not distinguishable from substance. Symbol is substance. And those symbols – ending Dublin's interference in Northern Ireland's affairs or ending British rule in Ireland – are ultimately worth fighting for. They are symbols of identity and that is precisely what politics in Northern Ireland is about – a struggle over identity. A supposed historic compromise with the enemy can never be seen as merely a symbolic gesture to satisfy the aspirations or concerns of the other side but rather as a substantial concession to the goal of that enemy. British policy, in its spurious quest for a balanced accommodation in Northern Ireland, has never understood the nature of that struggle. So therefore it is quite an impossible prospectus which claims that the Agreement can satisfy two mutually antagonistic positions. It cannot possibly be true that at one and the same time unionists can think that the Agreement means that Northern Ireland's place within the United Kingdom is safe and that nationalists/republicans can believe that the Agreement means that their objective of Irish unity is substantially advanced. Something – or someone – will have to give.

Indeed, the sort of emollient language of political civility which has formed the discourse of the pro-Agreement case – and which sounds so promising to British public opinion – is part of the new weaponry of communal warfare. The Agreement's advocates have become accomplished at trying to convince people that two competing opposites – unionism and nationalism – can make a single positive whole. The consequence of such logical absurdity will be a political disaster. And the absurdity of the pro-Agreement position is that it envisages Northern Ireland entering what the American novelist Kurt Vonnegut, in *The Sirens of Titan*, once described as a 'chrono-synclastic infundibulum'. A chrono-synclastic infundibulum is a place where the normal experience of political humanity – that there are some political issues about which people just cannot agree – can be overcome. A chrono-synclastic infundibulum is a place where all the different kinds of truth – in this case pro-Union and anti-Union – can fit together as neatly as the parts of a watch. A chrono-synclastic infundibulum is, of course, fantastic nonsense.

Therefore, the spirit of universal inclusiveness found in the Agreement, in other words, has lost touch with the hard choices of politics. And in practice, in their day-to-day experience of political affairs (if not during the hype of a referendum campaign), most sensible people receive the message of this sort of inclusiveness with incredulity. Democratic politics, they know, does not entail an equal chance for everyone. Democratic politics has its own exclusions and there should be no exception for those, like the paramilitaries, loyalist and republican, who want to govern people with a portfolio in one hand and a gun in the other.

Supporters of the Agreement latch on to such pronouncements and criticise them for being too pessimistic and reactionary. They denounce their opponents for having 'no alternative'. But they fail to identify the real logical gap in their own argument. The truth of the matter is that the alternative to signing up to a bad deal – and the Agreement is a bad deal – is simply this: do not sign up to a bad deal. There are a number of elements which together constitute the bad deal.

The first element is that the Agreement, however dressed up in fine phrases, really represents an appeasement of terrorism. And like all acts of appeasement it will be seen as a sign of weakness by the terrorists, who will come back and demand more. The reason for this is that the Agreement tries to do two things at once. It tries to establish the shape of a constitutional settlement. It also tries to resolve the conflict by making significant concessions to the demands of terrorists. In the end it will neither make for workable institutions nor will it encourage terrorists to give up for good. It will not make terrorists move exclusively into democratic politics because the British and Irish governments never satisfactorily identified what was required of them.

The Agreement tacitly accepts the terrorist view of conflict resolution. Republicans have argued that the model of conflict resolution appropriate to Northern Ireland is one of constitutional transformation as in South Africa or the Middle East. However, there are really no valid parallels between the Northern Ireland case and the conflicts in South Africa and the Middle East. In South Africa the minority white government negotiated with Mandela, the representative of the vast majority of the black people there. In the Middle East the Israeli government negotiated with Arafat, also the representative of the great majority of the people of Palestine. None of these factors apply in the Northern Ireland case. The citizens of Northern Ireland already enjoy full democratic rights. The reality is that the IRA has been conducting a subversive war against the constitutional status of Northern Ireland and loyalist paramilitaries have been conducting a campaign against those they assume to be sympathetic towards the IRA. This violence has been consistently condemned by large majorities in both communities and by the representatives of all main constitutional parties north and south of the border.

The conflict resolution model only flatters the campaign of the IRA by endowing it with retrospective legitimacy and raises the very grave danger of endorsing the view that violence works. That is tantamount to creating a rod for the back of democratic politics. The Agreement is in the process of achieving the worst of all possible results – a strengthening of the violent tradition in Irish nationalism and a sanctifying of the principle of armed struggle. And the lesson, one can be sure, will not be lost on loyalist paramilitaries and a wider circle of unionist opinion.

The truth of the matter is that you cannot get political stability by appeasing terrorists. In particular, you simply cannot trust Sinn Fein/IRA to deliver on its promises. The IRA broke its first ceasefire in February 1996 without warning. And it did this in order to force more concessions out of the British government. There is no clear evidence that the IRA will not do the same thing again (which is why it is so reluctant to hand over a single weapon from its arsenal). Moreover, there is something morally outrageous and politically corrupting in the concessions made in the Agreement to the terrorist agenda – on the early release of prisoners, on reform of the police force, on demilitarisation, on the equality agenda and, above all, on decommissioning (or rather, the lack of it).

The decommissioning of terrorist weapons is not a distraction from the main issue. It is the issue. It is the issue of whether private armies are willing to surrender to the principles of democratic procedure. If nothing is done about the military capacity of the IRA then the centre of gravity of politics is fundamentally skewed. Why? Because only states have armies and Sinn Fein, with its army *in situ*, takes on the character of a shadow state. Sinn Fein needs the arms of the IRA to remain un-decommissioned in order to retain that self-styled status. Under the terms of the Agreement there is no requirement on their part to disarm. Whatever disarmament takes place may only be token. That is why no right-thinking democrat can accept it.

Furthermore, a particular concern which is not at all addressed by those who support the Agreement is that the terrorist struggle will simply enter into a new phase precisely because the apologists for terror have been let into the citadel of democracy. The Agreement and its structures will now become the focus of a renewed campaign of destabilisation. This real concern is composed of a number of parts:

- The politics of revolutionary movements such as Sinn Fein/IRA is all about manoeuvre and manipulation, the intention of which is to weaken their opponents. No consensus on Northern Ireland's position can exist while such views are politically rewarded. And the institutions of the Agreement, far from providing a forum in which inter-communal bargains can be translated into collective stability, will become yet another site of sectarian disorder.
- Sinn Fein/IRA will try to subvert good government in its 'long march through the institutions'. Republicans will make no honest attempt to make the devolved Assembly work, but will only seek either to subvert or ignore

it, and try to make political gains from such subversion. This is unacceptable in a modern democratic society.

- Reform of the police force into local units and the reduction of security
  presence will allow paramilitary groups, republican and loyalist, to exert
  authority in certain areas of Northern Ireland. What is being officially sanctioned is the existence of political mafias. These mafias will enjoy the rules
  of democratic practice and the civilities of a liberal society while denying
  them to others. That contradiction is exemplified by a form of criminal
  behaviour. It tends to justify itself politically by proclaiming that the end
  justifies the means. The means are murder, intimidation, personation and
  extortion. The end is whatever the organisation decrees.

The second element of the bad deal is that the system of government for
Northern Ireland is such a Heath-Robinson contraption that it can never work
in practice. Indeed, it could be argued that the procedures for the operation of
the Assembly actually reveal the problem. If there were sufficient consensus
between unionists and nationalists/republicans about the government of Northern Ireland, then procedures of the Byzantine sort outlined for the Assembly
(see above) would be unnecessary. If there were not such a consensus then
arrangements of this kind would not work anyway. From this impossible
basis for sound administration, the following outcomes can be envisaged:

- The Assembly's Executive will not be able to form a coherent government,
  will have no negotiated programme and, because the parties are actually
  antagonistic, will encourage policy fragmentation and wasteful duplication.
- Since the d'Hondt procedure means that for Executive office neither the
  merit principle nor the electoral principle applies to the holding of office
  there will be no political consequences for bad government. This will lead
  to complacency and corruption.
- The political game will become one of shifting the blame. The parties will
  blame the Secretary of State for inadequate financial resources and other
  parties for failing to agree to their own favourite schemes. Add to this the
  presence of one or more parties with a vested interest in destabilising the
  state, and the prospects for good government are nil.

The third element of the bad deal is that the Agreement will undermine
the pillars of democratic culture in Northern Ireland. The prospect is not so
much nightmarish as Weimarish. Accepting the Agreement is tantamount to
accepting the suicide of public virtue which occurred in inter-war Germany.
For it is suicidal to confound the link between government and democratic
virtue. Bi-communalism – or what used to be called the 'institutionalisation of
sectarianism' – is the basis of the deal. Such politics, despite all the wonderful
claims made by supporters of the Agreement, will mean the sacrifice of political virtue in government to communal demands. This is an outcome of
despair. This will happen in the following ways:

- Despite the years of political violence and disruption, the Civil Service has ensured proper public provision and implemented, in a fair and equitable manner, government policy. Under the terms of the Agreement, civil servants will now operate in a political environment where it will not be so easy to bypass the sectarian impulse of local politics in the name of efficiency or of administrative expertise. Moreover, civil servants will come under tremendous pressure to sacrifice professionalisation for politicisation. Since their departmental political masters will be permanently in office, the careers of individual administrators will suffer if they are critical of the party line. This will lead to the demoralisation of the brightest and the best and the erosion of the public service ethic.
- Equally, the Royal Ulster Constabulary for the last thirty years has operated as a bulwark against anarchy and chaos. The commitment to subject it to thorough reform will demoralise long-serving police officers and weaken the ability to respond to the potential of renewed terrorism. Who will risk their lives in future to defend democracy if they know that the British government will treat them as dispensible?
- Finally, the stability of any society depends on those 'middling sort' of people whose way of life the terror campaigns of republican and loyalist groups have assaulted. Lose these people and you have lost the basis for a decent society. When the cost of the Agreement is finally recognised it is precisely these people who will be lost and angry.

Far from being 'as good as it gets', the Agreement will create the worst of all possible worlds. What is more, nothing in it is a necessary evil.

The Belfast Agreement

The case for

Strengths
- After intense, exhaustive and inclusive negotiations between the Northern Ireland parties and the British and Irish governments this is the best and fairest deal possible. There is no credible alternative.
- It will secure an end to violence and consolidate peace and security.
- It is an honourable compromise which maintains the unionist principle of consent for constitutional change but also provides for the nationalist aim to have institutional relationships with the Republic of Ireland.
- It establishes the institutions and procedures which can ensure that everyone has a say in the government of Northern Ireland and that everyone's rights and interests are acknowledged and protected.

- It provides the potential to end not only the conflict in Northern Ireland but also to improve relations on the island of Ireland and between the United Kingdom and the Republic of Ireland.

Weaknesses
- It envisages too rapid a transition from a condition of sectarian conflict to one in which old enemies are required to share together Executive power.
- It leaves too vague the need for parties associated with terrorist organisations to deliver the decommissioning of illegal weapons.
- The institutions are so full of checks and balances that it will be difficult to get effective government.
- The consequence of the principle of parity of esteem may not be a lessening of communal divisions but their entrenchment and intensification as unionists and nationalists fight for the distribution of public money.
- It has created a public mood which assumes that terrorists will be treated leniently and that concessions will continue to be made to those who threaten violence.

The case against

Strengths
- It is difficult to conceive of the range of opposed views co-operating in a power-sharing Executive.
- The complex arrangements may confuse lines of responsibility and accountability, making it difficult for electors to know what is going on and who is in charge.
- Although the Agreement is supposed to be the culmination of a 'peace process' there are still murder, punishment beatings and intimidation at the hands of terrorist organisations.
- The IRA and loyalist paramilitaries refuse to disarm, suggesting that the war is not over.
- There is still little trust in Northern Ireland politics that one's opponents will fulfil their side of the bargain.

Weaknesses
- The Agreement has democratic legitimacy, having been endorsed by 71 per cent in Northern Ireland, 95 per cent in the Republic of Ireland and together by 85 per cent on the island as a whole.
- There does not appear to be a credible alternative.
- The case against seems to provide no hope for the future.
- Many of the things which it opposes, such as reform of the police, could happen anyway, with or without an Agreement.
- Failure of the Agreement could lead to a loss of international support for, and economic investment in, Northern Ireland.

Reading

Hadfield, B. (1998) 'The Belfast Agreement, sovereignty and the state of the Union',
    Public Law, Winter.
Meehan, E. (1999) 'The Belfast Agreement and United Kingdom Devolution', *Parlia-
    mentary Affairs*, 52:1, January.
Mitchell, G. (1999) *Making Peace: The Inside Story of the Good Friday Agreement*, Alfred
    A. Knopf.
O'Leary, B. (1999) 'Assessing the British–Irish Agreement', *New Left Review*, no. 233,
    January/February.
Parliamentary Brief, 5:6, (May/June 1998) (special Northern Ireland edition on the
    Belfast Agreement).
The Agreement (Agreement Reached in the Multi-party Negotiations) (1998) Northern
    Ireland Office.

5

A people's Europe:
federal or pragmatic?

Colin Pilkington

The nature of EU membership

When Britain joined the European Community in 1972, most people's minds were occupied with the question as to whether Britain should be a member at all. By the 1990s, however, the important issue for most people had become, not membership itself, but the form taken by the European Union (EU) and the nature of British membership. Although opinion polls carried out in 1998 showed that over 50 per cent of the British people were now in favour of membership in general terms, they also showed that some specific European institutions such as the Common Agricultural Policy (CAP) remained extremely unpopular.

Over the years there have been at least two, often opposed, perspectives concerning the nature of the European Communities which have determined the degree of British commitment to the European ideal. The position on Europe adopted by individuals, parties, or even entire countries, does not follow a consistent pattern but tends to move according to the political and economic realities of the time. Thus the typical British attitude is pragmatic: the decision to join the European Communities is essentially based on self interest, within a system where pragmatists are members of the EU for what they can get out of it.

Pragmatists:
- believe the institutions of the Union only exist to satisfy the individual needs of member states;
- are unwilling to surrender any aspect of national sovereignty;
- believe in the supremacy of the centralised nation state over the supranational institutions of the EU and regard any form of regulation by Brussels as unwanted interference in the internal affairs of member states;
- belong to the EU, even while resisting moves towards integration, for the simple reason that it is more effective to co-operate than to face cut-throat

competition in the modern global market; however they want no more than the European Single Market without the need for any other aspect of the EU;

- for most of the time favour pure, self-interested nationalism.

Federalists:

- believe that the European movement is about much more than pragmatic self interest and ought to lead to such desirable outcomes as the elimination of war in Europe;
- believe that the national interests of component states should be subordinated to the general good of the EU as a whole;
- believe in a future political and economic union of Europe, with a federal structure, forming a political and economic entity that can compete on equal terms with the political and economic power of the United States as a major factor in the global economy;
- believe in a social and humanitarian dimension for the European movement beyond the merely practical and commercial that can only benefit the social welfare and civil rights of the people of Europe.

Critics often use the term 'Euro-centrism' to describe the federal viewpoint, implying an authoritarian role for Brussels, even though 'federalism' for other people means the very reverse of 'centralisation'. However, it has to be said that this wider view of Europe is far more typical of politicians and political theorists than the people as a whole. Popular opinion, in all member states of the EU, tends to remain nationalistically inclined.

Democratic deficit

Most criticism of Europe has either concentrated on issues of sovereignty, such as pragmatism or federalism, or has been critical of the cost of membership. Comparatively little attention has been paid to accusations that the EU is undemocratic. However, it has not been uncommon for the expression 'democratic deficit' to be used by critics of the EU in their attempts to undermine European institutions. By using the term 'democratic deficit' they are usually referring to:

- the unelected powers of the European Commission;
- the fact that an unaccountable Council of Ministers forms the legislature of the EU;
- the impotence of a European Parliament with no real control over legislation;
- a European Central Bank which controls the workings of European Monetary Union (EMU) but is not under the control of any democratic body.

There is, however, an anomaly in the situation in that it is largely the most pragmatic among national parliamentarians who take the lead in criticising the EU for its lack of democratic institutions – the so-called 'democratic deficit'. After all, there is a simple solution to accusations of non-accountability and that is to strengthen the powers of the European Parliament by either:

- making more European institutions answerable to the European Parliament; or
- opening up more European legislation to scrutiny by MEPs.

The anomaly, however, arises because proposals to democratise the EU through strengthening the European Parliament are bitterly opposed by national governments, since:

- to increase the democratic nature of the European Parliament would be to legitimise its activities, whereas now its actions can be contemptuously dismissed as being 'unrepresentative', allowing national governments to ignore its deliberations;
- to legitimise the European Parliament is to strengthen it in relation to national Parliaments, to the extent that it is not impossible that national Parliaments could become irrelevant in time.

So we end with the paradox that the very ministers who criticise the Union for being 'undemocratic' are the same people who, as members of the Council of Ministers, are being undemocratic in refusing to legislate for democracy within the EU.

Instead of resolving this paradox, the critics attempt to deal with these matters of sovereignty by making use of the term 'subsidiarity', which is the concept by means of which John Major and his advisers attempted to reconcile the federalist and pragmatic positions after Maastricht. The concept of subsidiarity agrees that EU policy decisions should be made at the centre but that the way those policies are implemented should be decided as close to the people as possible. In short, application of the subsidiarity principle means that EU policy is decided in Brussels but that each national government can then interpret that policy in the way which suits the individual state's interests.

Ironically, since subsidiarity was evoked to challenge federalism, that definition of subsidiarity is what many people would define as federalism.

Contrasting views of Europe

In March 1994, Martin Kettle wrote an article in the *Guardian* newspaper defining at least four different attitudes towards Europe:

- *Euro-enthusiasts*, as typified by the Liberal Democrats, welcome member-ship of the Union and are somewhat uncritical of European measures and moves towards integration. Conservative Euro-enthusiasts have either died out or keep a very low profile in the light of current thinking within the Conservative Party.
- *'Euro-phobes'* is the more accurate term for those more popularly known as Eurosceptics, usually Conservatives such as Norman Lamont and John Redwood. They are more than merely sceptical, being hostile to anything European and would probably welcome total British withdrawal from the EU.
- *Eurosceptics*, in the true sense of the term, are what Kettle calls 'people who rather dislike Europe but are prepared to put up with it'. They accept that the EU has its uses in areas such as the Single Market but are highly sceptical about European involvement in social policy, defence or internal security. This was the position taken by the Conservatives before the 1997 election when the Euro-phobes took over.
- *Euro-progressives* or *Euro-positives*, probably represent a majority of EU citi-zens. Once in the EU, they distrust change and would hate the disruption that would be caused by attempting to leave. These are the people who, in the UK, voted to remain in Europe in the 1975 referendum and would probably vote the same way today.

The Conservatives and their anti-European stance

The EU dominated the 1997 general election to the detriment of most other issues, with the main debate focusing on the question of EMU. However, for many of those involved in the debate, arguments over EMU were just a coded way of opposing the EU in all its aspects.

At the time of Maastricht, the UK won an opt-out clause in the Treaty which meant that Britain did not have to join EMU in the first wave if it did not wish to do so and could postpone any decision on the matter until such time as the economic climate was right for British membership. At the time that this opt-out was granted there was an economic recession and no one worried overmuch about a monetary union which might never actually hap-pen. As the UK economy improved, however, with Britain easily satisfying the convergence criteria, there were those – even in the Tory government – who began to contemplate the possibility of the UK joining EMU in the first wave. The mere prospect made the Euro-phobic wing of the Conservative Party demand that the party must rule it out by declaring against membership of EMU, at any time and under any conditions.

The result of this was a strange obsession with Europe that seemed to grip the Conservatives after the election. Just as the left wing of the Labour Party insisted after 1979 that Labour lost to the Conservatives through not being sufficiently socialist in its thinking, so now did the right wing of the Conservative Party insist that it had lost to Labour through not being sufficiently anti-European. This was carried to an extreme in the Tory leadership election when William Hague, having beaten all the other right-wing candidates, announced that if he won he would appoint no one to his shadow Cabinet who did not agree to a ten-year ban on Britain joining EMU. At the 1998 party conference Hague went so far as to hold a referendum of party members to endorse his 'no entry for two parliamentary terms' policy.

There are two main points to be made with regard to the Conservatives and Europe:

- The size of the Labour majority in 1997 means that the Conservatives are completely irrelevant, with all their energy, dynamism and activism concentrated on an issue about which they are totally impotent. Most importantly, the crucial decisions on Europe, including the decision as to whether or not to join EMU, will all have been taken before the earliest date at which the Conservatives could possibly regain power.
- Europe may have been a major issue in the 1997 general election but there is no evidence that the British people are as Euro-phobic as the right wing of the Conservative Party would like to think they are. The British are sceptical in the true meaning of the term: they dislike foreigners, particularly the Germans and French; they do not like the idea of 'losing the pound' and they can get very annoyed with 'nit-picking' bureaucratic measures from Brussels. However, abstract arguments over concepts such as national sovereignty come a very poor second to bread-and-butter election issues such as taxation or education.

New Labour and its relationship with Europe

Britain's position in Europe was a priority for the Blair government after the 1997 election victory. Within days of becoming Foreign Secretary Robin Cook had committed the British government to signing the Social Chapter and had agreed to extensions of majority voting in the Council of Ministers. Doug Henderson was appointed as the first specifically European minister at the Foreign Office and it was made clear that in future inter-governmental talks Britain would be represented by a minister rather than a civil servant, as had been the case under the Tories.

This new mood of give and take meant that other member states were more ready to accommodate British positions on contentious issues. With time the honeymoon effect has worn off and Europe has become more critical of Blair and his government. But any such criticism falls far short of the outright hostility engendered by the confrontational tactics so typical of Margaret Thatcher and John Major. Very shortly after his election victory Tony Blair announced that, just as he had modernised his party into becoming New Labour, he wanted to create a new kind of Europe: a People's Europe that would empower its own citizens. And Blair stressed the central role he wanted Britain to take in the creation of this new Europe. The main tasks of the EU in the late 1990s remain the enlargement of the Union through the accession of new member states to the east; and a more positive foreign, defence and security policy, together with the creation of some form of community accountability to remove the democratic deficit. And, as to the issue of EMU and the single currency:

- Economic union, as desired by France and Germany, has gone ahead regardless and it is quite clear from statements by the Chancellor and others that Britain will join when it is most convenient and most advantageous to British interests.
- Most British worries about early membership seem far less relevant now. The electoral victory for a wait-and-see approach means that EMU is no longer a problem as far as British domestic politics are concerned – except, of course, for the Tories.

Of all European measures, British Eurosceptics are most bitterly opposed to monetary union, which they believe represents the final surrender of British sovereignty. Sceptics use patriotism as a sentimental argument against monetary union, refusing to 'give up "our" pound' in favour of the euro. However, the retention of the pound is something of a red herring. The main argument of those opposed to EMU is that the existence of a European Central Bank would mean that a British Chancellor of the Exchequer could no longer control British fiscal policy.

Monetary union

During the last period of the Major government the Euro-phobes and Eurosceptics used to comfort themselves with the thought that the single currency could never happen. Among the scenarios they envisaged was one in which not more than one or two countries would be able to meet the convergence criteria and the planned union would be unable to go ahead. Another view envisaged the peoples of the EU turning on their leaders because of economic problems and forcing them to reject EMU before it started. The Eurosceptics were encouraged in their view by a largely hostile media in Britain which concentrated on those adverse economic factors which suggested that the economies of Europe were in such a mess that EMU could never come about. What the British media ignored was the fact that the foreign exchange markets were giving most trouble to those countries like Britain that remained outside the first wave of signatories.

On 1 May 1998 the largest ever currency union in financial history was created in Brussels. In the end it transpired that only one country – Greece – had failed to meet the convergence criteria. However, despite being qualified to join, Denmark and Sweden decided to side with Britain in exercising their right to opt out of EMU for the moment. It was therefore eleven countries which actually signed the agreement on 1 May.

It would be naive to think that, by refusing to enter with the first wave of signatories and saying that the UK would only enter EMU at some indefinite future date, the Eurosceptics had won this first skirmish. Once the euro became a reality on 1 January 1999, there was a sense in which British involvement became inevitable. Euro-phobes believe that Britain has won a great victory in preserving its own currency and refusing to have anything to do with the euro, and believe, equally sincerely, that these are the outcomes most ardently desired by the people. Despite these beliefs:

- Britain will inevitably use and trade in the common currency and the London financial markets will conduct an ever-increasing share of their business in the euro.
- The eleven EU members which have agreed to the common currency represent a trading bloc with which we in this country conduct 60 per cent of our trade.
- Even before the euro was introduced, firms such as British Steel, ICI and Marks and Spencer announced that they were ready to bill and be billed in euros by their suppliers.
- Vauxhall Motors actually settled a pay deal with its British workers at the euro exchange rate.
- British citizens can open euro bank accounts and pay their bills in euros.
- If Britons holiday in France, Italy or Spain, not to mention the Republic of Ireland, they will have to deal in euros and will hardly want to face bank charges and exchange bureau commission on their return.

There is a very real possibility that, by decision time at the next election, Britain will have already drifted into acceptance and usage of the single currency – almost by default!

Summary

In an article in the *Guardian* on 26 May 1999, Polly Toynbee pointed out two contemporary events which seemed to characterise attitudes towards Europe. On Thursday 27 May, Tony Blair was due to make a speech in Paris before the other European socialist leaders in which he would hail the coming triumph of social democracy as the much-vaunted 'Third Way' which would succeed in producing a truly progressive People's Europe. On the same day, elsewhere in Europe, a sub-committee of the European Commission was due to become involved in intense negotiations aimed at framing draft regulations on the restriction of excessive sound levels, particularly in respect of a variety of appliances such as domestic lawn mowers. The implication is clear that, whereas, along with most Euro-philes, the British Prime Minister favours a visionary approach to an integrated Europe, most Euro-phobes are highly critical of an organisation which is so attached to nit-picking bureaucracy that it can spend an inordinate amount of time and money in considering the noise made by a lawn mower.

If we ask ourselves which of these two visions of Europe we can possibly call a 'People's Europe', our first impression is that the federalists and Euro-philes are trying to adopt the intellectual high ground and thereby are occupying an elitist position since they imply that only they can understand the arguments for a federal Europe. Euro-phobes, on the other hand, would claim that the people's view of Europe is typified by a hatred of such bureaucratic niceties as the straightness of bananas or whether carrots are fruit. That this is the popular view of Europe is reinforced by a constant hostility shown to the European movement by the tabloid press. So convinced are they that the people are naturally hostile to Europe that the keenest advocates of a referendum on the subject of European membership are those Eurosceptic and Euro-phobic politicians who are so certain of the universality of their opinions that they believe the majority of people would vote against any form of European integration.

So the answer would seem to be that the federal view of Europe is an elitist position, argued over by academics and politicians but very far from popular support. Whereas the true People's Europe is the Europe of the pragmatic Eurosceptic.

Yet all the evidence produced by the 1997 election and the failure of Conservative Party attempts to make Europe into a major electoral issue, not to mention the apathetic response to European elections in Britain, seems to show that the People could not care less about Europe. The pragmatic view of Europe is just as much an elitist position as the federalist perspective because it is only the politicians and the press who can be bothered to discuss Europe. Most people will grumble about 'Brussels bureaucracy' when it does things like tell them that their lawn mower is making too much noise but they will equally take advantage of the Single Market when it means cheap food and drink on a cross-Channel shopping trip. As to the loss of sovereignty or the democratic deficit, the People cannot be bothered.

The real debate: stay or go?

During all the debates on federalism versus pragmatism, on the cost of British membership and the iniquities of the CAP, there was one constant. Even the most Eurosceptical of critics seemed to accept that Britain had to remain a member. There were reasons for this:

The arguments for membership

- With the Single Market in operation, British trade and industry are part of a very large internal market. Very few members of Britain's commercial and industrial community are ready to retreat from that, with the possible threat of European tariff barriers being raised against British goods and services.
- Britain has received a great deal of inward investment from the United States and elsewhere by firms which wished to set up a manufacturing base within the EU so as to avoid the external trade tariff. Withdrawal from the EU would mean the loss of these companies, with a consequent loss of investment, tax revenue and jobs.
- If Britain rejected its trading partners in Europe it is hard to see who would replace them. Commonwealth countries such as Australia and New Zealand have found new markets and the USA has made it clear that its interest in Britain is solely as a link with Europe.

Nevertheless, there are and always have been Euro-phobes who talk openly about withdrawal. At first this attitude was an emotive one among those whose thinking was largely guided by the tabloid press but, after the 1997 election, the most sceptical deepened their distrust of Europe. Their view is that they would like to reduce the EU to little more than a free trade area, with Britain having associate membership like Norway.

The arguments against membership

- European regulations such as the CAP have caused immeasurable damage to the British farming industry. The demands on the CAP represented by the addition of peasant economies such as Poland and other Eastern European countries would stretch the situation beyond breaking point.
- European countries such as Norway and Switzerland do very nicely through membership of the European Free Trade Association, having only associate status with the EU, and there is every reason to believe that Britain could flourish similarly. Breaking with the EU would allow Britain to resurrect old trading alliances within the Commonwealth and elsewhere.

- Social and employment policies imposed by Europe can harm Britain's economic competitiveness and hinder the country's recovery from recession. Membership of the EU is a retrograde step for industry that militates against efficiency, competitiveness, progress and development.
- In its growing inability to legislate without external regulation, or in the loss of freedom to make independent decisions over the direction of the economy, the sovereign rights of the British government are steadily being eroded and lost to direction from Brussels.

The possibility of leaving the EU, however, is by now so typical of Conservative right-wing opinion that it seems likely to become the entrenched position of the party in the foreseeable future. As the former Chancellor, Norman Lamont, pointed out as long ago as 1994, there are various alternatives to federalism but, if all these failed, the British government should not be afraid to accept the alternative. 'One day it may mean contemplating withdrawal. It has recently been said that the option of leaving the Community was "unthinkable". I believe this attitude is rather simplistic.'

Reading

Bainbridge, T. and Teasdale, A. (1995) *The Penguin Companion to the European Union*, Penguin.

Noble, S. (1996) *From Rome to Maastricht: The Essential Guide to the European Union*, Warner.

Pilkington, C. (1995) *Britain in the European Union Today*, Manchester University Press.

Rose, R. (1996) *What is Europe? A Dynamic Perspective*, Harper Collins.

Watts, D. (1996) *The European Union*, SHU Press for the Politics Association.

II

Debates on government

6

Should the Civil Service become fully politicised?

John Greenwood

Like many British institutions the Civil Service witnessed enormous change during the last quarter of the twentieth century. A host of factors, including the breakdown of post-war consensus, ministerial suspicion of Civil Service opposition to government policies and an increasing emphasis on efficiency, have all played some part in stimulating change. In the process traditional features of the Civil Service have been affected, not least the Service's political neutrality. This chapter examines the tensions surrounding Civil Service neutrality and asks the question, 'Should the Civil Service now be politicised'?

Traditional features of the Civil Service

Foremost among traditional features of the Civil Service is *political neutrality*. Some countries (e.g. the USA) have a partisan bureaucracy through a 'spoils system' which enables politicians in government to appoint political sympathisers to a wide range of public offices. Others, such as France, have a system of 'ministerial cabinets' whereby a small private staff chosen by the minister provide advice. Traditionally, however, Britain has avoided such arrangements; civil servants are politically neutral, serving ministers and governments of different political complexions. Their duty is to the government of the day regardless of private political beliefs. Thus many of the civil servants who served interventionist Labour governments of the 1970s subsequently implemented the Thatcher government's deregulation and privatisation policies. To safeguard this neutrality there are important restrictions: for example, senior civil servants cannot stand for Parliament and may not express views contrary to ministers.

It is important to recognise that other traditional features of the British Civil Service reinforce political neutrality. For example, civil servants are *permanent*, which enables them to work with different governments and to give advice without fearing dismissal. They are also *anonymous*. Their relations with, and advice to, ministers remain confidential and the convention of *ministerial responsibility* ensures that ministers answer for their civil servants' actions before public and Parliament. Anonymity prevents civil servants from being identified with particular actions or policies, which might otherwise compromise neutrality. Traditionally also the Civil Service was *unified*. Common pay scales, grading and recruitment, and frequent personnel transfers between departments all helped to develop a professional ethos transcending the political interests of particular ministers or governments.

These characteristics – permanence, anonymity, unity – all, therefore, reinforced Civil Service neutrality. They provided the basis upon which it was considered that constitutionally civil servants should work and the arrangement which would best characterise their role within British central government.

Political neutrality: an ill-defined concept?

While it is the job of civil servants to advise ministers about policy, provide information and implement ministers' decisions, neutrality is nevertheless a somewhat ambiguous concept. There are at least two interpretations:

- Civil servants should provide objective and impartial advice to ministers. From this perspective they should give honest advice, however unpalatable this might be to ministers.
- Civil servants should give advice in the spirit of government policy, throwing off the former government's policies and adopting those of the current administration. For example, before an election civil servants study the parties' election manifestos and advise a new government on how to implement its policies. From this standpoint civil servants should 'tailor' their advice according to ministers' political requirements.

While it may not appear difficult to reconcile these two interpretations, in fact it is. If civil servants have a duty to provide impartial advice, as the first interpretation suggests, this may not be supportive of ministers' policy preferences. Ministers may find their election pledges difficult to implement because 'impartial' Civil Service advice supports different solutions. Alternatively, if the second interpretation holds, and civil servants adapt their advice to their ministers' political outlook, this may compromise their impartiality and the policy advice which they give. The second interpretation allows less scope for civil servants to be guided by professional judgement, 'public interest' or ethical considerations, and locates their duty as first and foremost to their minister.

If neutrality is an ambiguous concept, in practice it can be difficult to apply. Politicians of both Left and Right have suggested that civil servants in practice sometimes undermine ministers' policies. While those on the Left have sometimes depicted top civil servants – recruited as they traditionally were from public schools and ancient universities – as part of the (anti-Labour) 'establishment', those on the Right (including Margaret Thatcher) sometimes identify them with the interventionist policies of 'big government'.

There have also been criticisms, from both sides of the political spectrum, that civil servants prefer consensus politics, which is hardly surprising as political neutrality is easier to practise when policy shifts only gradually when governments change. Both Tony Benn, a left-wing Cabinet minister in the 1970s, and Margaret Thatcher, leading a New Right government in the 1980s, have complained that civil servants tried to impose consensus policies on governments. According to Benn (1982, p. 50), the problem arises not because the Civil Service prefers one political party to another, but because it 'sees itself above the party battle, with a political position of its own to defend against all-comers'. Margaret Thatcher expressed it more bluntly. Civil Service attitudes, she believed, were influenced by 'a desire for no change' (Thatcher, 1993, p. 48), a desire not to reverse policies which they had previously pursued.

That civil servants are powerfully placed to influence policy is beyond doubt – they outnumber ministers, have more expertise, control information and implement policy, while ministers themselves are massively overloaded. Coxall and Robins (1988, pp. 279–80) identify several models of Civil Service/ministerial relationship: for example, the liberal-bureaucratic model (which sees a constant power struggle between ministers and civil servants); the power-bloc model (which sees civil servants as an establishment veto group); and the bureaucratic over-supply model (which sees civil servants motivated mainly by defence of their own interests regarding pay, pensions and jobs). The Whitehall model, by contrast, sees the relationship as more co-operative and there is much evidence to suggest that civil servants welcome a strong policy lead from ministers. What is significant here, however, is not the accuracy of these models but the existence of a debate about who rules – civil servants or ministers? And while this debate is not new, what is undeniable is that tensions between the two groups have increased in recent decades, leading in turn to tentative steps towards a more partisan bureaucracy.

Towards a partisan bureaucracy?: the 1960s and 1970s

As a response to ministerial concerns about Civil Service power, successive governments since the mid 1960s have adopted measures designed to supplement Civil Service advice.

Special advisers

In 1964 Harold Wilson's government appointed a small number of 'special advisers'. Although enjoying the status of temporary civil servants, special advisers were not neutral (being appointed for their political sympathies as well as their expertise), not permanent (usually retiring when 'their' minister left office), nor always anonymous (some, such as Thomas Balogh in Wilson's government were quite high profile). Subsequent governments also adopted this practice; indeed, the 1974–79 Labour governments allowed any Cabinet minister to appoint up to two special advisers, and at one time thirty-eight were in post.

The Central Policy Review Staff

In 1970 Edward Heath formed the Central Policy Review Staff, consisting of both outside experts and civil servants. It was charged with the job of strategic policy co-ordination across the whole field of government.

The Prime Minister's Policy Unit

Harold Wilson in 1974 introduced as part of the Prime Minister's Office a small Policy Unit, consisting of both outsider political appointees and civil servants from departments. This provided the Prime Minister with a policy unit capable of providing advice independently of formal Civil Service channels.

Margaret Thatcher's government also employed special advisers – and some, such as her economics adviser, Professor Sir Alan Walters, wielded considerable influence. Indeed, Walters' advice on European monetary policy brought Thatcher into conflict with the Treasury, leading to Nigel Lawson's resignation as Chancellor in 1989. She also retained the Policy Unit (which advised the Prime Minister alone), and in 1983 expanded it while disbanding the Central Policy Review Staff (which served the Cabinet collectively) – a move widely seen as strengthening the Prime Minister's position at Cabinet's expense. Margaret Thatcher also pursued other strategies which led some observers to ask whether the Civil Service was being politicised.

The Civil Service and Margaret Thatcher: Whitehall's political poodles?

David Richards (1997) who has examined the Civil Service under the Conservatives, intriguingly sub-titles his study, 'Whitehall's Political Poodles?' From the outset, several factors combined to make Margaret Thatcher's relations with the Civil Service somewhat controversial:

A radical policy shift

Margaret Thatcher offered a radical new policy agenda which broke sharply away from the post-war consensus characterised by social and economic intervention. This arguably posed a challenge to civil servants 'set' in the policy mould of her predecessors.

A threat to Civil Service interests

Margaret Thatcher's policies of public expenditure restraint and limited government threatened Civil Service jobs and pay. In 1981, following a period of industrial unrest in the Civil Service, she abolished the Civil Service Department and despatched its Permanent Secretary, Sir Ian Bancroft (Head of the Home Civil Service), into early retirement.

A Whitehall outsider

Unlike predecessors such as Wilson and Heath, Thatcher had never been a civil servant and was more likely to challenge established Civil Service norms and practices.

The drive for management efficiency

Margaret Thatcher's government was at the forefront of a worldwide drive towards efficient public sector management. Three main initiatives in particular can be identified:

- *The Rayner scrutiny programmes* In 1979 Margaret Thatcher appointed Sir Derek Rayner as her special adviser on efficiency. Part of her policy of bringing business management expertise into Whitehall, Rayner had previously worked for Marks & Spencer. He headed a new Efficiency Unit within Thatcher's Private Office, its main activity being a series of efficiency scrutinies within departments which by 1993 had reportedly produced savings of up to £1.5 billion.
- *The Financial Management Initiative* The Financial Management Initiative launched in 1982 involved reforms geared to providing taxpayers with Value for Money including: breaking down departments into cost centres; departmental management information systems; and measurement of performance against indicators of economy, efficiency and effectiveness (the 'three Es').
- *'Next Steps'* Originating from an Efficiency Unit report in 1998 (*Improving Management in Government: The Next Steps*), the Next Steps programme involved the creation of Executive Agencies (nicknamed 'Next Steps agencies') headed by ministerially appointed Chief Executives to deliver government services (e.g. issuing passports, processing welfare benefits) on business lines. Ministers determined the agencies' policy and budget, set performance targets and monitored performance but, freed from service delivery responsibilities, could focus more on policy matters. Although when Margaret

Thatcher resigned in 1990 there were only twenty-five agencies, her government pledged that within ten years three-quarters of civil servants would
be employed within agencies.

These managerialist innovations had a considerable impact upon the Civil
Service, including its traditional features of neutrality, permanence and anonymity. Many of its leading architects were outsiders brought temporarily
into government, and (like Rayner) were high profile rather than anonymous.
Many were also committed to Thatcher's vision of government, and some
came into conflict with career officials. One factor leading to Sir Ian Bancroft's
'retirement' was concern that Rayner's scrutiny programme should be supported more forcibly by civil servants.

These initiatives also emphasised the importance of management within
Whitehall. As Thatcher (1993, p. 47) saw it, 'Some Permanent Secretaries
had come to think of themselves as policy advisers, forgetting that they were
also responsible for efficient management of their departments.' This, in turn,
created in her mind a need to find and promote civil servants capable of
efficient management.

All of these factors were ingredients in an often troubled relationship
between ministers and civil servants in Margaret Thatcher's government.
Indeed, during the 1980s there were several highly publicised 'leaks' of confidential information by civil servants. In 1983 Derek Willmore, a civil servant
at the Department of Employment, leaked a minute which he felt revealed
inappropriate links between ministers and a senior judge. In 1984 Sarah Tisdall
was prosecuted for leaking information about cruise missiles arriving in the
UK and in 1985 Clive Ponting, a senior Ministry of Defence official, sent
documents about the sinking of the Argentine battleship *General Belgrano* to a
Foreign Affairs Select Committee member. Ponting was prosecuted under the
Official Secrets Act but the jury – despite the judge's claim that civil servants
had no duty other than to obey ministerial instructions – accepted his defence
that he had acted in the public interest.

The government's reaction to this crisis was twofold. First, following the
Willmore, Tisdall and Ponting cases, the Head of the Home Civil Service (Sir
Robert Armstrong) issued a *Note of Guidance on the Duties and Responsibilities
of Civil Servants in Relation to Ministers* (the Armstrong Memorandum). This
stressed that civil servants were servants of the Crown and had a duty first
and foremost to their minister. If in doubt they could consult more senior civil
servants, including ultimately the Head of the Home Civil Service, but if directed
must either obey instructions or resign. They could not claim wider duty to
the public interest or Parliament.

The Armstrong Memorandum's limitations were revealed shortly afterwards
by the Westland Affair, during which one civil servant, Collette Bowe, leaked
material damaging to Michael Heseltine, Defence Secretary, at the behest of
her minister, Leon Brittan. The Armstrong procedure proved unhelpful as

senior officials could not be contacted. The affair also raised issues of Civil Service anonymity, with key civil servants being identified both in Parliament and the media. Similar concerns were also voiced during the 'Spycatcher' affair, when the Cabinet Secretary, Sir Robert Armstrong, testified for the British government in the Australian courts.

Second, some observers suggest that Thatcher influenced top Civil Service appointments. Pyper (1995, p. 84) explains: 'Where previous premiers had usually adopted a fairly relaxed approach to Civil Service appointments, giving final approval to nominations forwarded by the Senior Appointments Selection Committee, Margaret Thatcher took pains to make her preferences clear to the Committee, through its chairman, the Cabinet Secretary.' This led to accusations that the higher Civil Service was being politicised by Conservative sympathisers, that it was being 'Thatcherised', and that only civil servants supporting Thatcherite neo-liberal, monetarist policies would be promoted. Several promotions aroused particular controversy, including accusations not only of politicisation but even of favouritism (allegedly, for example, with Peter Middleton, a committed monetarist, promoted to Permanent Secretary of the Treasury) and of prejudice (Donald Derx apparently passed over after 'standing up' to Thatcher about secondary picketing) (Hennessy, 1989, p. 634).

An investigation by the Royal Institute of Public Administration, however, effectively cleared Thatcher of such charges, while Hennessy (1989, p. 636) claims that, with few exceptions, it was difficult to see 'any . . . "one of us" figure benefiting from her preferment'. Richards (1997) also suggests that Margaret Thatcher did not support appointments on the basis of Conservative sympathies (although he does suggest that those impressing her may have improved their promotional prospects – which possibly encouraged some to give advice that ministers wanted to hear). Thatcher's lengthy premiership also probably produced a 'mind set' among civil servants, a 'mind set' which continued into the Major government.

Where Thatcher's intervention may have had an impact is in promoting 'managerial can-do' types capable of pursuing her managerial initiatives: '"doers" – good at implementing policy, concerned with good management and value for money – rather than . . . policy advisers' (Kavanagh, 1990, p. 252). Nevertheless, her premiership raised significant questions about Civil Service neutrality, questions which would prove no less pertinent during John Major's government.

The Major government and the Civil Service

John Major not only continued with many of Thatcher's reforms but accelerated their implementation and built upon them. Next Steps was expanded and by March 1997, 130 agencies had been established containing 387,000 staff (74 per cent of the Civil Service). Nine agencies had also been privatised and three had had all their functions contracted out. The Citizen's Charter, designed to promote quality within public services, was also introduced, along with market testing – which led to extensive contracting-out of agency and departmental functions to the private sector.

There were two other significant developments during Major's tenure:

- *More 'outsiders' in Whitehall*   While Major, unlike Thatcher, tended not to intervene in Civil Service promotions, his government sharply increased the number of 'outsiders' in key Whitehall posts. Two White Papers, *The Civil Service: Continuity and Change* (1994) and *Taking Forward Continuity and Change* (1995), included proposals both for seconding senior civil servants to the private sector and opening up competition for senior appointments. Altogether about 30 per cent of top appointments during Major's premiership went to 'outsiders'. These included not only appointments to specialist posts (such as Professor Alan Budd, from the London Business School to Chief Economic Adviser to the Treasury), but to agency Chief Executive positions (by 1997 67 per cent had been filled by open competition, with 31 per cent being recruited from outside), and even to Permanent Secretaries. (In 1995, Michael Bichard was appointed Permanent Secretary at the Department of Employment following open competition and shortly afterwards was preferred over internal candidates when the Employment and Education Departments were merged.)
- *Naming and blaming*   Major's government witnessed several cases where civil servants were 'named and blamed'. Mostly these concerned Next Steps agencies whose Chief Executives carried personal responsibility for performance (and normally also answered MPs' questions and letters on operational matters). In 1994 Ros Hepplewhite, Chief Executive of the Social Security Child Support Agency, resigned following criticism of the Agency's operations; and in 1995 Derek Lewis, Chief Executive of HM Prison Service Agency, was effectively sacked following high-security-prison escapes. This case was controversial as Lewis claimed the Home Office had constrained his managerial freedom. However, the Home Secretary, Michael Howard, refused to accept responsibility – other than for answering MPs' concerns in Parliament – claiming that the failures were purely operational.

If agency Chief Executives are outside the norms of ministerial responsibility, the same cannot be said of Permanent Secretaries. In 1992 Sir Peter Kemp, Second Permanent Secretary at the Office of Public Service and Science, and Project Manager of the Next Steps team, was effectively sacked by his minister, William Waldegrave. Waldegrave claimed to want a Permanent Secretary with different skills and secured Major's approval for the sacking. Contrary to previous procedure, no attempt was made to find Kemp another post.

While the above all have long-term implications for the Civil Service, one specific case led to particular concerns about Civil Service behaviour. The Scott Report, *The Export of Defence and Dual-Use Goods to Iraq and Related Prosecutions*, published in 1996, which examined the 'Arms to Iraq' affair, named and blamed several civil servants for such alleged failings as giving misleading answers to parliamentary questions and lack of frankness in assisting the inquiry.

Reflecting concerns about this and other developments, the *Nolan Report on Standards in Public Life* in 1995 recommended that ministers should not ask civil servants to carry out party political duties, and called for a Civil Service Code to clarify their duties and responsibilities. This followed earlier publication of a draft Code by the Civil Service First Division Association and a similar recommendation from the House of Commons Treasury and Civil Service Select Committee. In response the 1995 White Paper, *Taking Forward Continuity and Change*, accepted the recommendation for a Code. Re-stating the traditional view that civil servants should act with 'impartiality' in their public duties, the Code allowed civil servants to appeal to independent Civil Service Commissioners (and not, as under the Armstrong Memorandum, only to their Permanent Secretary and the Cabinet Secretary) if they felt their neutrality was being compromised. The White Paper also provided that the First Civil Service Commissioner should have a role in monitoring internal appointments.

While these provisions went some way to answering concerns about Civil Service neutrality, the Code significantly re-affirmed that civil servants giving evidence to select committees did so subject to ministerial instructions – which led to fears that such instructions might involve misleading Parliament. The government also rejected Nolan's view that the Code should have a statutory basis to provide legal protection for officials. Indeed, many observers were surprised that Major's government accepted a Code at all. Massey (1995, p. 23) suggests that what may have influenced this decision could have been the view that 'such a document was a way of demonstrating the Government's commitment to the traditional values of the Civil Service, while permitting the continuation of its managerial revolution'.

The Blair government and the Civil Service

Tony Blair's government has continued the managerial reforms inherited from its predecessors. Agencies are now a permanent feature of government. In March 1998, it was announced that the main task of creating new agencies was complete and that the emphasis in future would be on improving performance. The *Modernising Government* White Paper (March 1999), while emphasising public service values such as impartiality and objectivity, called for a 'less risk-averse culture' in government. Subsequently the *Wilson Report*

(December 1999) laid down specific targets for year on year increases in open competition into the service, for co-ordinated action to recruit external people in mid-career, and for 65 per cent of senior civil servants to have had outside experience by 2005. *The Times* (10 December 1999) described these as sweeping reforms to transform Whitehall 'along the lines of a thriving public enterprise', although some senior civil servants reportedly saw it as a 'smokescreen concealing very substantial politicisation imposed by the Prime Minister'.

The Blair government has also used outsiders to assist with policy development, many of them serving on 'task forces' and advisory groups (such as the 'Football Task Force' led by David Mellor, a former Conservative minister; and the Advisory Group on Citizenship, chaired by Professor Bernard Crick). By 2000 there were over 300 task forces involving about 2,500 members, many of whom had strong links with Labour. Significantly, too, Blair has increased the number of special advisers. Barberis, writing in 1996 (p. 16), suggested that following 'a bureaucracy serving without interruption one political party in office for almost a generation . . . corrective action' might be necessary by an incoming government. 'Such corrective action', he continued, 'could include a much greater influence for special advisers', which is the approach adopted by the new government. Blair's government has appointed over seventy special advisers, compared with thirty-eight appointed by Major. Two appointments were particularly controversial:

- Alistair Campbell, former *Daily Mirror* political editor, appointed as Prime Minister's Press Secretary. This was followed by the replacement of some departmental information officers with outsiders, amid claims that the government was politicising its information service.
- Ed Balls, appointed as economic adviser to the Chancellor of the Exchequer. He was previously leader writer for the *Financial Times* and adviser to Gordon Brown when Labour was in Opposition.

Other developments have not been uncontroversial. One ousted civil servant, for example, 'launched a strong attack on the politicisation of Whitehall [under Labour] and called for reforms to uphold the standards of the civil service' (*Daily Telegraph*, 6 December 1997). Nevertheless, there did seem to be a relatively smooth transition when Blair's government took office. One Permanent Secretary, Sir Patrick Brown, who had previously worked on water and rail privatisation, accepted retirement shortly after the election, and there were reports that Ed Balls, the Chancellor's economic adviser, had marginalised the influence of Treasury Permanent Secretary, Sir Terry Burns, who subsequently retired in 1998. Generally, however, there are few indications that officials have had difficulty working with the new government. To that extent fears about Thatcherite politicisation, and of a Conservative mind set within the service, appear groundless. The Blair government has also pledged to give statutory backing to the Civil Service Code.

Should the Civil Service become fully politicised?

Neutrality was a traditional feature of the Civil Service. Significantly, however, it developed in an age when policy making was less complex than today, when the media focused less sharply on government, and when politics was more consensual. Today the case for politicising the Civil Service is somewhat stronger.

The case for politicising the Civil Service rests on such claims as the following:

- First, in recent decades *policy making has become much more complex*, especially in fields such as foreign affairs and economic policy, and ministers may legitimately require advisers with alternative expertise to perform a role similar to French-style ministerial Cabinets. Wolmar (*Independent*, 4 June 1997) suggests that one reason why civil servants welcomed Blair's special advisers was because he had decided to retain the existing system rather than introduce a Cabinet system. Special advisers and Blair-type 'task forces' enable appropriate expertise, often not available through normal Civil Service channels, to be brought into the policy-making process. Politicisation would allow such expertise to be brought formally within the Civil Service.
- Second, the *influence of the media* has increased massively since the 1950s. Today ministers are concerned not just with policy making but with policy presentation. Ministers wish to present the best political 'spin' on policy, and neutral civil servants are not best placed to do this (and perhaps should not attempt to do so anyway). Sir Bernard Ingham, Margaret Thatcher's Press Secretary and a 'neutral' civil servant, often appeared to be closely identified with government policy, while an attempt by Major's Deputy Prime Minister, Michael Heseltine, to use civil servants as 'robust defenders' of government policy was vetoed by the Cabinet Secretary. Blair's replacement of many departmental information officers with political sympathisers reflects similar concerns.
- Third is the *breakdown of the post-war political consensus*. One former Prime Minister, Lord Callaghan, states, 'When you have a government like the government . . . in the 1980s, which emanates a very strong flavour, the Civil Service picks up the scent. Some are repelled by it, some are attracted by it, and I think the Civil Service has become more politicised as a consequence' (quoted in Barberis, 1996, p. 74). In other words, radical policy makes it harder for civil servants to remain neutral. In 1983 Ridley asked whether, in periods of radical politics, neutrality was still desirable. 'Perhaps', he suggested, 'the energetic pursuit of such policies . . . requires commitment – "conviction civil servants" as well as "conviction" politicians' (p. 40). If radical policies are to be pursued by governments, then perhaps radically committed civil servants are necessary to ensure effective implementation.

- Fourth, while senior civil servants have traditionally seen themselves as policy makers, with the drive towards *greater managerial efficiency* new skills, and perhaps new civil servants, have been required. It was to promote 'managerial can-do types' that Margaret Thatcher intervened in Civil Service promotions, and because ministers wanted the best available expertise to run agencies (and latterly departments) that open competition for senior posts was adopted. It was for similar reasons that Sir Peter Kemp was effectively dismissed. Developments such as these, potentially at least, threaten Civil Service neutrality. Indeed, the principle of appointing Chief Executives on fixed-term contracts, while it may be good management practice, is potentially corrosive of neutrality as officials seeking contract renewal are unlikely to give advice to ministers or to act in ways prejudicial to their re-appointment.

While, as yet, such developments are at an early stage, in the longer term their impact may be considerable. Butcher (1995, p. 42) quotes one Cabinet minister: 'Top mandarins in 30 years' time will be more likely to have spent long periods outside the Civil Service or to have joined after a career elsewhere.' Again Richards (1997, p. 232), reflecting on Kemp's dismissal, observes, 'it could be the precursor for future sackings . . . of senior civil servants by a government . . . if this were the case, then two of the fundamental . . . principles on which the Civil Service was founded, permanence and impartiality, would have been dismantled.' On this assessment the Civil Service is still essentially neutral, but whether it should remain so, and whether it will still be so in thirty years' time, is somewhat uncertain.

The case against politicising the Civil Service, however, remains a strong one:

- First, neutrality helps *develop a professionalism, an integrity and an ethical commitment* in government which could be lost if the Civil Service were politicised. Neutrality offers a valuable counterweight to the narrow political perspectives, expediencies and short termism which have often characterised British governments. It also contrasts favourably with foreign systems, which lack this professionalism. For example, is it likely that a neutral, professional Civil Service would have tolerated the excesses of Richard Nixon's presidency?
- Second, neutrality enables civil servants to give honest advice, rather than simply telling ministers what they want to hear. This ensures that civil servants' *expertise and professional judgement influence policy*, rather than the political considerations which might prevail if the service were politicised.
- Third, where a spoils system exists, politicisation requires changes in Civil Service personnel with each new government. The discontinuity which often accompanies such changes, and the loss of accumulated expertise,

are clearly disadvantageous. Under present arrangements, *because civil servants are politically neutral they can be permanent.*

- Fourth, a neutral Civil Service, like an independent judiciary and an official Opposition, is widely seen as *one of the hallmarks of the British political system.* Politicisation would erode other valued features of the Civil Service, such as anonymity and permanence.

Conclusion

There is a strong case for British civil servants to remain neutral. Nevertheless, under modern conditions impartiality is likely to be difficult to sustain and, therefore, the search for alternative arrangements is likely to continue. Such alternative arrangements, however, need not necessarily compromise, or even be seen as incompatible with, neutrality. Next Steps, for example, might be seen as an attempt to make agency Chief Executives personally accountable for service delivery while leaving neutral civil servants free to give policy advice in departments. Again, special advisers can be seen as protecting, rather than compromising, Civil Service neutrality. Blair himself suggests that bringing in outsiders to conduct political work protects Civil Service neutrality (*The Times*, 2 June 1997). Indeed, civil servants may welcome such developments. According to Hennessy (1997, p. 10), special advisers are 'warmly welcomed' and 'their role [is] well-understood in most departments'.

Perhaps, in keeping with Britain's evolutionary political system, special advisers have now become institutionalised within government. Although introduced only in the 1960s, they have developed under successive governments, Labour and Conservative, as a pragmatic response to ministers' needs for 'politically sympathetic' advice to complement that available through neutral Civil Service channels. In the same way Next Steps, and much that flows from it, separates policy making and administration to bring demands for managerial efficiency in line with the constitutional requirements of ministerial responsibility and Civil Service neutrality. Such developments go some way towards recognising the case for politicisation without abandoning the principle of neutrality which still overwhelmingly characterises the Service.

Despite the developments discussed above most civil servants are still unmistakably neutral, and still also permanent and anonymous. The tensions identified above mainly affect only the most senior civil servants – those advising ministers on policy, appearing before parliamentary committees, drafting answers to parliamentary questions, and so on – as well, of course, as agency Chief Executives. It is with civil servants at these levels that the neutrality debate is mainly concerned, and what seems clear – as the Whitehall managerial revolution continues to work through and ministers continue to feel the need for politically sympathetic advisers – is that this debate seems unlikely to abate in the foreseeable future.

Should the Civil Service become fully politicised?

The case for

- Policy making has become more complex. Politicisation would enable appropriate advice, not available through Civil Service channels, to be brought into the policy-making process.
- Politicisation would help policy presentation. Neutral civil servants are not appropriate, or best equipped, to put political 'spin' on policy.
- Politically committed civil servants may be more inclined to implement radical policies.
- Greater emphasis on management requires new skills. Margaret Thatcher allegedly intervened in Civil Service promotions to advance 'managerial can-do types'.

The case against

- Neutrality helps to develop professionalism, integrity and an ethical commitment.
- Neutrality enables civil servants to give honest advice.
- Neutrality reinforces Civil Service permanence.
- Neutrality is one of the hallmarks of the British political system.

Reading

Barberis, P. (ed.) (1996) *The Whitehall Reader*, Open University Press.

Benn, T. (1982) *Arguments for Democracy*, Penguin.

Butcher, T. (1995) 'The Civil Service in the 1990s: the revolution rolls on', *Talking Politics*, 8:3, Autumn.

Butcher, T. (1998) 'The Blair government and the Civil Service: continuity and change', *Teaching Public Administration*, XVIII:1, Spring.

Coxall, B. and Robins, L. (1998) *Contemporary British Politics*, Macmillan (3rd edn).

Hennessy, P. (1989) *Whitehall*, Fontana.

Hennessy, P., Hughes, P. and Seaton, J. (1997) *Ready, Steady, Go! New Labour and Whitehall*, Fabian Society.

Kavanagh, D. (1990) *Thatcherism and British Politics: The End of Consensus*, Oxford University Press (2nd edn).

Massey, A. (1995) 'Guidance to modern princes on how to choose their servants', *Parliamentary Brief*, February.

Modernising Government (March 1999) Report presented to Parliament by the Prime Minister and the Minister for the Cabinet Office, Cm 4310, The Stationery Office.

Pyper, R. (1995) *The British Civil Service*, Prentice Hall/Harvester Wheatsheaf.

Richards, D. (1997) *The Civil Service Under the Conservatives, 1979–1997: Whitehall's Political Poodles?*, Sussex Academic Press.

Ridley, F. (1983) 'The British Civil Service and politics: principles in question and traditions in flux', *Parliamentary Affairs*, 36.

Thatcher, M. (1993) *The Downing Street Years*, Harper Collins.

Wilson, Sir Richard (1999) *Wilson Report*, Report to the Prime Minister from Sir Richard Wilson, Head of the Home Civil Service, December.

7

Local government: could mayors make a difference?

David Wilson

Introduction

In its 1997 general election manifesto the Labour Party pledged to restore democratic city-wide government to London, with a mayor and an assembly, both directly elected. As John Prescott wrote in his Foreword to the subsequent Green Paper, *New Leadership for London*, (1997): 'The Government believes that this is essential to preserve and enhance London's competitiveness, to tackle London's problems and to speak up for Londoners and their interests.' Elected mayors were thereby pushed to the centre of political debate, the underlying argument being that such mayors could provide a focal point and driving force for a more dynamic and influential local government. Such executive leadership, it was argued, could revitalise local democracy. This chapter examines whether the introduction of elected mayors into UK local government really can enhance the position of local authorities or whether the associated dangers of elitist decision making means that caution should be counselled. It also warns against policy transfer or institutional transfer from one country to another without a thorough knowledge and understanding of the constituent political systems. Local government, via directly elected mayors, could indeed raise its public profile but in doing so could become less representative of grass roots needs.

The emerging idea

The 1990s opened with the arrival of a new Prime Minister, John Major, and a new Secretary of State for the Environment, Michael Heseltine. At the Department of the Environment (DoE) Heseltine immediately launched a wide-ranging review of the local government system, one element of which included an examination of internal management. It was in this context that elected mayors began to be seriously discussed as a possible model for local political leadership.

In July 1991 Heseltine produced his Consultation Paper, *The Internal Management of Local Authorities in England*, which put forward a range of alternative management models, most of which involved replacing the committee system (which Heseltine regarded as inefficient) with some form of either separate appointed or elected executive, thus splitting the executive and representational roles of the council.

The Consultation Paper did not put forward all the logical possibilities for further consideration. It bypassed the French model of nominated or indirectly elected mayors, thereby appearing to presume that any individual political executive should be elected directly and separately from the council. This reflected Michael Heseltine's much publicised personal enthusiasm for elected mayors.

The Conservative government's next move was to set up a joint working party of DoE nominees and representatives of the local authority associations which, in July 1993, produced a report entitled *Community Leadership and Representation: Unlocking the Potential*. One of the recommendations was that councils should consider the merits of more radical and experimental forms of internal management. Four specific examples were identified by the joint working party:

- *The single-party executive committee*   The council would delegate to a single-party policy committee certain powers of strategy and policy formulation, the council itself retaining control over, for example, the annual budget and planning decisions.
- *The lead member system*   The council would delegate powers to named lead members rather than to a collective political executive. The lead member – for example, the Chair of the Education Committee – would be free to take decisions in a way that would currently be illegal, but would be accountable to the whole council.
- *The Cabinet system*   The principle of delegation is extended to a single-party policy committee whose membership has *both* individual and collective executive powers. Decisions taken by this executive would be decisions of the council, and individual members would have delegated areas of responsibility. The full council would retain certain powers – such as setting the budget – and the right to overturn at least some decisions taken by the executive or lead members.
- *The political executive as a separate legal entity*   In this scenario there would be a separate – perhaps separately elected – political executive with its own legal powers, which would take control of the decision-making process on behalf of the council. The full council would become very largely a scrutinising and reviewing body.

Interestingly, the one option that did not receive much attention from the joint working party was that which had most attracted Michael Heseltine personally: directly elected mayors. The issue was, however, kept on the agenda by the independent Commission for Local Democracy (CLD) which, in its 1995 report, *Taking Charge: The Rebirth of Local Democracy*, put elected mayors centre-stage with its first recommendation: 'Local authorities should consist of a directly elected Council and a directly elected Leader/Mayor. Both Council and Leader/Mayor should be voted in for a term of three years but the elected Leader may only serve two full terms in office' (Appendix 1).

The CLD believed that a directly elected mayor was an important means of enhancing democracy in local government, by providing a focus of power which would be 'highly visible and thus highly accountable' (1995, para. 4.15), but at the same time it recommended a number of direct and indirect means of limiting the power of such executives, thus reducing the extent to which direct accountability would be achieved (see Pratchett and Wilson, 1996, ch. 12).

Jones and Stewart (1995, p. 8) reflected the scepticism of many involved with local government, arguing that the report's section on directly elected mayors was simplistic: 'It is as if the Commission regards it as a piece of magic which will automatically increase turn-out and build a vibrant local democracy. But the magic does not seem to work in the US. In 1991 in Phoenix – an authority with a city manager and directly elected mayor – only 17 per cent of the electorate voted, and that is of the electorate who bothered to register as voters.'

The Labour Party's 1997 election manifesto commitment to 'encourage democratic innovations in local government, including pilots of the idea of elected mayors with executive powers in cities' reflected widespread concern about local political leadership. The advent of elected mayors remains highly controversial, with strongly held views marshalled both for and against. Its advent in London (along with pilot experiments elsewhere) represents a radical innovation in Britain's local government system. Like many radical proposals the ensuing debate has frequently generated more heat than light.

Evidence from abroad

Advocates of elected mayors argue that such executives function well in other countries where local democracy is in a much healthier state than in Britain. Opponents argue equally strongly that we need to beware of uncritically adopting practices from elsewhere. All political systems have their own values, cultures and legal contexts; what works well in one country is not necessarily appropriate elsewhere.

The most frequently cited example of a directly elected local leader is that of the US mayor. The positive attributes of this system invariably focus on leadership capacity. To quote Stoker and Wolman (1992, p. 264): 'Especially in the management of relations with other government agencies, external interests and local citizens the mayor could provide a key focal point and driving force for a more dynamic and influential local government.' Against this, the potential narrowing of representation by the concentration of power in the mayor and a small group of around a dozen councillors is a frequently voiced criticism. In a similar vein questions are asked about sufficient people coming forward with the necessary skills to fulfil a mayor's role successfully. Powerful directly elected mayors are common in US cities, but governance in the USA is very different to that in the UK. Scrutiny of some experiences in Europe is more useful since, as Stoker (1996, p. 21) notes, countries such as Germany and Italy, both of which have recently moved towards directly elected local political leaders, 'have local welfare systems and a form of party politics that are in many respects close to the British case'.

In Germany the move towards directly elected executives needs to be seen as part of the process of democratisation within the country, part of a broader move towards greater political participation. It also has the virtue of providing 'a more direct influence for voters over its government leadership without going through the filter of the party groups' (Stoker, 1996, p. 21). There are a number of different mayoral systems within Germany but by 1999 virtually the whole of German local government will have some form of directly elected mayor.

The German experience has thrown up a number of questions. Should the assembly and the mayor (*bürgermeister*) be elected at the same time? Is the cost of the system too great? What is the appropriate term of office? Issues such as these require clear articulation in the UK context.

Turning to Italy, legislation in 1993 introduced directly elected mayors. Corruption had been a major problem in Italian local government; this, along with the move away from proportional representation systems towards majoritarian systems, is the stark backdrop against which the emergence of separately elected mayors took place. The two electoral rounds in Italy ensure that the winning candidate has the support of the majority of voters. Mayors have emerged as powerful figures but they are restricted to two four-year terms of office. The profile of mayors has been increased with the introduction of direct elections and greater political stability seems to have resulted from the change.

In Italy the mayor nominates the *Giunta* (Board) composed of 'assessors' (who cannot be elected councillors) which oversees the major policy areas such as education and environment. Mayors also have the power to sack the assessors. Stoker (1996, p. 28) sums up the Italian position thus: 'The administration of the system is effectively in the hands of the mayor, the chief executive and the assessors. They meet together in a management team. The business of the assembly is conducted through a mixture of commissions and standing committees. Each council has the right to decide how to conduct its affairs, so systems vary considerably.'

While useful lessons can be drawn from the USA and Europe, it is important not to copy directly or uncritically from such experience. Too often policy

'solutions' drawn from other countries are based on a partial understanding
of the operation of political systems elsewhere and of the conditions that contribute to their success or failure. As Page (1998, p. 1) has observed, 'Valid
lessons from cross-national experience can only be drawn on the basis of the
systematic application of knowledge about how policies and institutions work.'
As the same author emphasises, lesson drawing requires systematic evaluation of a number of factors:

- whether the different jurisdictions from which lessons are sought are the
  best or even appropriate ones;
- whether the institutions or policies compared are truly successful models
  to be emulated (or failures to be avoided);
- whether the conditions that make for their success are present in the different legal, political, social, economic and cultural contexts in which their
  application is contemplated.

Clearly, a proper understanding of the operation of elected mayors in Germany
necessitates a thorough understanding of the constitutional, political and
legal structure of that country. The transferability of policies or institutions
from Germany to Britain must take account of such differences or else they
are likely to be of very limited usefulness. To quote Page (1998, p. 1): 'To
draw valid and useful lessons requires more than a casual invocation of
experiences of other countries as, for example, has been demonstrated by
attempts to import economic planning from France or Japanese styles of
management into the United Kingdom.'

Much of the debate about elected mayors focuses on comparisons with
the USA. Judge *et al.* (1995, p. 12) provide a timely reminder that there are
certain fundamental contextual differences between Britain and the USA that
counsel caution. They identify five such differences:

- Differences in governmental structure that result in greater emphasis on
  spatial politics in the USA and party politics in Britain. The federal structure of the USA means that urban governments are in effect creatures of
  state governments. Party conflict and partisanship are central to the unitary British system. The weaker party politics of the USA creates greater
  scope for a local politics.
- The more direct role of central government in Britain (and greater local
  autonomy in the USA) provides less scope for British local government to
  engage in activity of its own choosing.
- A much more fragmented local structure in the USA that encourages
  economic competition among localities. The US system is incredibly more
  complex. There are some 80,000 local government agencies in the USA,
  approximately 200 times more agencies than there are elected local authorities in Britain.

- The lack of a focused local executive in Britain compared with the USA, where the elected mayor, or in some instances the city manager, has a prominent role in urban politics.
- A local fiscal system in Britain that substantially reduces incentives for local governments to compete against each other's tax base.

As Judge *et al.* emphasise (p. 12), 'cross-national research requires conceptual and theoretical rigour if comparison is to advance beyond description into the realm of explanation'. Nevertheless, as Hambleton has commented (1996, p. 2), good ideas do not need a passport to cross international frontiers: 'If the approaches of different local authorities in different countries can be juxta-posed in a reasonably organised way, it is possible to stimulate new insights which are grounded in experience.' It must always be emphasised, however, that uncritical policy transfer or an uninformed adoption of institutional arrangements that work well elsewhere is likely to be a recipe for disaster.

Enhancing democracy?

Advocates of directly elected mayors have drawn much ammunition from the depressed state of British local government in the 1990s. There is little inter-est in its activities. Turnout in elections is low – only 29 per cent in the 1998 local elections. Indeed, in a by-election for a ward on Tamworth Borough Council in December 1998, only 6 per cent of the electorate exercised their democratic right to vote. The 'first past the post' voting system distorts prefer-ences so a large number of local authorities are now 'one-party states' with no effective Opposition. In such contexts allegations of corruption have been rife: three examples from 1997 are presented below:

- *Renfrew DC, August 1997* Two councillors suspended by the Labour Party in an investigation into allegations that the community business FCB was a front for drug peddling and money laundering.
- *Doncaster MBC, February 1997* District auditor sparks off 'Donnygate' with a report criticising perks abuses. In March the police began criminal investigation and in July the Labour Party suspended four councillors at the centre of corruption allegations.
- *Glasgow City Council, February 1997* Leader Bob Gould alleges coun-cillors have traded support in return for junkets. Up to seventeen council-lors faced disciplinary action by Labour's National Executive Committee.

It seems that allegations of corruption are not the prerogative of cities with elected mayors. There is no reason why, with sensible safeguards, corruption should be any more likely with an elected mayor system than within the 'one-party states' which characterise UK elected local government in the late

1990s. At present it is not unusual for the strategic decisions in a local authority to be made in private by a majority group of thirty or forty individuals,
drawing on a manifesto compiled by an even smaller group of party activists
(or, in the case of the Conservative Party, by the Leader). Elitism, it seems, is
not restricted to cities with elected mayors.

Elected mayors probably provide the best chance of significantly increasing
electoral turnout; any such increase would help to undermine the widespread
criticism about local government's accountability. Likewise, the civic leadership role of local authorities would be enhanced through the visibility and
legitimacy of the mayor's position. Interestingly, though, a national survey of
nearly 3,000 people by Strathclyde and Glasgow Universities in 1995, carried
out as part of the ESRC Local Governance Programme, found that while over
70 per cent of the public supported the introduction of elected mayors only
16 per cent of councillors liked the idea. In a similar vein, a range of polls in
1998 showed that the public remain interested in the idea of elected mayors
even if councillors remained sceptical (table 7.1). Many councillors were
fearful that they would be marginalised if directly elected mayors emerged.
They feared the emergence of elitist decision making and a marked diminution
of their own spheres of responsibility.

Advocates of elected mayors do not accept this. On the contrary, they
maintain that a directly elected executive would in many ways strengthen
the role of councillors. Hodge *et al.* (1997, p. 26) outline a number of factors
which, they suggest, would increase the attractiveness of standing for council
membership:

- the explicit recognition that it was part time and hence compatible with
  full-time employment;
- the more realistic levels of remuneration;
- substantial reduction of time-consuming 'committee business' which has
  dominated councillor activity in the past and, in many authorities, still
  does;
- opportunity to specialise in a particular area of interest;

Table 7.1   *Making council membership more attractive*

Support for elected mayor	%
Arun District Council	63
Birmingham City Council	68
London Borough of Lewisham	58
West Sussex County Council	70

Source: Filkin *et al.*, 1999, p. 23.

- decreasing the domination of party politics in local government (given the increased likelihood of no overall control under the proportional voting system advocated by the authors).

Under a directly elected mayor system, local councillors would be on the side of local consumers and citizens; they would serve as voices for their local communities. They would be particularly important as policy scrutineers. The mayor might provide the bulk of the initiatives, but the council would determine whether services were actually delivered in the interests of local people. Linked with this could be greater participation by the local population via neighbourhood forums, focus groups, local scrutiny panels, citizens' juries and the like. Local democracy would thereby be enhanced. There could also be the development of technological facilities such as internet web sites, assisted computer access via terminals and even video conferencing. As Hodge *et al.* observe (1997, p. 27): 'We would expect the scrutiny role to be divided up so assembly members could pursue their specific interests. It would be likely, for example, that a small group of members would have a particular interest in artistic and cultural activities in the area. They could play a lead role in monitoring, scrutinising, and suggesting improvements in this policy area.' This would take place alongside their present representative role; they would still defend the interests of the ward they represent – their grievance-chasing role would in no way be diminished. An elected mayor would certainly not have the time (given his or her policy formulation, external representation and advocacy role) to deal with individual case-work. Elected councillors would still be centre-stage in this context. Indeed, as the role of assembly member would be unambiguously part time, it might be possible to attract a broader cross-section of the population than at present to stand as representatives. If this proved to be so then the enhanced competition for nomination would strengthen local democracy.

Critics of the elected mayor scenario argue that if the mayor was from a different party to the party controlling the assembly, government would be impossible. Conflict and policy stagnation would result. Even under the present system there are frequently strong factions *within* the majority group which, equally, can provide conflict and division. In November 1995, for example, two majority group leaders – Stewart Foster in Leicester and Valerie Wise in Preston – were overthrown on the same day, following votes of no confidence by their respective Labour groups. In practice the mayor/assembly division can be handled, but if a Single Transferable Vote system is adopted for the elections of mayor and assembly (who are elected at the same time) such a discrepancy becomes very unlikely anyway. What becomes most likely is a mayor working with a hung assembly; such hung councils are relatively familiar in British local government. In 1997/98, for example, some 134 authorities (30 per cent) had no overall control. There were few signs of such authorities failing to face up to policy challenges.

Conclusion

At the 1997 Labour Party Conference, Hilary Armstrong, Local Government Minister, observed: 'I want every council, every Labour group, to come forward with local experiences of democratic modernisation. I want them to demonstrate how they will encourage local people to exercise their democratic authority. I want them to transform the rhetoric of empowerment into the reality of power.' Those who are currently advocating elected mayors see them as part of the regeneration of local democracy. As Hodge *et al.* (1997, p. 1) argue, 'It's not the only way forward. Neither is it a complete response to the problems we face in revitalising local government. However, as part of a package of reforms it is one exciting option which offers great potential for delivering local democratic renewal.' Controversy is never far away from the elected mayor concept. Speaking at a workshop in June 1997 Labour MP Margaret Hodge cited the 'low calibre' of many elected members as a reason for introducing elected mayors. But John Fletcher, Labour Leader of Coventry City Council, was not impressed: 'what I object to is Margaret Hodge muscling in on this debate in order to give a 25 minute piece of propaganda in favour of elected mayors'. Two leading members of the same party were clearly at odds. Fletcher argued that Coventry was keen to co-operate with the government on welfare work, regeneration of cities and best-value services, but in his view elected mayors were irrelevant to these (*Local Government Chronicle*, 27 June 1997). The debate goes on.

In this context, in November 1997 Lord Hunt introduced his private members' Local Government (Experimental Arrangements) Bill, which aimed to give councils the freedom to experiment with new management structures – from elected mayors to Cabinet-style executives. Despite the Blair government providing its support for the Bill it was 'talked out' by the Conservatives in the House of Commons in March 1998. This meant that the government brought forward its own legislative proposals based on the White Paper, *Modern Local Government: In Touch with the People* (July 1998). In March 1999 the government published a draft Local Government (Organisation and Standards) Bill as part of a Consultation Paper, *Local Leadership, Local Choice*. This Bill requires all local authorities to make proposals for new political leadership at local level. It puts forward three models with which local authorities' proposals must conform: (1) directly elected mayor with Cabinet; (2) Cabinet with a Leader; and (3) directly elected mayor and council manager. It allows the Secretary of State to add further models later. The Bill also requires local authorities to hold a referendum where their proposal includes a directly elected mayor, where 5 per cent (originally 10 per cent in the White Paper) or more of the council's electorate petition for such arrangements. Executive political leadership is integral to the Labour government's plans for a modernised local government system.

Gerry Stoker (1998, p. 8) argues strongly for a change to systems which provide directly elected mayors. He outlines three advantages:

First it would create a leader with some independence. The legitimacy of direct election would create a figure more confident in their ability to speak and act for the public than under the current system. This is the particular attraction of direct election. Second a directly elected leader will create a well-known and accountable figure. The assembly would also have an enhanced profile as supporters and opponents of the leader's actions use it to make their case. This higher profile should make for a greater local dimension to policy-making. It could increase turn-out in local elections. By playing up personality and leadership, nationally orientated party politics will be downgraded. Fun, excitement, and community spirit could be injected into local politics. Finally, the elected mayor or leader would provide a steering capacity within and beyond the locality. A French mayor or German burgermeister are notable players in their political systems. We need similar 'big-hitters' in our local politics.

While the adoption of elected mayors is likely to remain controversial they seem likely to emerge as part of a mosaic of experiments focusing on developing both representative and participatory democracy. Andrew Adonis (*Observer*, 14 December 1997) predicted that within ten years 'most of Britain's major cities will have elected mayors. The mayoralties will be more sought after than membership of the House of Commons, and they may come to wield greater power than all but a handful of Westminster politicians.' Such a development would undoubtedly raise the profile of local authorities but this must never be at the expense of democratic values and grass roots needs. A generally low turnout – shown in the 34 per cent poll in May 1998 for the referendum on plans for a London mayor and assembly – was not an encouraging signal for ministers' drive to modernise local government.

Directly elected mayors

The case for

- More visible political leadership.
- Streamlines decision making.
- Direct accountability to electorate.
- More powerful political leadership with some independence.

The case against

- Backbench councillors marginalised.
- Decision making becomes more elitist.
- The possible advent of 'personality' policies.
- Greater propensity for corruption.

Reading

Commission for Local Democracy (1995) *Taking Charge: The Rebirth of Local Democracy*, Municipal Journal Books.

Department of the Environment (1991) *The Internal Management of Local Authorities in England*, HMSO.

Department of the Environment (1993) *Community Leadership and Representation: Unlocking the Potential*, Report of the Working Party on the Internal Management of Local Authorities in England, HMSO.

Department of the Environment, Transport and the Regions (1998) *Modern Local Government: In Touch with the People*, Cm 4014, HMSO.

Department of the Environment, Transport and the Regions (1999) *Local Leadership, Local Choice*, DETR.

Filkin, G. with Lord Bassam, Corrigan, P., Stoker, G. and Tizard, J. (1999) *Starting to Modernise: The Change Agenda for Local Government*, New Local Government Network for the Joseph Rowntree Foundation.

Hambleton, R. (1996) *Leadership in Local Government*, University of the West of England, Faculty of the Built Environment, Occasional Paper, No. 1.

H. M. Government (1997) *New Leadership For London*, Green Paper, HMSO.

Hodge, M., Leach, S. and Stoker, G. (1997) *More than the Flower Show: Elected Mayors and Democracy*, Fabian Society, Discussion Paper 32.

Jones, G. and Stewart, J. (1995) 'Directly elected nightmayor', *Local Government Chronicle*, 7 July.

Judge, D., Stoker, G. and Wolman, H. (eds) (1995) *Theories of Urban Politics*, Sage.

Labour Party (1997) *New Labour – Because Britain Deserves Better*, Labour Party Publications.

Page, E. C. (1998) *Future Governance: Lessons from Comparative Public Policy*, Draft proposal to ESRC, University of Hull.

Pratchett, L. and Wilson, D. (eds) (1996) *Local Democracy and Local Government*, Macmillan.

Stoker, G. (1996) *The Reform of the Institutions of Local Representative Democracy: Is there a Role for the Mayor–Council Model?*, Commission for Local Democracy.

Stoker, G. (1998) 'Local political leadership: preparing for the 21st century', Strathclyde University, mimeographed paper.

Stoker, G. and Wolman, H. (1992) 'Drawing lessons from US experience: an elected mayor for British local government', *Public Administration*, 70:2, 241–67.

8

Quangos: are they unloved and misunderstood?

Tony Stott

Introduction

In the 1970s and again in the 1990s, non-elected bodies, or quangos as they are more popularly known, were the subject of high-profile political controversy. Perhaps unfairly, they acquired a public image as disreputable, sleazy, unaccountable and undemocratic institutions. Quangos were unloved by Opposition parties and the media, which painted a picture of them as rather dubious and secretive organisations, wielding great power and packed full of the government's 'friends and supporters'. A party political game emerged as Opposition parties, first the Conservatives in the 1970s and then Labour in the 1990s, attacked the growth of an 'unelected state' as a means of discrediting the government (Stott, 1995a). Quangos, however, are loved by politicians when in office, irrespective of what they may have said when in Opposition. In government, both the Conservative and Labour Parties have established a variety of non-elected national, regional and local bodies. Governments of both major parties have recognised that non-elected bodies play an essential part in the formation, implementation and delivery of public policies. As an important element of the governmental and administrative structure in Britain, they are vital for helping governments achieve their political and public sector managerial objectives and policies.

Confusion, ambiguity and misunderstandings surround quangos. The word 'quango' has become an ill defined but popular catch-phrase. There are important issues about accountability, openness of decision making and democratic participation that have led many to question the legitimacy of quangos as public decision-making bodies. However, political debate has become clouded by myths and political symbolism and distorted by popular, but negative, generalisations, such as those that alleged that all quangos were full either of Conservative or Labour supporters. In all this, the positive contribution that non-elected bodies make to government and administration in Britain has not been widely acknowledged.

There are arguments for and against the use of quangos as instruments of government. There are also conflicting interpretations about the extent to which a 'quango state' has supplanted democratically elected institutions. There are no clear unambiguous answers to the complex and complicated issues surrounding their use. This chapter can only set out and review some of the arguments about the role of quangos in the government of Britain. Much of the debate and misunderstanding of their position stems from the lack of a clear and agreed idea of what quangos really are. The chapter will therefore begin by reviewing what is meant by the term 'quango' and how reliance on different definitions has led to conflicting conclusions about the extent of the 'quango state' today. The chapter will then go on to put the positive case for quangos, explaining why governments favour their use. Finally, the case against quangos as presented by their critics is outlined.

Quangos and their development

What are quangos?

The word 'quango', which began life in the late 1960s meaning 'quasi-autonomous non-governmental organisation' and transformed in the 1970s into 'quasi-autonomous national government organisation', has become an umbrella term beneath which a tremendous variety of organisations shelter. The widespread and popular use of the term has meant, as Weir and Hall (1994, p. 6) note, that 'there is no satisfactory nor universally agreed definition of quango':

- *Narrow definition*   Government, through its publication, *Public Bodies*, produces a list of non-departmental public bodies (NDPBs). An NDPB is defined as 'a body which has a role in the processes of national government, but is not a government department, or part of one, and which accordingly operates to a greater or lesser extent at arm's length from Ministers' (Cabinet Office, 1997a, p. iv). This is a narrow definition that has produced a relatively low number of quangos and a count that has since 1979 recorded a reduction in the number of non-elected bodies (table 8.1). There are two major types of NDPB. Executive NDPBs carry out a wide range of operational, regulatory and commercial functions while advisory NDPBs, which are usually composed of experts in a particular sphere, advise government. In this definition, quangos are NDPBs and are 'quasi-autonomous national government organisations'.
- *Wide definition*   An alternative and wider definition of quangos as 'extra-government organisations' (EGOs) was put forward by Weir and Hall (1994, p. 8). EGOs were defined as 'executive bodies of a semi-autonomous nature which effectively act as agencies for central government and carry out

Table 8.1   *Narrow definition of 'quango': numbers of NDPBs, 1979, 1982, 1990 and 1993–98*

	Executive NDPBs	Staff[a]	Expenditure £m[a]	Advisory bodies	Tribunals	Boards of visitors	Total NDPBs
1979	492	217,000	6,150	1485	70	120	2167
1982	450	205,500	8,330	1173	64	123	1810
1990	374	117,500	11,870	971	66	128	1539
1993	358	111,300	15,410	829	68	134	1389
1994	325	110,200	18,330	814	71	135	1345
1995	320	109,000	20,840	699	73	135	1227
1996	309	107,000	21,420	674	75	136	1194
1997	305	106,400	22,400	610	75	138	1128
1998	304	107,800	24,130	563	69	137	1073

Note: [a] For executive NDPBs only.
Source: *Public Bodies (1998)*.

government policies'. This definition excluded advisory NDPBs but included executive NDPBs as well as NHS bodies. The authors widened the definition of 'quango' by including what they called 'non-recognised bodies'. These were the newer non-elected bodies, such as grant maintained schools, Training and Enterprise Councils, housing associations and Further and Higher Education Corporations, that had been created following the restructuring of different parts of the public sector in the late 1980s and early 1990s. However, a later report (Hall and Weir, 1996, p. 4) recognised that 'there are two species of quangos – executive and advisory' and, as a result, the advisory NDPBs were added into their quango count (table 8.2).

- *Local spending bodies*   These 'non-recognised' bodies were called 'local public spending bodies' by the Nolan Committee, which defined them as ' "not for profit" bodies which are rarely elected and whose members are not appointed by Ministers. They provide public services, often delivered at local level, and are largely or wholly publicly funded' (Committee on Standards in Public Life, 1996, p. 1). These bodies have been recognised by the new Labour government. For the first time, *Public Bodies 1997* made reference to these bodies as a collective group and, according to this report (p. vii), there were 4,651 local public spending bodies in 1997 with 69,813 Board members.

The development of quangos since 1979

From the perspective of the narrow definition, it would appear that the 'quango state' is receding as the number of NDPBs has been declining steadily since 1979 (table 8.1). The wider definition, however, points to a growth and proliferation of government by non-elected bodies (table 8.2).

Table 8.2   *Wider definition of 'quango': numbers of EGOs, 1993 and 1996*

Organisation	1993	1996
Executive NDPBs	358	309
NHS bodies	629	788
Advisory NDPBs	not counted	674
Non-recognised EGOs	4534	4653
Career service companies	–	91
Grant maintained schools	1025	1103
City Technology Colleges	15	15
Further Education Corporations	557	560
Higher Education Corporations	164	175
Registered housing associations	2668	2565
Police authorities	–	41
Training and Enterprise Councils	82	81
Local enterprise companies	23	22
Total	5521	6424

Source: Weir and Hall (1994), Hall and Weir (1996).

- *The 'quango state' is proliferating*   The proponents of this view argue that the public sector managerial reforms, instituted by the Conservative government, have led to a large-scale expansion and unacceptable growth of the 'quango state'. Critics have suggested that the creation of a wide range of new non-elected local bodies has shifted power away from democratically elected institutions to appointed bodies. Professor John Stewart (1992) argued that a 'new magistracy', or new non-elected local elite, which had colonised these newly created local bodies, had taken over responsibility for the delivery of many important local services. As Jones and Stewart (1992) argued, 'elected representatives are being replaced by a burgeoning army of the selected', who are unaccountable to local communities and beyond the reach of any local democratically based decision-making bodies.
- *The 'quango state' is receding*   Conservative ministers and their supporters denied that they had presided over a vast expansion of the 'quango state'. They pointed to the decline in the number of NDPBs after 1979 and argued that the government had cut back the 'quango state'. Their argument was based on the narrow definition of quangos as NDPBs and on the popularised version of the term as meaning 'quasi-autonomous *national* government organisation'. Therefore, bodies that were not national organisations clearly were not quangos. This enabled William Waldegrave, in a House of Commons debate in February 1994, to argue that the government had cut the number of quangos from 2,167 in 1979 to 1,389 in 1994 (*Hansard* (Commons), 24 February 1994, cols 464–6).

Types of quango

Quangos, either as executive or advisory bodies, are now central to the processes involved in the formulation, implementation and delivery of public policies at national, regional and local level in Britain.

- *Moving from the periphery* Prior to the 1980s, quangos tended to be confined to areas on the periphery of government and to operate with specific and narrow executive or advisory tasks at arm's length from government. The character of the quasi-governmental sector, however, changed substantially during the 1980s and 1990s. As Stoker (1999, p. 42) has argued, 'quasi-governmental agencies have moved from the periphery of the policy process to become major agents of new policies and approaches'. According to Weir and Beetham (1999, p. 192), 'executive quangos moved under the Conservatives from the "arm's length" margins of government to become major agents of government policy and action'. In addition, there has been an increasing recognition of the powerful influence now exerted by advisory quangos or advisory NDPBs on government policy. Advisory quangos are 'of major significance to an understanding of the way in which government is informed and policy shaped' (Skelcher, 1998, p. 3). There are different types of executive and of advisory quango (table 8.3).
- *Executive quangos* Executive quangos generally have operational responsibilities for the delivery of different aspects of government policy or public services as regulators, funders or providers. Weir and Beetham (1999, p. 203) suggest that there are two types of executive quango: arm's length and agency type. Arm's-length bodies, such as the Commission for Racial Equality and the Equal Opportunities Commission, are created because they need to be insulated from political interference. During the 1980s and 1990s, the restructuring of the public sector involved the establishment of non-elected bodies as agents of government. Some agency-type bodies were 'strategic' quangos, such as the Further Education Funding Council and the Housing Corporation. Their task was to channel government funding to, and supervise, local public spending bodies. These bodies, such as Further Education Corporations or registered housing associations, together with other executive NDPBs, such as Urban Development Corporations, were direct service providers and acted as agents for government.
- *Advisory quangos* A significant network of advisory bodies, committees and task forces that advise government has developed. Weir and Beetham suggest that there are two major types of advisory quango: judicial-type bodies and advisory bodies. First, judicial-type bodies, such as the Committee on Safety of Medicines and the Advisory Committee on Releases to the Environment, perform 'monitoring, scrutiny, licensing and regulating roles for government ministers on issues which involve specialist knowledge and potentially high risks to the public' (Weir and Beetham, 1999, p. 219). Second, advisory bodies are a source of information and views from experts

Table 8.3   *Types of quango*

Executive Quangos Agency		
Arm's length	**Strategic**	**Agents**
• Commission for Racial Equality • Equal Opportunities Commission • Environment Agency • Civil Aviation Authority • Arts Council • Horserace Totalisator Board (The Tote)	• Higher Education Funding Council • Further Education Funding Council • Funding Agency for Schools • Housing Corporation	• Higher Education Corporations • Urban Development Corporations • Grant maintained schools • Training and Enterprise Councils
Advisory Quangos		
Judicial	**Advisory**	**Investigative**
• Committee on Safety of Medicines • Advisory Committee on Releases to the Environment • Spongiform Encephalopathy Advisory Committee	• British Overseas Trade Board • Overseas Projects Board • Review Board for Government Contracts	• Royal Commission on Environmental Pollution • Football Task Force • Better Regulation Task Force • Disability Rights Task Force • Skills Task Force

Source: Weir and Beetham (1999), *Public Bodies 1998*.

or representatives of different sectors of society. They can be seen as part of networks of 'governing institutions' that influence government activity. For instance, Weir and Beetham (1999, p. 220) identified the existence of a network of business-oriented advisory bodies that included the British Overseas Trade Board. A third type of advisory NDPB, such as the Royal Commission on Environmental Pollution and the Football Task Force, are largely investigative bodies.

The case for and against quangos

It is clear that quangos no longer occupy a place on the periphery of government but are centrally involved in the formulation and implementation of public policies and the delivery of public services. Governments love non-elected bodies because they 'provide an appealing and managerially efficient solution to the problems of governing a complex society' (Skelcher, 1998, p. 2). However, as non-elected bodies, they take decision-making responsibilities out of the direct ambit of democratic institutions. Hence the case against them is that they undermine democratic accountability. The debate can thus be seen, in stark terms, as one of managerialism versus democracy (Skelcher, 1998, p. 5).

The case for quangos

Non-elected executive and advisory bodies provide governments with flexible institutional mechanisms for the political management and handling of public issues and for the management of public services. There are a number of overlapping managerial and political reasons for creating quangos that include:

Putting areas of decision making at arm's length from the political arena   According to the government's Consultation Paper, *Opening up Quangos*, 'there are a number of Government functions which need to be carried out at arm's length from Ministers' (Cabinet Office, 1997b, p. 8). Functions that have a 'judicial' character, such as regulation, and those that relate to the adjudication of claims for funding for areas such as the arts or research, applications for licences and commercial activities, are given to 'autonomous' arm's-length bodies. For example, the Environment Agency has responsibility for regulating pollution while the Civil Aviation Authority grants various licences to airlines. The Arts Councils distribute funding to the arts, while the Horserace Totalisator Board provides a commercial betting service. In addition, responsibility for developing and implementing sensitive areas of public policy, such as racial and gender discrimination, where government seeks cross-party and widespread public consensus, are likely to be given to arm's-length bodies, such as the Commission for Racial Equality and the Equal Opportunities Commission (table 8.3).

Political insulation is a motive for creating arm's-length bodies. The use of independent bodies to make funding and licensing decisions ensures that they are not a vehicle for promoting partisan political interests. They can help to create consensus on sensitive and controversial issues. The legitimacy and public acceptability of decisions are enhanced if they are made, or seen to be made, by bodies that are not subject to political interference. In terms of the overall debate, independent arm's-length quangos provide an important mechanism for depoliticising and managing politically or publicly sensitive governmental activities.

Incorporating experts and stakeholders into public decision-making processes Quangos, especially advisory bodies, give government access to expert advice, information and views on technical, scientific and specialised issues. These include the safety of medicines and drugs, BSE, releases of genetically modified materials into the environment and the development of genetically modified plants (table 8.3) (Weir and Hall, 1995). From the late 1980s, the Spongiform Encephalopathy Advisory Committee played an important role in helping to develop the government's response to the BSE crisis by providing it with expert advice based on an assessment of scientific and medical data and research.

Other bodies have a stronger investigatory role. The Royal Commission on Environmental Pollution, despite its title, is a long-standing and investigative advisory NDPB. It has produced a number of reports, based on its own independent investigations, which have resulted in changes to government policy. In recent years, governments have used advisory bodies increasingly as instruments for conducting fact finding and review investigations. Since 1997, the Labour government has created temporary or short-lived task forces, composed of businesspeople and others with expertise, to investigate a multitude of issues (Rowe, 1998; Ungoed-Thomas and Barot, 1998). Some of these, such as the Football Task Force, Better Regulation Task Force, Disability Rights Task Force and Skills Task Force, have now become permanent advisory NDPBs and thus fall within the narrow definition of 'quango'. The Football Task Force studies issues relating to racism in football, access for the disabled, ticket prices and the increasing commercialisation of football (Cabinet Office, 1998b).

The argument for these quangos is that they help to improve the quality and effectiveness of policy deliberations and governmental decision processes. They provide a forum for contributions from nationally recognised experts and stakeholders associated with different interests that are not involved in the political arena. The status of the members of these advisory bodies, as recognised experts independent of government, helps to give credibility and legitimacy to government decision making. They assist government in managing and making decisions for a society that involve increasingly complex scientific and technical issues.

Improving the management of the public sector   Executive quangos have long been seen as an organisationally and managerially beneficial way of providing services and delivering public policies. According to Skelcher (1998, p. 48), 'notions of efficient management have constantly informed the case for appointed bodies'. In the 1980s and 1990s, non-elected executive quangos, especially local public spending bodies, were seen as important agents for the introduction of 'innovative new management practices largely derived from the private sector' (Flinders, 1999, p. 34). Central to this process was the transfer of functions from traditional and bureaucratic public sector organisations, such as local government, to separate single-purpose executive bodies that were responsible for the delivery of a particular service or activity (table 8.2). Single-purpose and focused organisations can concentrate on the efficient and effective delivery of their assigned tasks that would have a higher profile than if they were subsumed within a wider organisation.

Government now sees quangos as an essential element in the restructuring and reform of the public sector and in the development of a new 'reinvented' form of governance. It was argued that better managed, more effective and customer-oriented public services would result from the creation of single-purpose delivery bodies, such as NHS Hospital Trusts and Further Education Corporations. The separation of the management of service delivery from policy making allows central and local government to concentrate on policy making and, as an enabler, on ensuring that public services are provided. In the parlance of Osborne and Gaebler (1993, pp. 34–7), government could concentrate on 'steering' the public sector while entrusting the delivery of services to executive quangos that act as its agents.

Creating 'flexible friends' or agents to act for government   Weir and Beetham (1999, p. 196) suggest that quangos are the 'government's flexible friends'. As flexible organisational instruments, government can fashion, re-fashion and tailor quangos to meet its specific and changing policy and management needs. In this way, new types of non-elected body, which are 'agents' of government, emerged as part of the restructuring of the public sector. A two-tier hierarchy of providers developed that consisted of local public spending bodies as frontline service-providing agents and strategic agents that supervised their activities. This structure reflected the twin desires of the government to delegate managerial responsibility to frontline providers while at the same time retaining central policy control.

Managerial decentralisation and central control have been at the heart of the creation of educational quangos since 1988. The government argued that the new self-managed educational provider organisations would be better oriented to improving educational standards, providing skills relevant to a modern globally competitive economy, and meeting the needs of its customers and stakeholders. Separate Higher and Further Education Corporations and grant maintained schools became self-managed local public spending bodies and took over responsibility for what are now the new universities, further education colleges and opted-out schools from the Local Education Authorities. This devolution of managerial responsibility has been matched by an increase in central controls. Strategic quangos, such as the Higher Education Funding Council, the Further Education Funding Council and the Funding Agency for Schools, each with substantial budgets (Cabinet Office, 1998b), act as agents for the government and supervise, monitor and channel funds to the local public spending bodies engaged in education. Other quangos are also instruments of central control and provide a mechanism for indirect government intervention and influence (Johnson and Riley, 1995, p. 287). The Qualifications and Curriculum Authority is the latest body to formulate detailed requirements on behalf of government regarding the national curriculum and testing of children.

Assisting government with political management of public issues   For government, quangos are an instrument for managing public issues. There are two different aspects to this. First, quangos are used to increase and consolidate government control. They have been established to bypass existing bodies, such as local authorities, which central government considers inadequate or politically unacceptable. The Urban Development Corporations and the Housing Action Trusts were established to bypass local authorities and to carry out urban and housing regeneration schemes directly.

Second, government distances itself from issues that are too 'hot' or too difficult by delegating responsibility for handling them to a quango. For example, in the early 1990s the task of reviewing the structure of local government in England and of assessing the competing claims of county and district councils was given to the Local Government Commission for England (Skelcher, 1998, p. 2). Public confidence on an issue may be rebuilt if responsibility for decision making is transferred to a body that is at arm's length from the political arena. Following a number of high-profile miscarriages of justice, the Criminal Cases Review Commission was established to make it easier to scrutinise cases when miscarriage was alleged (Flinders and Smith, 1999, p. 9).

The case against quangos

In principle, quangos, as non-elected bodies, appear to be incompatible with elected, representative and democratic government. They are unloved by academic and political critics because they are seen in particular respects to conflict with these principles. The arguments against them include:

Undermining democratically elected institutions and creating a democratic deficit
Employing non-elected bodies to undertake public decision making and service management functions undermines the position of democratically elected and representative institutions. Their members do not have the democratic legitimacy that comes from having been elected. Important areas of public affairs are taken out of the ambit of democratic and representative decision processes. Democracy and public confidence are undermined because, as Skelcher (1998, p. 181) suggests, the 'democratic deficit reflects a fundamental weakness in the ability of citizens to be involved in the structures with which society governs itself'.

The transfer of powers to quangos has weakened elected institutions. It is only in the last few years, starting with the reports of the Nolan Committee (Committee on Standards in Public Life, 1995, 1996), that the democratic issues arising from this development have been given any attention. More recently, the Labour government, through its Consultation Paper, *Opening up Quangos* (Cabinet Office, 1997b), and subsequent White Paper, *Quangos: Opening the Doors* (Cabinet Office, 1998a), has put forward proposals to reduce the democratic deficit. It wanted to make quangos more accountable, open and better understood, with improved links to elected bodies, especially local authorities, thereby creating greater public confidence.

Fragmenting and undermining public accountability   Another aspect of the case against quangos is their lack of public accountability. Stewart (1992) argued that there was no way in which the new non-elected elite of quango members, or 'new magistracy' as he called them, could be locally accountable. They are largely unknown locally and there is no obligation for them to hold open meetings, give the public or local councillors access to information, or subject themselves to local scrutiny. The growth of the 'new magistracy' has resulted in the fragmentation of local channels of accountability. Their accountability is to central government and not local people.

Quangos operate in varying degrees in secret and behind closed doors. Weir and Hall (1995) focus upon the secrecy and lack of accountability of significant advisory NDPBs that deal with crucial issues, such as the safety of medicines (table 8.3). They operate in a twilight world around government where commercial confidentiality operates and the requirements for political accountability and openness are minimal. Weir and Hall (1995, p. 10) noted that 'all advisory quangos meet behind closed doors' and 'are not obliged by law to publicise their work, or to consult and inform the public'. Consequently, it is difficult for them to be held accountable for their advice and decisions.

The Labour government Consultation Paper, *Opening Up Quangos*, recognised that 'there is no obvious mechanism by which quangos can be held to account for their activity' (p. 6). Previously, Conservative ministers, such as William Waldegrave, had argued that accountability to the public had increased as a result of establishing clear standards of service, identifying who was responsible for that service and creating more effective complaints procedures. This argument emphasised accountability to service users and did not address the lack of political accountability. Prior to 1997, there had been some measures to require quangos to be more open, publish annual reports and accounts, hold public meetings and strengthen procedures for dealing with complaints. With its White Paper, *Quangos: Opening the Doors*, the Labour government proposed to extend these measures. More information was to be made available by NDPBs about their meetings and decisions through media such as the Internet. In addition, links between NDPBs and local authorities were to be increased and NDPBs were to be subjected to more focused parliamentary scrutiny by select committees. So far, these moves have been limited in terms of political accountability. Access to the framing of the policies set by national or local quangos is still minimal. To this extent, the use of quangos continues to undermine democratic government.

Creating a patronage state   In the 1970s there were stories of Labour supporters being appointed to quangos and similar stories highlighted Conservative appointments in the 1990s. As each party appeared to appoint its 'friends', allegations of partisan bias and abuse of power emerged. With a lack of systematic information, from a democratic point of view, appointments seemed to be biased, unrepresentative and drawn from a narrow range of interests. In 1993, the *Financial Times* concluded that 'if there is a new elite running Britain's public services . . . it appears the best qualifications to join are to be a businessman with Conservative leanings' (cited in Stott, 1995b, p. 125). Anecdotal evidence suggests it is now Labour-leaning businessmen that assist the Labour government (Rowe, 1998; Ungoed-Thomas and Barot, 1998). It is not surprising that every government will want to have people sympathetic to its views and policies placed in organisations that are key agents for the delivery of its policies and the provision of public services.

While appointments to advisory NDPBs tend not to be tainted with party political bias, there is, according to Weir and Beetham (1999, p. 223), 'commercial penetration of advisory quangos' because many expert or specialist members have professional connections with the industries that they are judging. Without members representing other interests to act as a counterbalance, the decisions of these bodies may be biased to commercial interests. This undermines the argument that advisory NDPBs provide independent and expert advice for government.

Until the 1990s there were no rules to govern or to subject quango appointments to public scrutiny. In addition, very little information was collected systematically or made available publicly (Weir and Hall, 1994, p. 21). Following the first report in 1995 of the Nolan Committee on standards in public life, a Public Appointments Commissioner was appointed to deal with executive NDPBs. Some appointments are now advertised and more information on members of these bodies has been collected, published and placed on the Internet. The Labour government is now proposing to extend the remit of the Commissioner to cover advisory NDPBs and to open public appointments to a wider field of candidates, including more women and members of ethnic minorities who have been under-represented in the past.

Fragmenting governmental institutions Fragmentation of the governmental structure is a consequence of transferring public policy and service management functions to separate single-focus quangos. While these individual quangos may be well suited to their particular tasks and may carry them out effectively, they have a narrow and particular perspective. The creation of smaller specialised provider units means that integration and co-ordination of policies and services no longer occur within multi-purpose organisations such as local authorities. The capacity of local authorities to act as agents for the integration of public policy has been weakened by the creation of local public spending bodies, especially as many of these are not locally accountable. Thus part of the case against quangos rests upon a concern about the lack of policy and managerial integration and co-ordination. Duplication, waste and reduced efficiency, which are signs of inadequate integration, can negate any benefits that arise from the use of single-purpose specialised bodies.

Manipulating the public agenda   Quangos provide governments with useful instruments for manipulating the public agenda. By creating particular quangos and by making favourable appointments to them, governments can dictate the way policy issues are handled. For instance, by creating Urban Development Corporations and bypassing Labour local authorities in the 1980s, the Conservative government was able to institute a more market- and private sector-oriented approach to urban regeneration. In this case, the position of democratic elected institutions was weakened by the way the agenda was manipulated. The ability of the government to take issues out of the ambit of democratic and representative institutions results in some interests in society not being represented in public decision making.

Conclusions

The position of quangos in British politics and public administration continues to be misunderstood. Despite the availability of more information in the last decade, confusion and ambiguity remain. Disagreements continue about defini- tions, numbers and about whether quangos are proliferating or receding as

---

The case for and against quangos

Arguments for

- Decision making at arm's length from the political arena.
- Incorporation of experts and other stakeholders into public decision making.
- Improvement of the management of the public sector.
- 'Flexible friends' or agents to act for government.
- Assist government with political management of public issues.

Arguments against

- Democratically elected institutions undermined and 'democratic deficit' created.
- Public accountability fragmented and undermined.
- 'Patronage state' created.
- Governmental institutions fragmented.
- Manipulation of the public agenda.

---

instruments of government. They are unloved by critics and Opposition parties, and are seen by them as powerful, undemocratic and unrepresentative bodies that place enormous power in the hands of governments. However, governments of all parties love them because they provide them with flexible instruments through which they can govern and manage a complex society. Quangos can and do play a positive role in public policy making and service provision, but without proper democratic safeguards, abuses occur. The developments of the last twenty years suggest that non-elected bodies will continue to be an essential feature of the governmental structure of Britain. The key issue remains one of ensuring that they support rather than undermine elected and democratic government.

Reading

Cabinet Office (1997a) *Public Bodies 1997*, The Stationery Office.

Cabinet Office (1997b) *Opening up Quangos*, Cabinet Office. (*Also available at:* http://www.open.gov.uk/m-of-g/consult97/qufore.htm)

Cabinet Office (1998a) *Quangos: Opening the Doors*, Cabinet Office. (*Also available at:* http://www.cabinet-office.gov.uk/central/1998/pb/open/index.htm)

Cabinet Office (1998b) *Public Bodies 1998*, The Stationery Office.

Cole, M. (1998) 'Quasi-government in Britain: the origins, persistence and implications of the term "quango"', *Public Policy and Administration*, 13:1.

Committee on Standards in Public Life (1995) *Standards in Public Life, Vol. 1: Report*, Cm 2850-I, HMSO.

Committee on Standards in Public Life (1996) *Local Public Spending Bodies, Vol. 1: Report*, Cm 3270-I, HMSO.

Dynes, M. and Walker, D. (1995) *The New British State*, Times Books.

Finkelstein, D. (1995) 'Hail the quangocracy, bane of interfering politicians', *The Times*, 31 January.

Flinders, M. (1999) 'Quangos: why do governments love them?', in M. Flinders and M. Smith (eds), *Quangos, Accountability and Reform*, Macmillan.

Flinders, M. and Smith, M. (eds) (1999) *Quangos, Accountability and Reform*, Macmillan.

Hall, W. and Weir, S. (eds) (1996) *The Untouchables*, The Scarman Trust for Democratic Audit.

Jenkins, S. (1995) *Accountable to None*, Hamish Hamilton.

Johnson, H. and Riley, K. (1995) 'The impact of quangos and the new government agencies on education', *Parliamentary Affairs*, 48:2, April.

Jones, G. and Stewart, J. (1992) 'Selected not elected', *Local Government Chronicle*, 13 November.

Osborne, D. and Gaebler, T. (1993) *Reinventing Government*, Plume (Penguin Books).

Rowe, M. (1998) 'Task Force: a quango by any other name', *Independent on Sunday*, 18 January.

Skelcher, C. (1998) *The Appointed State*, Open University Press.

Stewart, J. (1992) 'The rebuilding of public accountability', Paper to European Policy Forum Conference, December.

Stoker, G. (1999) 'Quangos and local democracy', in M. Flinders and M. Smith (eds), *Quangos, Accountability and Reform*, Macmillan.

Stott, T. (1995a) '"Snouts in the trough": the politics of quangos', *Parliamentary Affairs*, 48:2.

Stott, T. (1995b) 'Evaluating the quango debate', *Talking Politics*, 8:2, Winter.

Ungoed-Thomas, J. and Barot, T. (1998) 'Revealed: Labour's "quangocrat" army', *Sunday Times*, 11 October.

Weir, S. and Beetham, D. (1999) *Political Power and Democratic Control in Britain*, Routledge.

Weir, S. and Hall, W. (eds) (1994) *EGO Trip*, The Charter 88 Trust for Democratic Audit.

Weir, S. and Hall, W. (1995) *Behind Closed Doors*, Channel 4 Television and Democratic Audit.

III

Debates on democracy

9

Are the media the enemy
of democracy?

Bill Jones

Introduction

'Democracy depends on information circulating freely in society', said Katherine Graham, publisher of the *Washington Post* and a key figure in the exposure of the 1972 Watergate conspiracy. Sir Thomas Inskip MP contributed another thought on the subject of the media and politics when he said, 'Dictators have only become possible through the invention of the microphone.' Britain's political system is clearly no dictatorship but some commentators have suggested that, modern media systems notwithstanding, information does not circulate as freely as it should in a properly functioning democracy. This chapter looks at the arguments for and against the modern media as facilitators of democracy, making necessary distinctions between the printed and broadcast media which operate in qualitatively different ways. The debate between the free market and public service is addressed via a box, as is the argument between those Marxist-inclined critics who claim the media are no more than a mouthpiece of the ruling class rather than a bulwark of pluralistic democracy.

Background

Democratic ideas first developed in ancient Greece and the mode of communication was necessarily the spoken word. This remained the case for several hundred years until the invention of the printing press in the fifteenth century. This gave a huge impetus to books and pamphlets as conduits for political ideas and potential stimulants for political action. Next came the development of the press in the nineteenth century, both the broadsheet precursors, including *The Times*, and the early tabloids such as the *Daily Mail* and *Daily Express*. Then came the microphone early in the twentieth century and the radio during the inter-war years, utilised brilliantly by such politicians as Roosevelt,

Baldwin, Adolf Hitler and, incomparably, Winston Churchill. Television became important in Western countries after Richard Nixon used it successfully
in 1952 to clear his name of sleaze allegations and unsuccessfully when he
debated Kennedy in the 1960 presidential elections. In Britain its salience
increased immensely after television coverage of the 1953 Coronation of Elizabeth II was seen by some 20 million via the little box which was destined to
dominate politics from the 1959 election onwards. In 1997 the general election was so heavily covered by television that polls revealed the public was
saturated with it and was beginning to withdraw from the contest as a result.

To contribute towards a healthy pluralist democracy the media should
provide sources of information about the political system and current issues
which are:

- accountable: this includes government accountability to the voters and
  media accountability to the public;
- plentiful and varied;
- relatively unbiased;
- easily accessible;
- not excessively concentrated in terms of ownership;
- factually reliable;
- characterised by a high value on political content.

These, then, are the democratic criteria by which the media need to be judged
for this question to be debated and answered.

The press and democracy

The press comprises some ten national daily newspapers – three tabloid and
two 'mid-market' tabloids plus six broadsheets. In addition there are nine
Sunday papers. Though Britain has a thriving regional press, two-thirds of
the country's 57 million regularly read a national newspaper and slightly more
a Sunday one. In all 185 million newspapers are sold each week in the UK.

The case for the press

Accountability

As long ago as the eighteenth century the press was described as 'the fourth
estate' which functioned as a check on government through reporting, analysing and criticising its actions. Good journalists can often trip up politicians
at press conferences and investigative journalism can reveal scandals such as
the 'cash for questions' affair of 1996–97 or the Mandelson loan in 1998.

Plentiful and varied

The British press boasts a large number of dailies and Sundays as well as local/regional papers providing choices for all tastes and political views.

Relatively unbiased

Most newspapers do tend to take a clear position on issues but these can stimulate thinking and overall the contrasting biases tend to cancel each other out. Moreover, while newspaper proprietors can influence editorial policy on certain issues, many leave such matters purely to their appointed editors.

Easily accessible

Newspapers are for the most part very cheap and within the pocket of virtually every kind of consumer or voter. The declining cost of printing has opened up a new kind of market for magazines of all kinds and political hues. However, the big press battalions have moved in on these too, and the most dynamic and successful are currently being bought up.

Ownership and control

Ownership may be concentrated but even Murdoch controls only 35 per cent of daily circulation and there is a wide choice available.

Factually reliable

Occasionally tabloids have taken liberties with the truth but, taken overall, these can be seen as anomalies; all newspapers respect a duty to report only the truth and all are vulnerable to legal action if they do not.

Political content

The tabloids cater for a different audience to the broadsheets but they do cover most serious political stories, if in a more concise and focused fashion. One additional factor has to be noted: the sheer size of newspapers has expanded enormously since the last war when they were thin and contained only minimal political content. Now daily newspapers can be three or four times as big and many more times on Sundays.

The case against the press

Accountability

The press cannot make politicians realistically accountable as their function is to report and comment at some time removed. Politicians can easily evade questions from the press and their spin doctors – that modern political actor who wields such power – frequently massage the messages reaching readers so that they fail to offer any threat to the government of the day.

The press is not accountable to the public in any real fashion. The Press Council, set up in 1954, was no more than a gathering of the industry's own and was in any case toothless. The Press Complaints Commission, which was set up in 1991, was broader based in membership but still relatively toothless.

Plentiful and varied

UK citizens have a wide choice of newpapers but over the years the number of titles has fallen. In 1900 there were 21 national dailies: the present-day total is 10. In 1923 there were 14 Sunday papers; in the present day only 8. The number of provincial and regional papers has also fallen; from 134 in 1921 to 87 in 1992. In 1900 London had 9 daily evening newspapers; now it has 1.

However, with five broadsheet dailies the UK compares very well with comparable developed countries. The UK has one of the highest newpaper-reading publics in the world, with some 40 million reading a daily paper (it is usually reckoned that three people read each newspaper purchased). Some commentators have been concerned at the fact that the *New Statesman*, a long-established intellectual journal of the Left, has been struggling to survive while the *Spectator*, its equivalent on the Right, has been thriving.

Relatively unbiased

This criterion is not fulfilled by the press as most major newspapers pursue a policy of supporting one or other of the major political parties and otherwise endorsing related sets of political principles. In 1945 the balance of reader-ship favoured the Conservatives, with 6.7 million daily readers of right-wing-leaning papers compared with 4.4 million for Labour. The real swing to the Right, though, came in the 1970s when the *Herald* metamorphosed into the right-wing tabloid the *Sun*. Its owner, Rupert Murdoch, also stiffened the right-wing stance of the press by buying up *The Times* and *Sunday Times*. By 1992 only three dailies supported Labour and the reader ratio had skewed to 8.7 million Conservative readers to 3.3 million Labour.

Between 1992 and 1997, however, a huge dealignment of press sym-pathies occurred as a result of the Conservatives' perceived poor performance in government. By 1997 six of the ten dailies and five of the nine Sundays plumped for Labour in their end-of-the-campaign editorials (see table 9.1). It could be argued that the press fails to support a democratic system when it sides so emphatically with one major party or the other, incidentally leaving the Liberal Democrats without a single major supporter in the press. The broad-sheets tend to strive harder than the tabloids to steer an unbiased course,

Table 9.1   *Newspapers' political allegiances and circulations (figures in millions)*

Daily papers	1997		1992	
Sun	Labour	(3.84)	Conservative	(3.57)
Mirror/Record	Labour	(3.08)	Labour	(3.66)
Daily Star	Labour	(0.73)	Conservative	(0.81)
Daily Mail	Conservative	(2.15)	Conservative	(1.68)
Express	Conservative	(1.22)	Conservative	(1.53)
Daily Telegraph	Conservative	(1.13)	Conservative	(1.04)
Guardian	Labour	(0.40)	Labour	(0.43)
The Times	Euro-Sceptic	(0.72)	Conservative	(0.37)
Independent	Labour	(0.25)	None	(0.39)
Financial Times	Labour	(0.31)	Labour	(0.29)
Sunday papers	**1997**		**1992**	
News of the World	Labour	(4.37)	Conservative	(4.77)
Sunday Mirror	Labour	(2.24)	Labour	(2.77)
People	Labour	(1.98)	Labour	(2.17)
Mail on Sunday	Conservative	(2.11)	Conservative	(1.94)
Express on Sunday	Conservative	(1.16)	Conservative	(1.67)
Sunday Times	Conservative	(1.31)	Conservative	(1.17)
Sunday Telegraph	Conservative	(0.91)	Conservative	(0.56)
Observer	Labour	(0.45)	Labour	(0.54)
Independent on Sunday	Labour	(0.28)	None	(0.40)

Source: Audit Bureau of Circulation.

with the latter being openly partisan during elections; the *Sun*, for example, on election day in 1992 exhorting the last person leaving the country to 'turn out the lights' if Labour were elected into government.

Easily accessible

Most newspapers are so cheap that it can be argued that they are all easily accessible but the price war between Murdoch's *Times* and the competing broadsheets, the *Telegraph* and the *Independent*, suggests price is a factor for even middle-class newspaper purchasers. Moreover, sales dipped in the early 1980s when the huge increases in unemployment made even newspaper purchase a luxury beyond the reach of many.

Ownership and control

There has long been an oligopolistic tendency in the British press. Press barons such as Northcliffe at the turn of the twentieth century owned over half of the national dailies and most of the Sundays but, by 1983, the big three equivalents, Murdoch, Maxwell and Rothermere, owned an even larger share of both markets. Moreover, by the latter date the biggest five companies owned a larger share of the local and regional press (54 and 72 per cent, respectively) than they had in 1945. The four biggest press owners are:

- *Rupert Murdoch*: the Australian US citizen who runs News International and therefore owns the *Sun*, *The Times* and *Sunday Times* (plus their supplements), *News of the World* plus a portfolio of other media interests in the UK and world-wide.
- *Associated Newspapers*: owns the *Daily Mail* and *Mail on Sunday*.
- *Mirror Group*: owns the *Daily Mirror*, *Sunday Mirror*, *Sunday People* and *Daily Record*.
- *United Newspapers*: *Daily* and *Sunday Express*, *Star* and *Evening Standard*.

Most of the big newspaper owners also have substantial interests in television, magazines, books, films and local radio. They are often part of international business conglomerates which operate across a wide gamut of business activity; for example, Berlusconi in Italy and Springer in Germany, as well as Murdoch who operates in the USA, UK, Australia and most of Asia. The Press Commission of 1977 wrote: 'Rather than saying that the press has other business interests, it would be truer to argue that the press has become a subsidiary of other interests' (quoted in Budge *et al.* 1998, p. 336). The Press Complaints Commission has been dominated by fears that the press is too intrusive into the private lives of public people, especially the Royals.

Factually reliable

The broadsheets are for the most part very careful about what they print; they have a reputation for accuracy and fear law suits if they publish wrong information. The tabloids, however, can be less scrupulous and there are examples of the *Sun* publishing interviews with people who did not exist as well as using devices which stretched the truth in order to make something more newsworthy. For example, in December 1998 the *Sun* published photographs of Peter Mandelson – recently revealed as gay – and Nick Brown, similarly revealed once a newspaper threatened to expose a gay affair. The headline was 'Outed' and readers might reasonably have expected a sex exposure story. Instead the headline story related to their support of the single currency, something which the *Sun* hotly opposed.

Some critics argue that the press is not allowed to publish the whole truth because the libel laws in Britain are so favourable to the rich and powerful who can prevent stories being run and use their wealth to fund expensive libel actions against intrusive journalists. Ironically, one of the most persistent post-war litigators in this field was not a politician but a press baron himself: Robert Maxwell.

Political content

Broadsheets devote columns and columns to political features, including long editorials, biographical profiles and news stories. The tabloids tend to minimise their political content, and major news stories relating to policy or international events are often relegated to a few column inches while those relating to soap stars and trivia are given front-page treatment.

News values

As table 9.3 at the end of this chapter shows, the broadsheets tend to support pluralistic democracy while the tabloids tend to work against it. Clearly the mass-selling tabloids, or 'redtops' as they are sometimes called, operate in the mass market, selling more to the less well educated, and create content on the basis of different values from the broadsheets, or 'unpopulars' as Kelvin Mackenzie, legendary editor of the *Sun*, used to describe them. What are these values? They would appear to include the following:

- stories about personalities (easy to understand and accessible to millions) rather than policies (difficult to understand and of interest to a limited number only);
- racy stories about sex and financial misdoings – 'sleaze' – especially if they involve people in the public domain, such as the Royals, politicians or, indeed, actors and television personalities;
- revelations or things which someone or some group of people – for instance politicians – have tried to keep secret;
- disasters or tragedies in which readers seem to have a morbid interest.

Sales of tabloid newspapers more or less prove that, given a preference, British readers will choose to read such stories rather than serious political ones.

Broadcasting and democracy

The British Broadcasting Corporation was set up in 1926 and under John Reith sought to fulfil a mission to 'inform, educate and entertain' in that order. The BBC maintained its monopoly over broadcasting until 1955, when independent television offered competition to the establishment-oriented BBC; BBC2 emerged in 1964. Commercial radio arrived in 1973 and in 1982 another independent television channel in the form of Channel 4. Satellite broadcasting started in 1989, though it took several years for Murdoch's enterprise to start making profits. In 1997 Channel 5 offered another terrestrial option to television viewers. News and current affairs programming is such that every regular watcher of the medium – and on average each British person watches twenty-five hours a week – imbibes a fairly large diet of it.

Public service versus the free market*

Public service

Traditionalists revere the public service ethos of the original BBC which, in a reflection of its formidable first Director General, saw itself as having a mission to serve the public. They see 'spectrum scarcity' – the limited wavelengths available to broadcasters – as a factor which makes the medium a public resource to be treasured for all society. It follows from this that broadcasting should be regulated by the state in terms of creating either a monopoly corporation, such as the BBC during 1926–55, or issuing licences to companies which operate under a system of agreed rules. These would include: accurate and fair news and current affairs coverage; no political advertising or opinions espoused by broadcasters over the air; accountability of broadcasting to the public; broadcasting to serve the whole nation and not particular social strata or geographical regions; and funding from public sources. Public service advocates say that if left to the free market, broadcasting would cater to the lowest common denominator – the equivalent of tabloid journalism – and encourage the worst kind of journalism.

Free market

Free market supporters tend to be on the Right and argue that there should be an open market in broadcasting just as there is for any other commodity; so news programmes would compete with like and the competition would improve the quality of what resulted. This way the public would get what it wanted and not what the university-educated elitists who run broadcasting think they might want. The plenitude of opportunities provided by cable and now digital broadcasting remove the limits of spectrum scarcity and enable broadcasters to operate competitively in a free market. Introducing the free market to the medium would also eliminate the insidious effect of government control of the media which, because it undermines freedom of speech, is even more dangerous than that of media moguls. The free competition between ideas which would ensue from such an arrangement, claim some free marketeers, would produce the victory of the 'best' set of ideas.

* Material for this box was drawn from Budge *et al.* (1998), pp. 330–1.

The case for broadcasting

Accountability

News conferences in the UK are not televised as in the USA and it is the current affairs programme, such as *Today* on Radio Four and *Newsnight* on BBC2, which puts the politician on the spot even more effectively than Prime Minister's Questions on a Wednesday afternoon. Politicians find it very hard to escape the probing interrogations of the likes of John Humphrys, Jim Naughtie on *Today* or the formidable Jeremy Paxman on *Newsnight*. Paxman once famously asked an evasive Michael Howard, then Home Secretary, the same question fourteen times and each time Howard did not give a straight answer. These programmes reveal politicians to us in all their strengths and weaknesses and enable us to 'know' them in a way never before possible.

Relatively unbiased

The broadcast media are obliged by statute – the Broadcasting Act of 1981 – to be politically unbiased and to provide equal coverage of the parties or candidates during election campaigns. According to surveys, two-thirds of voters regularly believe this ideal to have been achieved by this branch of the media.

Easily accessible

Virtually every family now has a colour television; the BBC requires a licence of over £100 per year but independent terrestrial channels are funded by advertising and are free to the viewer. In addition satellite or cable, and now digital, channels provide even more viewing time at a cost which a growing percentage of viewers find acceptable to their finances.

Concentrations of ownership

The publicly owned BBC represents a concentration of ownership but as this is 'public' there is less danger of it taking a partisan line as a result. Moreover, there is strict legislation to ensure that there is no political bias in television and radio news or current affairs broadcasting (see below).

Factually reliable

The BBC has a world-wide reputation for accuracy and tends to be very wary about broadcasting anything but the double-checked truth. Other broadcasting channels reflect a similar respect for the truth and in consequence over two-thirds of voters respect such sources as reliable compared with only one-third regarding the press. Harold Wilson, the Labour Prime Minister, used to say that broadcasting was 'our medium' as the press belonged to the Conservatives. He may have changed his mind after David Dimbleby's *Yesterday's Men* programme in 1972 poured scorn on the Labour Shadow Cabinet.

Political content

Reithian traditions at the BBC placed a high value on current affairs and this emphasis is replicated by most major broadcast outlets, depending on the specialisms concerned. Radio Four, for example, has the *Today* programme, listened to every morning by the nation's top decision makers; the *World at One* and the *PM Programme*, as well as scores of news broadcasts and documentary programmes. Radio One plays popular music but also provides regular news bulletins. Even commercial pop-music stations carry regular news programmes provided by an independent agency. On television all the major terrestrial channels provide extensive news coverage and most seek to provide substantial current affairs coverage in the form of regular discussion or investigative programmes such as *Dispatches* or *World in Action*. The BBC's *Question Time*, watched by several million viewers, provides an approximation to a national discussion forum with its mixture of government, Opposition and independent participants, as well as a vocal and critical audience.

The case against broadcasting

It is not possible to argue that television is either inaccessible or not varied and plentiful. It is a universally cheap medium and even unemployed people can afford to have a set or even two. Moreover, since the arrival of cable, satellite and digital television there is no shortage of choice, with twenty-four hour *Sky News* matching the similar service which the BBC currently offers to cable viewers. However, the critical case is on firmer ground regarding some of the other criteria.

Accountability

Broadcasters are in theory accountable to the people via government but for many this merely defines the problem as it is the government which is the source of anti-democratic tendencies. There is no direct accountability of broadcasters to the public except for occasional programmes such as *Feedback* on Radio Four. Many claim that the accountability of broadcasters to the government is merely an opportunity for the government to exercise control in its own political interests. Campaigners for freedom of the media were outraged during the 1980s when the Conservatives launched attacks on the BBC for alleged left-wing bias and were scarcely reassured by the Labour government in December 1998 when it too attacked the BBC for alleged bias towards the Conservatives. The Conservatives appointed a right-wing Chairman of the BBC in the form of Marmaduke Hussey in an attempt to correct its perceived left-wing leaning. It is also the case that the government sets the parameters of how the broadcasters operate and can apply pressure through threatening to change these guidelines; for example, the rules affecting the positions of companies operating under the Independent Television Commission or the cost of the licence which entitles viewers to watch or listen to BBC programmes.

Relatively unbiased

Both major political parties argue about the BBC and both have accused it in the past of being biased one way or the other. Most members of the public tend to believe it is unbiased, in accordance with its statutory duty. It is an odd fact that the BBC is not legally obliged by the 1954 and 1981 Broadcasting Acts to be unbiased in its political coverage, although it voluntarily agrees to abide by the rules by which independent companies are formally and legally bound. However, some media researchers, based at Glasgow University, argue that television, through its packaging, editing and presentation, subtly reinforces those dominant values which reinforce the position of the ruling economic groups in society (see 'Dominance versus pluralism' box).

Table 9.2 *Dominance and pluralism models compared*

	Dominance	Pluralism
Societal source	Ruling class or dominant elite	Competing political social, cultural interests and groups
Media	Under concentrated ownership and of uniform type	Many and independent of each other
Production	Standardised, routinised, controlled	Creative, free, original
Content and world view	Selective and coherent: decided from 'above'	Diverse and competing views responsive to audience demand
Audience	Dependent, passive, organised on large scale	Fragmented, selective, reactive and active
Effects	Strong and confirmative of established social order	Numerous, without consistency or predictability of direction, but often 'no effect'

Source: McQuail (1983), p. 68.

Dominance versus pluralism

The Frankfurt school of social theorists argued that Marx was fundamentally correct when he said that 'the ideas of the ruling class are in every epoch the ruling ideas'. In a capitalist society it would therefore be the ideas which suited the interests of the property owners – the bourgeoisie – which would, through myriad subtle ways, permeate society at all levels. In this way those basic rules would be provided which constituted society's view of 'common sense'; on how the economy should be run, on how workers should be paid, and so on. This Marxist analysis goes on to argue that in modern capitalist societies the ruling class exercises such control that a uniform world view is disseminated to its passive and uncritical audience; news is interpreted and presented in a way which reinforces the existing social order; and the ignorance of the mass audience is maintained through a plethora of light entertainment such as sport, soap operas, game shows and the like.

Against this, defenders of the modern media insist that they take take their position as one of the competing forces in society, seeking, through their many outlets, to offer contrasting views of the world according both to the independent views of those in charge of the media and the requirements of the range of audiences which comprise a modern developed society. Table 9.2 summarises the different positions. Which is closest to the truth? It cannot be denied that the BBC has tended to support establishment positions – for example, Reith admitted during the General Strike in 1926 that ultimately his corporation would not be 'really impartial'. However, in the current day the media have developed a strong sense of independence which they guard jealously – witness the fights over programmes such as *Death on the Rock* in 1988. This is the programme which the Conservative government tried but, despite intense pressure, failed, to ban; a retrospective inquiry by an ex-government minister further embarrassed his former colleagues by completely exonerating the programme. Further strong anti-establishment messages break through in other ways: via programmes such as *Rough Justice*, which exposed the innocence of the Guildford Four; via soap operas which regularly deal with radical issues; and via satirical programmes such as *Spitting Image* and Rory Bremner, which poke fun and ridicule politicians, however high, mighty and powerful they may be. On balance, though the media's messages may be distorted by the bias of the press, the tendency of the television to reflect consensual views and the news management efforts of the government, the media's role and nature accord more closely to the pluralist model than the Marxist one of sinister control and passive audience acceptance.

Concentration of ownership

The print media moguls have also made huge inroads into ownership of broadcasting. The most obvious is Murdoch, who owns BSkyB as well as holding substantial interests in other media companies. In theory such magnates are restricted from intruding too deeply into such business areas lest they become too powerful for the health of the country's democracy. However, few checks have been placed on Murdoch's progress; his merger of Sky with British Satellite Broadcasting in 1990, for example, was not even referred to the Independent Broadcasting Authority. Moreover, since the sale of independent television franchises in 1992, a number of mergers have occurred – for example, Granada and London Weekend. These developments would appear to suggest that concentration of ownership is likely to continue in the foreseeable future.

Factually reliable

Television is perceived as being the most reliable of all the media in terms of accuracy, but some point out that:

- Some documentaries and guests on chat shows on independent stations have been proved to be faked.
- The role of spin doctors has raised question marks against some of the news coverage regarding the extent to which it has been massaged and altered by politicians' media advisers. Occasionally such spin can be counter-productive, as when Peter Lilley's spinners heralded his speech on funding the welfare state in April 1999 as a 'break with Thatcherism'. It was received as such and precipitated an almighty row with the right wing of the party which William Hague found difficult to calm down.
- The amount of time television gives to politicians has declined enormously. As in the USA, Britain has been taken over by the tendency of political leaders to speak in 'sound bites', aiming for a memorable quote to be featured in news broadcasts and the headlines of the print press. In consequence much of politics seems to have been reduced to meaningless slogans incompatible with the real understanding a functioning democracy requires. Moreover, a whole news broadcast would fill only two columns of a broadsheet newspaper, raising the question of whether television, with all its immediacy and colour, can really fulfil the needs of a sophisticated democracy.

Political content

Some independent companies have been criticised for not fulfilling their 'public service' obligations regarding news and current affairs, and others, including the BBC, have been upbraided for 'dumbing down' their news coverage with 'tabloid' news values, and focusing on non-political human interest stories and sensational topics such as scandal and sleaze.

Conclusion

The media are essential to democratic political activity. They are the blood which circulates around the body politic and enables it to work. To argue therefore that they are anti-democratic seems contradictory. However, the media can be the instrument of a tyrannical system of government and some commentators perceive in developed capitalist countries some of the symptoms of such malign political control becoming manifest. They argue that the media are easily manipulated by government and its clever media advisers; witness the famed spin doctors of Labour: Mandelson, Campbell and Whelan. They also argue that concentrated ownership enables media tycoons to exert unfair control of what is presented to the people as well as put undemocratic pressure on the government of the day. Table 9.3 reveals how the different

Table 9.3   *The 'democrativeness' of media elements*

Democratic criterion	Broadsheets	Tabloids	Radio		TV	
			BBC	Commercial	BBC	Commercial
Easily accessible	+	+	+	+	+	+
Plentiful and varied	+	+	+	+	+	+
Concentration of ownership	–	–	–	–	–	–
Factually reliable	+	–	+	+	+	+
High value political content	+	–	0	–	+	+
Accountability 1 (Government)	+	–	+	–	–	–
Accountability 2 (Media)	–	–	–	–	–	–
Low bias	0	–	+	–	+	+

Notes:
Accountability 1 = the tendency for the media element to facilitate democracy.
Accountability 2 = degree of accountability of medium to public.
+ = high tendency to encourage democracy.
– = low tendency to encourage democracy.
0 = neutral effect (i.e. '0' is given for BBC radio as most of its five channels are music based and '0' for the bias of broadsheets as they tend to give space to alternative opinions to their editorials).

elements of the media score as facilitators of democracy. The pluses indicate positive forces for democracy, the zeros a neutral influence and the minuses a negative influence. The most positive element therefore seems to be television and radio, though the broadsheets also score well on most criteria. Least contributive to democratic politics are the tabloid press, and some critics of the media claim the news values which this branch of the press espouse are insidiously affecting the broadsheets as well as television and radio. However, Stuart Higgins, the former editor of the *Sun*, the leading tabloid, declared he would take his publication more 'up market' to cater for the improving educational standards of his working-class readership. David Yelland, his successor, has decided to pursue the same direction. What is perhaps ignored in such discussions is that the media themselves are not accountable in any democratic fashion. The press operates in the open market, so a kind of accountability exists in that people who dislike what it does can switch to another publication. Broadcasters are even less constrained. Independent broadcasters can be shunned by the viewing public but they do not have to answer for their decisions in any political fashion. Given the danger of political controls over television perhaps this is just as well.

Reading

Budge, I. *et al.* (1998) *The New British Politics*, Longman.

Curran, J. and Seaton, J. (1991) *Power without Responsibility: The Press and Broadcasting in Britain*, Routledge.

Glasgow University Media Group (1976) *Bad News*, Routledge & Kegan Paul.

McQuail, D. (1983) *Mass Communication Theory: An Introduction*, Sage.

McQuail, D. (1992) *Media Performance: Mass Communications and the Public Interest*, Sage.

Negrine, R. (1995) *Politics and the Mass Media*, Routledge.

Newton, K. (1997) 'Mass media and politics', in L. Robins and B. Jones, *Half a Century in British Politics*, Manchester University Press.

Seymore-Ure, C. (1974) *The Political Impact of the Mass Media*, Constable.

Watts, D. (1997) *Political Communication Today*, Manchester University Press.

10

Would fixed-term Parliaments enhance democracy?

Philip Norton (Lord Norton of Louth)

The Parliament Act of 1911 provides for each Parliament to have a maximum life of five years but it is rare for any Parliament to go its full term. Elections occur within the five year limit whenever the Prime Minister recommends one to the Monarch.

Recent years have seen a growing demand for fixed-term Parliaments; that is, with elections for Parliament taking place on a set day once every so many years (a four year term is popular among advocates), with the Prime Minister of the day having no scope for bringing the date forward.

Support for fixed-term Parliaments was notable among Opposition politicians – that is, politicians drawn from the parties losing out under the current arrangements – during the period of Conservative government from 1979 to 1997. In March 1983, Labour MP Austin Mitchell introduced a ten minute rule Bill 'to dissolve the present Parliament immediately; and to provide for general elections to be held at intervals of not more than four years unless a majority of the House of Commons votes for an earlier dissolution' (*House of Commons Debates (HC Deb.)*, vol. 19, cols 841–4). In February 1987, another Labour MP, Tony Banks, also utilised the ten minute rule Bill procedure to introduce a Bill 'to make provision for a fixed five year term for the duration of Parliament' (*HC Deb.* vol. 109, cols 1003–4). In May 1991, Liberal Democrat peer, Lord Holme of Cheltenham, initiated a debate in the House of Lords to call attention to the case for fixed-term Parliaments (*House of Lords Debates (HL Deb.)*, vol. 529, cols 244–62). The same year, the proposal was included in a programme of constitutional reform by the Institute of Public Policy Research and endorsed at the Labour Party Conference by the party leader, Neil Kinnock. In March 1992, Tony Banks again introduced a Bill, this time under the unballoted Bill procedure, to provide for fixed-term Parliaments (*HC Deb.*, vol. 205, col. 744), and in the general election of that year the Labour manifesto, as well as that of the Liberal Democrats, included fixed-term Parliaments as a policy proposal. Labour MP Jeff Rooker – who had opposed Austin Mitchell's Bill in 1983 – introduced a Bill in February 1994, under the unballoted Bill procedure, to give effect to the policy, supported by former Labour leader Neil Kinnock (*HC Deb.*, vol. 238, col. 658).

None of these proposals got anywhere. Austin Mitchell was denied leave to introduce his Bill by 130 votes to 42. Opponents of Tony Banks' 1987 Bill did not force a vote, thus allowing Banks leave to introduce the Bill, but the Bill made no further progress. Only Banks and Austin Mitchell served as the Bill's sponsors. The debate in the Lords was not subject to a vote and the remaining Bills introduced in the Commons were introduced formally but, because of the procedure under which they were introduced, were not debated. Neither of the parties committed to fixed-term Parliaments – Labour and the Liberal Democrats – won the 1992 general election.

During the period of Conservative government, ministers stood fast in support of the existing arrangements. Opposition MPs questioning ministers on the issue were usually given short shrift. When Liberal MP Archy Kirkwood asked the Prime Minister, Margaret Thatcher, in December 1986 if the government would introduce legislation to provide for fixed-term Parliaments, he got a monosyllabic response: 'No' (*HC Deb.*, vol. 106, col. 729W). When Labour MP Andrew Mackinlay asked a similar question of Margaret Thatcher's successor, John Major, in May 1992, the answer was longer but the import was identical: 'I have no plans to do so. The present system serves the country well' (*HC Deb.*, vol. 208, col. 493).

The election in May 1997 of a Labour government committed to a programme of constitutional reform has not resulted in any move to introduce fixed-term Parliaments. The case against tends not to be made by Conservative or Labour politicians as such but rather by politicians who are in power, or some who expect to be in power. Those who are the most enduring advocates of fixed-term Parliaments are those who are perennially the 'outs' of politics. Those engaging in the debate thus lay themselves open to the charge of self interest, but in engaging in the debate they have advanced arguments of principle and practicality.

What, then, are the principal arguments for and against having fixed-term Parliaments?

The case for

The arguments for fixed-term Parliaments are essentially twofold.

Equity

The principal argument is that they would provide a greater degree of equity, or fairness, in the nation's electoral arrangements. At present, the law stipulates the maximum lifetime of a Parliament. Within that statutory maximum, it is a Crown prerogative as to when Parliament is dissolved. The Monarch now acts on the advice of her government and so the date of the election is determined, in practice, by the Prime Minister.

The Prime Minister is a political animal and chooses a date most likely to ensure the return of his or her party to office. Margaret Thatcher was especially effective in choosing dates that favoured the return of her Conservative government. The Conservative Party was in office from 1979 to 1997 but the Conservatives did not enjoy a lead in the opinion polls continuously throughout that period. At one point in 1981, the party actually fell to third place in the polls. The party trailed Labour in the polls during the Westland crisis in 1986 and in the Spring of 1990 the party trailed Labour by more than twenty points. Margaret Thatcher made sure that when she asked the Queen to call a general election it was at a time most propitious for the Conservatives to win another term in office: that is, when the party was leading in the opinion polls. Her successor, John Major, led a party that rarely enjoyed a lead in the opinion polls and so chose dates that he thought would do least damage to the party.

Advocates of fixed-term Parliaments argue that allowing the Prime Minister the power to choose the date of the election is unfair on the other political parties – which have no say in the matter and which lose out under the arrangement – and unfair on electors in that the decision as to when they vote rests with the leader of a political party. The point was argued by Lord Holme in opening his debate in the House of Lords: 'General elections are about renewing the power and re-establishing the legitimacy upon which democratic government rests. So in a very real sense, elections should belong to the voters rather than in any sense belonging to or being manipulated by the Prime Minister and the Government' (*HL Deb.*, vol. 529, col. 245).

Furthermore, the power to determine the date of the election can permit the Prime Minister to engage in a political cat-and-mouse game with the Opposition parties, keeping them guessing as to when an election will be held. Opposition parties have difficulty planning for an election if they do not know when it is to be held and may waste time and money on party promotion if the Prime Minister sends out signals an election is imminent but then decides not to call an election. Providing for a specific date on which each general election will take place removes the privileged position of the Prime Minister and of the party in office.

Certainty

The second argument in favour of fixed-term Parliaments is one of certainty. Knowing precisely when an election is to be held has beneficial effects both politically and economically. Politically, election campaigns will be geared to the known date of the election. This, it is argued, would get rid of the long and sometimes phoney election campaigns that can occur under the existing system, parties anticipating an election a year or so before it actually takes place. As Prime Minister, John Major let the 1987–92 Parliament virtually go its full term and then did the same with the succeeding Parliament. Given that few Parliaments go their full term (the last was that of 1959–64), political parties engaged in what was effectively an election campaign a year or so before the actual election. If the date of the election is fixed, campaigns will be geared to that date. Phoney campaigns – which are a drain on party resources and electors' patience – will be at an end.

Knowing when an election is to be held will also have economic consequences. According to critics of the existing system, the uncertainty of the election date means that companies and investors cannot plan ahead. Long campaigns generate uncertainty. The point was developed by a company Chairman and former Chairman of the National Coal Board, Lord Ezra, in the 1991 House of Lords debate: 'The present position is that for at least a year before the term of a government expires, speculation begins and uncertainty is generated. While that may be of interest to the bookmakers, such uncertainty and speculation are of no interest whatever to business. Uncertainty weakens confidence and therefore business operations suffer' (*HL Deb.*, vol. 529, col. 245). An allied point is that governments are prone to manipulate the economy in the run-up to a general election. Introducing a fixed term may encourage government to engage in greater long-term planning, since it would not be able to wait to see the effects of short-term manipulation of the economy before calling an election.

Proponents of fixed-term Parliaments contend that these are powerful arguments. Furthermore, they point out that having fixed-term Parliaments would bring the United Kingdom into line with many other European nations, including Germany, the Netherlands, Sweden and Norway. Indeed, they can also point out that fixed-term elections are not unknown within the United Kingdom. Local government elections take place on a fixed-term basis, as do elections to the European Parliament. Fixed-term elections have also been introduced for the new Scottish Parliament and the Welsh Assembly. Flexible election dates for Parliament are thus the exception within British electoral practice.

Advocates of fixed-term elections do, though, concede that there are circumstances in which the life of a Parliament may need to be cut short. If a government has difficulty governing – perhaps because of splits within its own ranks or a minuscule or non-existent parliamentary majority – should the Parliament necessarily have to complete its full term? Supporters of fixed-term Parliaments have come up with various suggestions to meet this point. The most straightforward is to provide for an election if the government loses a vote of confidence in the House of Commons. This, it is argued, provides for some degree of flexibility while at the same time taking the power to call an election out of the hands of the Prime Minister and giving it to the House of Commons.

The case against

The case against fixed-term Parliaments is that they would introduce inflexibility and excessive electioneering.

Inflexibility

A strict application of the concept of fixed-term Parliaments would mean that there was little or no provision for an election before the stipulated – that is the fixed – date. A Parliament would run its fixed term regardless of what circumstances befell the Parliament or the government. As we have seen, supporters of fixed-term Parliaments concede that a general election may be triggered before the fixed date by the House of Commons passing a vote of no confidence in the government. Some also argue that an election may be triggered by a simple motion passed by the House agreeing to an election. There are provisions for such a premature dissolution of the Parliament in various European countries with fixed-term Parliaments. Opponents of fixed terms argue that there are circumstances, other than the government losing the confidence of the House, when a new general election may be desirable. The most obvious, but not the only, example they cite is that in which a government has no overall majority. Should the Parliament continue, leaving a weak minority government or one forced to do deals with other parties, or should it be dissolved, allowing voters to decide what should happen? 'Is it better for a government unable to govern to go to the country to try to obtain a new mandate or for the same government to spend their time fixing up deals in which the unfortunate electorate has no say whatsoever? . . . The people not the parties should decide who governs' (Lord Waddington, Leader of the House of Lords, *HL Deb.*, vol. 529, col. 260).

If the scope for a premature dissolution of Parliament is extended beyond that of the government losing a vote of confidence, then one soon ends up in a situation that is not greatly dissimilar to that which presently exists in the United Kingdom. If the House can pass a motion agreeing to a premature election, or some discretion is vested in the head of state, then the situation would not vary greatly from what exists at the moment. The issue then becomes one, not of whether one has a fixed-term Parliament or not, but rather of where the power rests in calling an election. Indeed, as one proponent of fixed-term Parliaments has conceded, once one goes beyond a vote of no confidence as a triggering mechanism for an early dissolution of Parliament, the value of fixed-term Parliaments is lost: 'it is only under a fixed-term arrangement subject to No Confidence motions as proposed that one could hope to keep early dissolutions free from political manipulation by the government, and ensure electoral timing was determined by reasons of genuine constitutional need, as opposed to pure party political advantage' (Blackburn, 1995,

p. 63). The choice is thus between creating a largely inflexible system, with no provision for an early election other than as a consequence of a vote of no confidence, or one that permits of some degree of political manipulation. The former is the one generated by a strict application of the concept of fixed-term Parliaments.

Supporters of the present arrangements contend that flexibility is an aid rather than a hindrance in democratic terms. If a government is returned with a small or non-existent majority, and/or later slips into a minority in the House of Commons, there is nothing especially democratic about forcing it to stagger on as a minority government or force it to do some deals with other parties, deals that have no electoral sanction. Allowing the government to call an election – and let the electorate decide whether it should continue or not – is a far more democratic option.

Even if a government is returned with a clear overall majority, supporters of existing arrangements see no objection to the Prime Minister advising the Monarch as to when to call an election. The government is seeking a renewal of its mandate from the people and, if the people do not wish to renew that mandate, then they are free to deny the government another term in office. The political manipulation involved in determining electoral dates is seen as preferable to the inflexibility that would be injected by fixed-term Parliaments.

Excessive electioneering

If the date of elections is fixed, there is the danger of long drawn-out election campaigns. As we have seen, long campaigns are possible under the present system. Opponents of fixed-term Parliaments claim that under this system such long campaigns will be the norm rather than the exception. Once one election is over, then the campaign for the next one gets under way. Parties can plan ahead and may attempt to steal a march on their opponents by campaigning early. Though parties may not wish to engage in long campaigns – they are expensive and put tremendous strain on party resources – the ratchet effect of election campaigns (once one party starts early, the others have to follow so as not to lose out) may mean that they have no option. The result would be more attention to fund raising and to campaigning, placing not only an undue stress on party resources but also on electors' patience.

The extent to which long campaigns would become the norm is not clear. Campaigns in local government elections, with fixed-term elections, are short. Opponents point to experience in the USA, with rigid fixed-term elections, where there is virtually a continuous election campaign, especially at national level. They contend that, so long as there is a possibility of such a situation being replicated in the UK, fixed-term elections are best avoided.

Conclusion

In terms of enhancing democracy, fixed-term elections are claimed by supporters to be beneficial in that they remove the opportunity for political manipulation by the party in power. The choice of election dates becomes neutral. Fixed terms are seen by opponents as undermining democracy in that, by reducing or eliminating the prospect of an early election, voters are denied a say in what should happen after a government runs into trouble, the decisions being taken by politicians and not by the electorate.

Supporters of fixed-term Parliaments are able to call in their aid popular support. In the MORI *State of the Nation* polls in 1991 and 1995, a majority of respondents supported 'fixing the length of a Parliament so removing the power of Government to choose the date of an election'. In 1991, as can be seen from Table 10.1, 56 per cent of those questioned either 'strongly' supported or 'tended' to support the statement; in 1995 the figure was 57 per cent. In 1991 only 23 per cent opposed the statement; in 1995 the figure was 18 per cent (MORI, 1995, p. 10). However, there is little evidence that this popular support has been translated into significant pressure for change. In the MORI polls, those 'strongly' supporting fixed-term Parliaments never exceeded 23 per cent and supporters do not appear to be prominent in pressing their case in Parliament. The issue of fixed-term Parliaments does not appear to rank high on voters' or politicians' lists of priorities. The outcome of the 1997 general election may have pushed the issue further down the list of priorities. The 'out' party for eighteen years was voted in by the electors. The existing arrangements for calling elections did not prevent the electors turning the incumbent party out of office and doing so decisively. The new party in office may not give a high priority to change now that it controls the levers of power.

Table 10.1   *Fixed-term parliaments*

	1991 (%)	1995 (%)	Change 91–95 (%)
Strongly support	21	23	+2
Tend to support	35	34	−1
Neither support nor oppose	16	18	+2
Tend to oppose	18	12	−6
Strongly oppose	5	6	+1
Don't know	5	6	+1

Source: MORI (1995).

Fixed-term Parliaments

The case for

- Would introduce fairness in electoral arrangements, taking power out of the hands of the Prime Minister.
- Would give electors and parties greater certainty in knowing when elections will be held.
- Would introduce greater certainty for those firms and investors wanting to plan ahead.
- Would bring the UK into line with many of its continental partners.
- Would enjoy popular support.

The case against

- Would introduce inflexibility into the political system.
- Would create the potential for weak and unstable governments.
- May force parties to enter into bargaining and coalitions not sanctioned by the electorate.
- Would, or may, allow lengthy election campaigns.
- Are not regarded as a priority by political parties.

Reading

Blackburn, R. (1995) *The Electoral System in Britain*, Macmillan.
MORI (1995) *State of the Nation*, MORI.

11

Should citizenship education be compulsory?

Lynton Robins and Vivien Robins

Labour's interest in promoting citizenship has been reflected in a variety of constitutional reforms – from devolution, bringing home a Bill of Rights and electoral reform through to introducing citizenship education in schools. However, the idea of universal citizenship education is not new and there is a long history of reformers promoting citizenship education under a variety of labels, such as 'civic education', 'political education' and 'political literacy'. Furthermore, the case that citizenship education has any beneficial impact upon school pupils is contested. This chapter places the contemporary debate into context and explores the main arguments for and against compulsory citizenship education.

Old wine in a new bottle?

The idea that citizenship education in schools might provide a more enlightened and civilised democracy is not new. For example, the emergence of fascist regimes in 1930s Europe, together with the threat of fascism becoming popular in British politics, led a number of liberal intellectuals to set up the Association for Citizenship in Education in 1934. It was argued that if British schoolchildren were taught about democracy they would reject fascism, unlike their counterparts in Spain, Italy and Germany. Until then, citizenship education had been restricted to a public school elite where it was the ethos of the school rather than the classroom curriculum which was seen as crucial in preparing the young for their future role of leadership in society. The Association for Citizenship in Education was concerned, however, not with the public school elite but with the children of the masses who, it was felt, could be manipulated either safely towards democracy or dangerously towards some authoritarian alternative.

Despite the support of prominent intellectuals of the day, such as G. D. H. Cole, Kingsley Martin, Sir Henry Hadow and Sidney Webb, the Association failed in its objectives. Final defeat came with rejection of their idea of putting citizenship into the curriculum by the Norwood Report of 1943. Norwood argued that it would be the positive character-building life of the school which would prepare young pupils for their future roles as citizens, not lessons in politics.

The second campaign dedicated to the cause of universal political education, the Politics Association, was established in 1969. Once again, a relatively small group of educationalists was concerned about the low levels of political awareness displayed by young people alongside high levels of alienation towards Britain's national political symbols. The latter concern was reinforced by the findings of political socialisation research by American academics, led by the respected Jack Dennis. In a comparative study, published in the *British Journal of Political Science*, he and his colleagues found that English schoolchildren exhibited such a degree of antipathy towards politics that they felt justified in speculating about a future crisis of legitimacy afflicting British politics.

General interest in political education was intensified by an initiative from the Politics Association and Hansard Society – led by Professor Bernard Crick and funded by the Nuffield Foundation – the Programme for Political Education (PPE). It was proposed that within this curriculum programme initiative 'politics' be taught to pupils through 'issues' rather than 'institutions'; that all pupils should benefit from 'political literacy' and not just the privileged few; and that the programme's focus should be on development of political skills rather than political knowledge. Any public anxiety about political bias or indoctrination being introduced into the classroom was eased by underpinning the whole process by specific 'procedural values' – namely, freedom, toleration, fairness, respect for the truth and respect for reasoning.

The report of the PPE, published in 1978 and edited by Bernard Crick and Alex Porter (a newly appointed lecturer in political education at the London Institute) was savaged. Most destructive was the attack by John Vincent in the *Times Literary Supplement*. His attack on the sloppiness of the report's presentation ranged from its typographical errors, incorrect page numbering and meaningless diagrams, and then continued to attack the sloppiness of the very notion of political education. While probably not deserving the full weight of Vincent's criticism, the PPE report was naive. In retrospect, many of the illustrative lesson plans would have resulted in classroom mayhem had they been implemented in most schools. Nevertheless, despite being unrealistic in much of what was recommended, the PPE represented a first attempt at developing a curriculum together with an anticipation that improvements would follow in any future attempt.

Brave New Right world

Individuals identified with the New Right of the 1980s did not approve of political education in any shape or form, from black studies, women's studies, world studies, peace studies or even the patriotic 'Crown, constitution and Conservatism' version of political education supported by more liberal-minded Tories. Roger Scruton frequently led the attack on proposals such as political literacy and citizenship education. He was inadvertently assisted in this task by the Inner London Education Authority-appointed 'Authorised Member for Political Education', Labour Councillor George Nicholson, for on more than one occasion the councillor was reported as saying that he saw universal political education as a force which could change society. Each statement had the effect of driving another nail into the coffin of school-based political education. In London's local elections Conservatives campaigned on 'Pupils before Politics', promising parents the comforting option of a 'back to basics' curriculum as their alternative to George Nicholson's platform of political education and social engineering.

In the face of the prevailing right-wing political climate, the campaign for political education went into a slow decline. In a survey of political educators conducted in 1985, Alex Porter reported that political education in schools remained in 'dynamic equilibrium at a low level' (Reid, 1985, p. 4). A book edited by the second appointed university lecturer in political education, at Birmingham, Clive Harber, was published in 1987. Here political education in schools was described as being a 'low status, high risk area of the curriculum' (p. 176). In other words, to all intents and purposes the 1970s experiment with political education was now dead.

Rising levels of crime and anti-social behaviour during the 1980s, however, led some Conservatives to start addressing the meaning of citizenship in contemporary society. Douglas Hurd, for example, saw the need for more 'active citizens' to encourage responsible and civilised behaviour. Citizenship was becoming the politically fashionable solution to the moral, social and criminal crises of the day. Following a Speaker's Conference on citizenship, the National Curriculum Council announced that 'education for citizenship' would be one of five cross-curricular themes taught to all pupils. It was proposed that eight essential components be included: community; a pluralist society; being a citizen; the family; democracy in action; law and the citizen; work, employment and leisure; and the public services.

It was an illusion, however, to believe that the National Curriculum had resuscitated citizenship education and given it a place in the school curriculum. It emerged that the citizenship cross-curricular theme was not to be part of the 'entitlement curriculum'. Put simply, it was voluntary. If schools wanted to incorporate citizenship into the curriculum then they could do so. At the same time, schools were also free to decide against such a move. In reality, it was obvious that very few headteachers would devote scarce resources to a voluntary part of the curriculum which would require complex co-ordination and which would not be tested through examination and hence contribute nothing to their schools' position in league tables. As expected, the citizenship cross-curricular theme became dormant.

New Labour has taken a much greater interest in developing citizenship than the preceding Conservative administrations, mainly through constitutional reform and a 'new deal' in welfare. It was inevitable that the school curriculum would once again be seen as providing an opportunity to inculcate the values of citizenship to successive generations. A government task force led by Bernard Crick collected evidence and recommended that citizenship should be part of the curriculum of all school pupils. It was proposed that citizenship education should take up about 5 per cent of lesson time and, like a cross-curricular theme, some aspects could be taught through existing subjects. Alternatively, other aspects might be taught in regular citizenship lessons. Extra resources would be needed to train teachers. However, the end result would include the benefits of having a school population taught about socially and morally responsible behaviour and the value of community, as well as being equipped with the political skills of effective participation and compromise.

The final report, *Education for Citizenship and the Teaching of Democracy in Schools*, was better received than earlier reports. It went further than its predecessors in recommending that citizenship education should be in existence by Key Stage 1. In other words, a five-year-old should be able to 'take part in a simple debate and vote on an issue'. In his review of the National Curriculum the Secretary of State for Education and Employment, David Blunkett, accepted the main thrust of the report and gave citizenship statutory status in secondary education. From 2002 it will be compulsory for citizenship to be taught to pupils from the age of eleven, while primary schools would be encouraged to develop appropriate aspects of citizenship education.

Can citizenship education in schools contribute towards producing a better society, or is citizenship education (along with its variants of political education, political literacy and civics education) simply a 'quick fix' for politicians to latch on to whenever they are short of other solutions to reduce crime, revive interest in local government or promote specific forms of social behaviour? What is the evidence for and against the likely impact of compulsory citizenship education?

The case for citizenship education

The main argument in favour of having compulsory political education or citizenship education in the school curriculum is that it is effective. In other words, it works. At the very least, sound teaching about politics will combat the widespread political ignorance among school pupils; at best, it will produce more democratic attitudes among pupils.

A number of surveys have revealed alarmingly high levels of political ignorance among young people. Many teachers were shocked by the findings of a survey, 'The Political Awareness of the School Leaver', published in 1977 by the Hansard Society. Ten years later a report, *What Next?*, edited by Harry McGurk, revealed not only widespread indifference to, and misunderstanding of, politics, but also a growth in support among young people for fascist parties which reached 30 per cent in some inner-city areas.

Can teachers combat political ignorance and political extremism through teaching about politics and citizenship? The findings of a research project conducted by David Denver and Gordon Hands concluded that those pupils who were taught politics had greater factual knowledge and an awareness of issues and ideologies than pupils who did not study politics. In addition, the researchers found that pupils who were taught politics had a stronger 'participative orientation' and lower levels of political cynicism than those who were not (Denver and Hands, 1990). In other words, teaching politics was proven to have a beneficial impact on both the knowledge and attitudes of school pupils.

Recent evidence has suggested that young people are becoming increasingly alienated from mainstream society. A survey conducted in 1995 by the National Youth Agency (Wilkinson, 1995) estimated that over a hundred thousand young people formed an underclass which had hardly attended school after the age of twelve and which had received no education likely to help secure employment. Around 10 per cent of the young people interviewed had no substantial contact with society and many of them were caught in a vicious circle of truanting from school, crime, bad childhood experiences, drug abuse, poverty and homelessness. Another report published in 1995, from Demos (Wilkinson and Mulgan, 1995), found that more than a third of the 'Thatcher generation' of young people were alienated, living in an environment of considerable personal freedom mixed with relationship instability and an inclination towards lawlessness. Schools had failed these young people, but need this have been the case?

Schools differ enormously, but the right school setting can reduce feelings of alienation and contribute towards developing a democratic culture among pupils. Not all political or citizenship education is accomplished through the means of formal teaching. Much of it takes place through the 'hidden curriculum' of classroom climate, the nature of teacher–pupil interaction, the values reflected in the organisation of the school, and the style of teaching and learning.

Put another way, schools are micro-political systems organised to produce certain outcomes. If schools are modelled on something along the lines of the old East Germany – with the three Rs being rules, regulations and routines – then they will produce pupils who are passive and conforming. Under the surface, however, many of these pupils might feel anger, alienation and other negative attitudes. If, on the other hand, schools are based on a more democratic model then they will produce more active and participative pupils. The constant theme of a study edited by Byron Massialas, *Political Youth: Traditional Schools*, was the transfer value of pupil participation in school life to wider political education. According to the evidence, aspects of school organisation, such as formal teaching styles or the streaming of pupils in terms of academic ability, do not contribute towards developing positive political attitudes (although there may be other advantages). In contrast, differentiated school power structures and pupil-centred teaching methods result in feelings of greater political trust and political competence on the part of pupils.

The evidence suggests that democratic schools provide education for democracy. For political literacy is not only *taught* in the formal curriculum but also *caught* from the hidden curriculum of values promoted by schools. A first step to combat the alienation experienced by many young people reported above would be their integration into school life which, together with political education, could provide them with the 'routemap' necessary for them to find their way around society as adults and to operate as politically competent adults.

An argument which develops from the points made above is that not only should citizenship education be compulsory but also that it should exist throughout education, starting in the primary school. In the past it has been argued that citizenship education is 'suitable' only for pupils aged fourteen or above because younger pupils are unable to cope with the abstract ideas involved. Very crudely, it was commonly argued that a child's thinking went through various stages at different ages. This 'ages and stages' perspective often led reseachers into underestimating the significance of their findings. For example, one researcher stressed the confusion in the mind of a five-year-old Australian who described the US President as the 'king of America' rather than marvel at the reasoning displayed. In 1978 Robins and Robins published transcriptions of mixed-ability eight- and nine-year-olds discussing whether children should have the vote and whether all workers should receive equal pay. The results showed enormous potential for formal citizenship education being conducted at the primary stage with children displaying an ability to think in abstract terms about society. Although still opposed by some for either political or educational reasons, more and more people support the view that citizenship education is appropriate for pupils from their earliest years in school.

As well as primary pupils being able to handle political topics, the primary school generally provides the type of setting conducive to the development of positive political attitudes. Although there are exceptions, primary schools are rarely the tough type of institution characterised by some secondary schools. They are smaller in scale, with pupils having much greater contact with one teacher. Most teachers spend considerable time instilling social skills which are embryonic citizenship skills: getting children to think about each other and to help and support each other; getting children to accept differences; encouraging children towards being independent. And in the typical primary school, this is achieved in a classroom climate shaped by care, help, support and trust. In short, if many secondary schools provide a setting likely to promote alienation among a significant number of pupils, the typical primary school provides a setting for the development of positive political attitudes.

The case against citizenship education

Opponents of citizenship and political education customarily raise fears about extremist teachers indoctrinating their pupils. This argument has no basis in practice, and there are far more persuasive arguments against imposing compulsory citizenship education. The real case against citizenship and political education is that, to date, it has been totally ineffective and teachers have little or no idea about how it might be successfully taught in the future.

Researchers have found that citizenship education has no impact on pupils' political attitudes. The best known study is that of Langton and Jennings into civics courses in US high schools. In the pages of the *American Political Science Review*, they reported that they had 'found not a single case . . . in which the civics curriculum was significantly associated with students' political orientations' (Langton and Jennings, 1968, p. 852). Similar findings have been reported subsequently by other researchers.

What of the positive correlations found in the research mentioned above conducted by Denver and Hands? It must be stressed that they investigated the impact of teaching A-level Government and Politics to sixth-formers, not universally taught citizenship courses. Of course, A-level Politics students will know more and have different attitudes towards politics than their peers who are studying other subjects at A-level. It is what common sense would suggest. (In a similar way it might be expected that students studying A-level Maths have more knowledge and hold different attitudes about Maths than their peers studying other subjects.)

Denver and Hands found that teaching Politics to a relatively small A-level elite has a positive impact. Their findings do not contradict Langton and Jennings, who found that civics courses taught to all pupils had no impact. It is the latter finding that relates to citizenship education.

The strongest argument against compulsory citizenship education is that political educators have no idea how it might be accomplished. They are able to devise schemes of work, lesson plans and so on for academically able pupils but are bankrupt when it comes to ideas regarding how to teach the rest of the school population.

The experiment with citizenship education in the 1970s, the PPE, helps prove this point. Professor Fred Ridley had already criticised the approach adopted by the PPE as totally inappropriate for disadvantaged inner-city children, a point which was reinforced by the ideas for lessons contained in the handbook. It was suggested, for example, that History would be a gripping subject for delivering political education to pupils and that studying arguably remote topics such as the election of Banbury's MPs from 1830–80 or the role of the Plebeian in Ancient Rome would provide material for suitable lessons.

The editor of *Teaching Politics* attempted to make good the deficiency of realistic teaching ideas applicable to all pupils during the 1980s by inviting teachers to contribute to a series of short articles which outlined the structure, content and method of successful courses or lessons. In the event it proved to be a remarkably short-lived series. Another attempt to elicit ideas on how to deliver a political education was made by the Politics Association following the news that the National Curriculum was to include a cross-curricular theme on citizenship. It was decided that teaching guidance should be provided in a book, *Political Understanding Across the Curriculum*. The editor, Frank Conley, an established textbook author and respected teacher, faced the same desperate task as a co-author of this chapter had on the previously mentioned occasion; namely, assembling a realistic set of practical ideas which could be translated into devising successful citizenship education. The book contained a few thoughtful general essays but failed miserably whenever contributors attempted to tackle the classroom realities of how to provide political education. For example, the novels of Shaw, Chesterton, Huxley, Orwell, Koestler, Lessing, Burgess, Sillitoe and Drabble were among the recommended reading for English teachers planning to deliver part of the citizenship cross-curricular theme in their lessons. No doubt the works of these authors would provide excellent material for some pupils, but it is hard to imagine many connections being made with the multiply disadvantaged pupils which were the concern of Fred Ridley.

Finally, there is no substantial agreement on whether citizenship education is best provided through having separate 'citizenship lessons' or through topics contained in other subjects on the school timetable, such as English, History, Science and PE. It is argued that the already crowded school timetable makes the former difficult, but the fragmentation of the latter undermines, and then destroys, the very identity of citizenship education.

Conclusion

The arguments for and against compulsory political or citizenship education have to be assessed before any sort of conclusion can be reached. In order to do this, a number of questions have to be asked. What is the quality of the evidence used to support the differing conclusions? Are all the surveys reasonably up to date, methodologically sound, with findings which are reliable? Are the findings in one country, such as the United States, transferable to another country, such as Britain? How important are the impressions and opinions of individuals which are based simply on their own personal experience? How logical are the arguments in terms of moving from one point to the next until they reach a conclusion?

The starting point is to ask whether there is a need for young people to have citizenship education as a compulsory part of their school curriculum. The evidence from a considerable number of surveys consistently portrays a picture of schools containing a large proportion of pupils who are politically unaware, having little knowledge and understanding of politics, and who feel that they have and will have no influence in shaping the political system. In this sense, the case in principle for providing compulsory citizenship education in order to remedy this situation seems self evident. Britons live in a devolved parliamentary democracy in which opinions can be expressed, support can be mobilised and, from time to time, favourable decisions can be won. The existence of widespread political ignorance both limits the lives of the unaware by restricting their potential to advance and defend their true interests, while at the same time posing a danger to the interests of the politically educated who will lose if the fabric of democracy is risked through the intolerance, injustice or unfairness of others.

The debate is not about the *principle* of citizenship education, but the *possibility* of providing it in practice. It is not plausible to argue against the aspiration of all schools instilling good citizenship, but it is plausible to argue that in practical terms the chances of this happening are so slim that it is not worth the effort. This is the crux of the debate. For while some believe that it will be possible to include a successful citizenship education in the school curriculum, others look at past experience as well as experience abroad and do not believe that it will be possible.

There is no persuasive evidence to support the argument that effective universal political or citizenship education has ever been provided in schools. Indeed, the evidence suggests that whenever teachers have attempted to devise a practical curriculum for citizenship or related political topics, they have ended up with ideas and schemes more suited to the needs of a minority comprising the most academically able pupils rather than suited to all pupils from the least to the most able. In the hands of professional teachers, therefore, citizenship education became an experience which was accessible only to pupils who were already destined to become the most powerful in society. In practice, political and citizenship education has been elitist in nature and because of this it has worked against democratic values rather than in support of them.

A more positive case for compulsory citizenship education in practice can be made if the focus is moved from the formal to the hidden curriculum. Although the evidence is not overwhelming, there are anecdotal accounts of successful democratic political education where the wider school experiences of pupils are congruent with and reinforce their formal learning about politics. If pupils learn about the benefits and frustrations of living in a democracy from their experiences as pupils in school, then citizenship education becomes a viable proposition. Under these circumstances the importance of the formal curriculum, with which teachers have grappled unsuccessfully in the past, is

---

Compulsory citizenship education

The case for

- Builds the foundation for a democratic society, defending it against fascism and racism.
- Many schools already provide successful citizenship education.
- Research suggests that certain school 'climates' provide a better context for successful citizenship education than others. Primary schools generally provide the most suitable context.
- Society is becoming increasingly complex, with increasing European integration as well as devolution and other reforms. Future citizens will need extra guidance to cope with this complexity.

The case against

- More time on citizenship lessons will mean less time on literacy and numeracy. Standards will fall even lower.
- Not taken seriously by either staff or pupils. Citizenship lessons fail.
- Research has shown that civics teaching has had little or no impact on pupils' attitudes. Schools are too authoritarian to teach democracy.
- Pupils who would benefit most from citizenship education are the least likely to absorb democratic values. Many are already alienated or attracted by anti-democratic values.

---

reduced as other sources of political learning become more important. The conclusion of the Norwood Report was too close to the truth for the comfort of many supporters of citizenship education. For if citizenship education is to flourish then its success appears more dependent upon democratic schools than on lessons in citizenship.

Reading

Brighouse, T. (1991) *What Makes a Good School?*, Network Educational Press.

Citizenship Advisory Group (1998) *Education for Citizenship and the Teaching of Democracy in Schools*, Qualifications and Curriculum Authority.

Crick, B. and Porter, A. (eds) (1978) *Political Education and Political Literacy*, Longman.

Denver, D. and Hands, G. (1990) 'Does studying Politics make a difference? The political knowledge, attitudes and perceptions of school students', *British Journal of Political Science*, 20.

Harber, C. (ed.) (1987) *Political Education in Britain*, Falmer Press.

Heater, D. (ed.) (1969) *The Teaching of Politics*, Methuen.

Langton, K. and Jennings, M. (1968) 'Political socialization and the high school Civics curriculum', *American Political Science Review*, 62.

Massialas, B. (ed.) (1972) *Political Youth, Traditional Schools*, Prentice Hall.

Reid, A. (1985) 'An outsider's view of political education in England', *Talking Politics*, 14.

Ridley, F. F. (1980) 'Politics and political education', *Teaching Politics*, 9.

Robins, L. (1979) 'Political literacy: caught or taught?', *International Journal of Political Education*, 2.

Robins, L. and Robins, V. (1978) 'Politics in the first school: this year, next year, sometime . . . never?', *Teaching Politics*, 7.

Stradling, R. and Noctor, M. (1981) *The Provision of Political Education in Schools: A National Survey*, University of London CRU.

Whitmarsh, G. (1981) 'Change and tradition in the teaching of politics in schools', *Teaching Politics*, 10.

Wilkinson, C. (1995) *The Drop Out Society*, National Youth Agency.

Wilkinson, H. and Mulgan, G. (1995) *Freedom's Children: Work Relationships and Politics for 18–34 Year Olds*, Demos.

12

Towards a more responsive democracy: referendums or electoral reform?

Duncan Watts

Democracy literally means 'rule by the people'. From the time of the Ancient Greeks through until the nineteenth century, democracy was generally meant to imply some form of direct government through majority rule, an idea little changed since the time of the early philosophers. Today, in vaster and more complex societies, such direct involvement is impossible, and the mass of people could not make all important political decisions. The form of democracy which has developed over the last century in Western countries is indirect or representative democracy, a situation in which representatives of the people, freely elected, make decisions subject to popular control.

In effect, the few govern on behalf of the many, so that democracy as it now operates is a form of oligarchy or elitism. The electorate are vote casters at election time, but in between they have little say. In these circumstances, it may be seen as particularly important that those who exercise power are representative of the popular will and are responsive to the views of those who elected them. Electoral reform and referendums are two means by which elected politicians are kept more closely in contact with public opinion and made more accountable to it.

Electoral reform

The term 'electoral reform' implies no particular system of election, merely that there is a move from one system to another. For a politician in the Irish Republic (where a variety of proportional representation (PR), the Single Transferable Vote (STV), is in use), this may mean a change to the British system of voting, First Past The Post (FPTP). For someone in Britain, it implies a move to another majoritarian method or else to a semi/proportional one.

Electoral reform in Britain has long been advocated by the Electoral Reform Society, by the Liberal Party in its various guises and by many other small parties whose members believe that the dice are loaded against them. Their demands began to be taken more seriously when the Liberals and the nation-alist parties between them gained a significant number of votes in the 1970s; in February 1974, between them they gained 25 per cent of the votes and yet won only 5.8 per cent of the seats. Since then, the Liberals/Alliance/Liberal Democrats have regularly scored a sizeable third-party vote, peaking at 25.4 per cent in 1983. However, what really moved the issue up the political agenda was the failure of the Labour Party to win a general election between 1979 and 1992, causing some of its members to wonder whether the only way of getting back to power was via a different electoral system and some embrace of coalition politics. As long as the Lib Dem–Lab vote was divided, the Con-servatives were able to gain power on a gradually diminishing share of the national vote (see table 12.1). Indeed, even the Labour leader, Neil Kinnock, who had shown no previous inclination to take up the subject, was moved to observe in 1988 that 'If, by changing the system of election, we could assure a perpetuation of justice and reasonability in government, there would not be a single argument against PR.'

Under pressure from elements within the Labour Party, Kinnock's suc-cessor, John Smith, moved Labour policy forward to take up the idea of a referendum on the issue of voting reform. Tony Blair, famously 'unpersuaded' about the case for abandoning FPTP, nonetheless honoured a pre-1997 election agreement with the Liberal Democrats, and set up a commission of inquiry under the centrist Lord Jenkins (hereafter, the Jenkins Commission) to recommend a new system which could then be put before the electorate in a referendum. Meanwhile, Labour had committed itself to the use of a more proportional voting system for elections to the European Parliament, its pro-posed Scottish and Welsh assemblies, for the new Northern Ireland assembly which emerged as a result of the Good Friday Agreement, and for the Mayoralty and Council for Greater London, as well as envisaging that in any reformed second chamber there might be at least an element elected under a more proportional system.

Before we concern ourselves with the arguments put forward, it is worth briefly considering the results in 1997, when the swing to Labour across Great Britain was greater than in any previous post-war election, provid-ing that party with a higher total of MPs than it had ever secured before

Table 12.1 *The Conservative success in British elections, 1979–92*

Year	Anti-Conservative vote (Labour/Lib/Lib Dem) (%)	Conservative vote (%)	Conservative seats (%)
1979	50.7	43.9	53.4
1983	53.0	42.4	61.0
1987	53.5	42.3	57.8
1992	52.2	41.9	51.6

(table 12.2). Yet again they illustrate some of the idiosyncrasies (many would prefer the term 'anomalies') of the FPTP system:

- The winning party again failed to win 50 per cent of the popular vote. Indeed, in 1970, for a similar percentage of the vote, Labour lost the election and secured only 287 (45.6 per cent) seats.
- The Liberal Democrats won forty-six seats – the highest total of any third party for many years – despite experiencing a drop in their popular vote since 1992. North of the border the Lib Dems took ten seats on the basis of only 13 per cent of the vote. Yet overall, in the UK, they still came off badly. For 16.8 per cent of the vote, they gained only 6.8 per cent of the seats, still a much lower figure than the 106 to which they might have felt entitled. Table 12.3 illustrates the scale of their under-representation.
- There are many areas in which one party won the bulk of the seats but where the second party gained no recognition at all, or only very limited success. Labour and the Liberal Democrats did particularly well in Scotland, but the Conservatives suffered a 'wipe-out'. Their 17.5 per cent of the vote went totally unrewarded. In Wales, they gained nothing for scoring 19.6 per cent. In the West Midlands, 33.7 per cent of the popular vote

Table 12.2   *The 1997 election at a glance: the performance of the parties*

	Votes	% share	Candidates	MPs elected
Labour	13,516,632	43.2	639	418
Conservative	9,602,857	30.7	648	165
Liberal Democrat	5,242,894	16.8	639	46
Scottish National Party	621,540	2.0	72	6
Plaid Cymru	161,030	0.5	40	4

Turnout 71.7%, the lowest since 1935.

Table 12.3   *Votes required to elect one MP*

Liberal Democrat	115,958
Scottish National Party	103,586
Conservative	57,979
Plaid Cymru	40,258
Labour	32,326

Note: Figures attained by dividing total number of votes acquired across the UK by number of seats won by the party.

earned them 23.7 per cent (14/59) of the seats, whereas Labour's 47.8 per cent was rewarded with 44 seats.

- Many MPs were again elected on a minority basis. For instance, in Old Bexley and Sidcup, 28,780 of those who turned out cast their vote against Sir Edward Heath, yet he was elected.
- Minorities are under-represented in the House once again, though this time more women were elected than ever before (120) and ethnic minority representation increased.
- Under any other electoral system, the outcome would have been very different, as shown in table 12.4.

The Jenkins Report

The terms of reference for the inquiry were mapped out by the Home Secretary, Jack Straw, who set out certain guidelines, namely that the Commission would 'observe the requirement for broad proportionality, the need for stable government, an extension of voter choice and the maintenance of a link between honourable members and geographical constituencies' (Report of the Independent Commission on Voting Systems, 1998, p. 1).

The Jenkins Commission reported in October 1998. Its report proved to be a treasure trove of electoral data, including several tables illustrating how the result might have been under a different system. The drawbacks of the present system were clearly set out and discussed, and several alternatives – known by their initials such as AMS, AV, FPTP and STV – were all assessed. The actual recommendation of the inquiry team was for a scheme labelled 'AV Top-Up' (sometimes referred to as 'AV Plus' or 'Amended AMS'), in which the bulk of seats would be fought on a single-member constituency basis, as now, using the Alternative Vote, while a top-up of additional members would provide for a greater measure of proportionality in the outcome.

Table 12.4   *The 1997 result: how it might have been*

	FPTP	Alternative vote	STV	Additional members system (50/50)	List
Conservative	165	103	193	207	208
Labour	418	436	340	303	300
Liberal Democrat	46	91	89	111	113
Others	29	29	35	38	38

Source: Adapted from Curtice and Steed (1997). For STV, the calculation is based on using relatively small multi-member seats, returning 4 MPs. Larger ones (of about 8 MPs) would not have yielded a majority for Labour, which might have won around 317 seats, compared with the Conservatives' 195 and the Lib Dems' 110.

The case for electoral reform in Britain

The Jenkins Report listed several arguments against the present FPTP system, noting that the deficiencies identified derived largely from a natural tendency of the system to disunite rather than unite the country, a situation which manifests itself in several ways:

- FPTP exaggerates the movements of opinion within the electorate, and when they are strong produces mammoth majorities, as in 1983 and 1997; 'landslides' are now often won on the basis of an ever-diminishing share of the popular vote.
- Third parties suffer badly, and this factor has become more important. It was a negligible problem in the era after 1945, but is today more apparent. The Scottish National Party and the Greens have suffered in recent years, as well as the Liberal Democrats.
- FPTP is geographically divisive between the two leading parties, even though each of them can from time to time be rewarded with a jackpot. Thus in 1997 the Conservatives were wiped out in Scotland, Wales and the large English provincial cities. In the same way, Labour suffered in the rapidly growing and more prosperous southern half of the country in the 1980s and fared badly in rural English constituencies: 'This bifurcation has recently become increasingly sharp . . . such apartheid in electoral out-come is a heavy count against the system which produces it' (p. 8).
- FPTP fails to allow voters the freedom to choose in both the selection of a constituency representative and the determination of the government of the country. It forces the voter to give priority to one or the other, and the evidence is that in the great majority of cases he or she deems it more important who is Prime Minister than who is member for their local con-stituency. As a result, the choice of which individual is MP effectively rests not with the electorate but with the selecting body of whichever party is dominant in the area.
- FPTP narrows the terrain over which the political battle is fought, and also – an associated although not an identical point – excludes many voters from ever helping to elect a winning candidate: 'The essential contest be-tween the two main parties is fought over about a hundred or at most 150 . . . swingable constituencies . . . Outside the chosen arena, voters [in 1997] were deprived of . . . the visits of party leaders, saw few canvassers, and were generally treated . . . as either irrevocably damned or sufficiently saved as to qualify for being taken for granted' (p. 9).
- As a consequence of the above, many voters spend their entire lives with-out ever voting for a winning candidate, and cast their vote without any realistic hope of influencing a result: 'These people are the inhabitants of electoral deserts for the two main parties, places where they cannot ever have a realistic hope of success' (p. 7).

- Often, more than half of the voters vote against rather than in favour of the victorious candidate. There is also the matching 'perversity' of governments winning elections when they fail to achieve the majority (50.1 per cent) of the votes or in many cases as many votes as their opponents. (It was conceded that other electoral systems can also produce occasional irrational results.)
- FPTP is not usually as good at producing parliamentary representation for women and ethnic minorities as other systems. Since the introduction of a more proportional system in New Zealand, there has been a marked increase in the percentage of women elected (now around 30 per cent) and Germany also produces better representation for women. However, the use of a system of PR in the Republic of Ireland has not had this effect, and women are less well represented there than in the United Kingdom.
- FPTP produces long periods of systemic bias against one or other of the two main parties, and these are difficult to correct in the short term. Third parties are familiar with this bias against them but the two main parties have been affected at different times. Bias arises when 'a given number of votes translates into significantly more seats for one party than the other'. It has various causes, including the over-representation of Scotland and Wales at Westminster, inequality in the size of English constituencies, the impact of third parties and low turn-outs in inner cities. In the period until 1970 the Conservative Party generally did well under the present system, while Labour piled up large unneeded majorities in its heartland seats and failed to pick up a full share of the key voters in the marginals. In the 1970s and 1980s, Labour generally fared better from the operation of the system. However, in the last two elections that advantage became more significant. In 1992 the Conservatives received a similar number of votes to that achieved by Labour five years later – yet their success provided them with only a shaky and erodable majority of twenty-one.

Fundamental to the case of the Jenkins team and other electoral reformers is the fact that the results do not reflect the way in which people have voted. Indeed, in 1997, only 30.9 per cent of the eligible electorate voted for the victorious Labour Party. This not only leads to powerful, unrepresentative government. In the eyes of some writers it contributes to a lack of democratic legitimacy. The point was well made by Professor Ridley when he wrote about the British residing 'at the bottom of the democracy league' (*Guardian*, 10 August 1987). His figures related to the period prior to August 1987, and when updated they carry significantly less force today than they did even a few years ago. There are more administrations in Europe today which are based on a low level of popular support, some even lower than that in Britain. But of course none of them have a government with a landslide parliamentary majority, so that there is some support for the second part of Ridley's basic thesis, namely that: 'Our Government has less electoral support than any other government in power in a European democracy . . . Britain seems to have the most powerful and least representative system of government in Western Europe.'

Professor Ridley's figures revealed the proportion of voters at the most recent election which had backed the parties then forming, or officially supporting, a government (table 12.5).

The case, then, is not just about justice for the Liberal Democrats, though some would see unfairness to small parties as a key argument for change. It is about fairness to voters, those effectively disenfranchised people who in parts of the country have never cast a vote that has elected an MP or, indeed, had any influence on the outcome of an election. It is about legitimacy and the right to govern. It is about employing a system which emphasises the politics of agreement and co-operation, rather than confrontation. In sum, it is about the better government of the UK.

Support for electoral reform is, then, support for democracy. If governments are supposed to represent the people, ours clearly does not. If we started again from scratch, no one would opt for such a system, for it corresponds to no known democratic ideal. It is significant that few countries employ it, and the ones that do are those with strong Anglo-Saxon links. Indeed, in the new

Table 12.5 *Proportion of votes won by governing parties*

Country	1987	1999
Switzerland	77.5	(73.9)
Luxembourg	68.4	(55.7)
Italy	57.4	(43.0)
Germany	55.8	(47.6)
Austria	52.9	(59.2)
Netherlands	52.0	(62.7)
Denmark	52.0	(42.0)
Belgium	50.2	(49.3)
Sweden	50.0	(36.4)
Norway	49.0	(26.1)
Finland	48.9	(62.8)
Ireland	47.3	(44.0)
Greece	45.8	(41.5)
France	44.9	(44.5)
Spain	44.1	(44.8)
Portugal	44.0	(42.9)
UK	42.3	(43.2)

Note: Updated figures are from January 1999 and are adapted from those provided by the Electoral Reform Society, the help of which is gratefully acknowledged.

democracies of Central and Eastern Europe much thought was given to devising fairer voting systems, and Britain was not an example to which they turned.

The case against electoral reform in Britain

Yet the argument over electoral reform is not one sided and defenders of FPTP are certain to mount a strong counter-attack in support of its retention. Many of them are to be found in the Labour Party as well as among Conservatives. They note the plethora of parties in countries with PR and see it as being associated with unstable and weak government. They tend to deride the experience of some countries which employ a variant of PR; often they choose Italy, but other cases from the Republic of Ireland to Israel are used to illustrate their case.

The sceptics doubt the quality of government produced in a situation where coalition governments are frequent or even the norm, and feel that the voters should be able to vote for explicit policies as set out in the manifesto, and see them implemented. Indeed, Britain's democratic tradition demands no less. They worry also about the disproportionate power of small parties in such a situation, a case advanced by George Cunningham MP, several years ago:

> If we were to have PR . . . the Liberal Party would sell its support to whichever of the other two parties it wanted to see in government. The Labour and Conservative parties might alternate as they do now, but the Liberals would always be there. A Liberal can be forgiven for wanting that to happen, but let him not say that it is democratic when the middle of the see-saw is always in power simply because it is the middle of the see-saw. (*House of Commons Debates*, 1977, vol. 2, col. 1257)

Opponents of change challenge a central assumption of electoral reformers, namely that it is important to have a legislature which is a mathematical reflection of the way electors vote. Of course the system needs broadly to reflect changes in the public mood, as indeed the British one does. But elections are primarily about choosing a strong, effective and accountable government.

In recognition of this, those who oppose the adoption of any more proportional method of voting point to the 'solid' virtues of FPTP, among which they observe that:

- It usually leads to the formation of strong, stable, single-party governments with an overall majority; coalition government other than in times of emergency is virtually unknown. Such administrations are said to be capable of providing effective leadership for the nation. This is viewed as more important than achieving a proportional result. In Britain, we know who is to form the government immediately after the election is over. There is no need for private deals to be done by politicians who bargain in smoke-filled rooms, away from the public gaze; it is the voters directly who choose which party is in office.

- Because we have single-member constituencies there is a close relationship between the MP and his/her constituency. The one Member alone has responsibility for that area which he/she can get to know well. Once elected, the MP represents all who live in the area, not just those who voted for one particular party; all citizens know who to approach if they have a problem or grievance needing resolution. This is very different from what happens under some more proportional systems in which several elected members represent a broad geographical area.
- Finally, the system is easy to understand, especially for the voter who marks an X on the ballot paper. It has the merits of simplicity and familiarity and, as such, is widely accepted.

Lord Jenkins himself referred to the 'by no means negligible' merits of the present system. In addition to the points above, the commissioners made the point that it enables the electorate sharply and cleanly to rid itself of an unwanted government; in other words, it is easy to punish those directly responsible for their errors.

The case considered

The choice of electoral system to elect a particular assembly is a question of great importance in our democracy. To a significant degree electoral systems define how the body politic operates. As Farrell (1997, p. 2) points out, 'they are the cogs which keep the wheels of democracy properly functioning'. The choice of system raises issues about the nature of representative government and the purpose of elections. Representative government is based on the idea that the legislature (the House of Commons) represents the will of the people. For some, it is crucial that the House should reflect the voters' wishes as closely as possible and so cater for minority opinion. Any new Parliament is then a microcosm or mirror image of society. Out of the resulting chamber, a government will be formed.

Currently, the Westminster Parliament is a very inaccurate mirror image of the electorate, being overwhelmingly white, male and middle class. Important sections, most obviously women and ethnic minorities, are under-represented, and the House of Commons only loosely reflects the voters' wishes as expressed in the last election. However, even if it were possible to have an electoral system which produced a more representative assembly, this would only apply at the time of the election. There is no guarantee that it will continue to do so unless elections are held very frequently. It is unrealistic to expect that we shall ever achieve a House of Commons sensitive to every shade of opinion.

Supporters of the present arrangements place less emphasis on having a system which mathematically reflects the way electors vote and more on the need for one which produces strong government. They want governments to have an effective majority, so that they can develop coherent and consistent policies without facing the risk of regular parliamentary defeats. The emphasis here is on stability, so that governments, once chosen, can get on with their job. Yet strong government does not necessarily mean effective government, and stability is not only achieved by having a single party in control of affairs. Several continental countries have had governments which have been effective and stable, but which have also been coalitions of two or more parties.

An ideal system?

There is no perfect electoral system, appropriate to every country at every time. Indeed, it is quite possible to have different types of election within a particular country. FPTP may well be seen as inappropriate for elections to the European Parliament, to the new Scottish or Welsh assemblies or to an elected second chamber, should one ever materialise. That does not necessarily mean that there has to be a change at Westminster, for the way in which we vote in general elections.

Much depends on what the electoral system is supposed to achieve. Obviously, it is desirable that it produces an outcome which is intelligible and acceptable to as many people as possible, so that when they vote they feel comfortable with the arrangements made and accept that the outcome on polling day is fair and legitimate. Beyond that, there are other possible functions which those interested might expect any system to fulfil, the accurate representation of the popular will and/or the production of effective, strong governments among them.

In devising any new method of voting, different priorities are relevant in different situations, hence the diversity in the systems across the world. It is a matter of preference about what values and outcomes are important for the smooth operation of an effective democracy. It is perfectly possible to be a good democrat and support electoral reform or the status quo. Arguments about democracy are not one sided, which is why an impressive array of speakers can be fielded on either side of the argument.

The referendum

Electoral reform is concerned to get the right people and the right parties elected, by ensuring that those in the House, and more especially those who take key decisions, are representative of the people. By contrast, those who advocate a referendum – with or without an initiative (see below) – are concerned with the way in which decisions are taken. They want to see more direct public involvement, so that those in power, whether or not they got there via a fair electoral system, act in accordance with the express wishes of the electorate.

The *referendum* has been defined by Magleby (1994) as a 'vote of the people on a proposed law, policy or public expenditure'. In other words, it is a vote on a single issue, allowing people to respond in a simple 'yes'/'no' fashion to the question asked.

An *initiative* is a device through which an individual or group may propose legislation by securing the signatures of a required number of qualified voters. In most countries that have referendums, there is also provision for the right of popular initiative.

In recent years referendums have been much more widely used in most parts of the world. A growing number of American states have used them to decide on contentious moral issues, from the use of cannabis for treatment of the sick to the right to 'death with dignity' via euthanasia; on social issues such as the rights of minorities and health reform, and on constitutional issues such as term limits for those who serve in positions of political power. Some member states of the European Union have used them to confirm their membership or to ratify some important constitutional development. In Switzerland, they are built into the regular machinery of government, and are held on a three-monthly basis. The new democracies of Central and Eastern Europe, particularly the fifteen republics of the former USSR, have used them to decide a range of issues relating to the form of their new governments.

In the past, referendums were often associated with dictatorial systems, such as that of Nazi Germany, or democratic ones with authoritarian overtones, such as the Fifth French Republic of Charles de Gaulle. Often they were known as plebiscites. It is the memory of such past experience which troubles some democrats who fear the purpose and management of such means of consultation with the public. Such overtones have today largely disappeared, and initiatives and referendums are now used with increasing regularity in countries and states which have impeccable democratic credentials. Yet Britain has until recently had very little experience of voting on a single issue.

The case for referendums

- The basic case for referendums is that a democracy rests upon the people's will; a referendum is the most direct and accurate way of getting their verdict. Such an exercise in direct democracy has an intrinsic appeal, for the idea of 'letting the people have their say' appears to gel with the usual understanding of what democratic government involves. Those countries which also use the initiative capitalise on this idea. A *Guardian* editorial (4 March 1993) recognised this aspect when it discussed the idea of a vote on electoral reform. It noted that Britain suffers from an enormous and increasing 'democratic deficit' and saw a need to encourage politicians to go out and persuade people of the merits of their case: 'Imaginative means have to be sought to redress the imbalance . . . [a referendum] would generate an urgent civic discussion which will never take place with such purpose in any other way.'

- General elections have their limitations as a means of consultation, in that:
  1 They occur only every four or five years, so that for many people their political involvement occurs very infrequently; referendums offer the possibility of more regular participation.
  2 They are essentially an overall verdict on the performance of the government, and do not show the strength and extent of feeling on particular issues.
  3 They are usually won on a minority basis, which casts doubt upon claims that the government of the day is acting with popular backing in pursuing its policies.
- Referendums are also useful for the government in that it can strengthen its authority as it seeks to deal with difficult issues. France and Australia have provision to resolve a political impasse by using such direct questioning, and there are occasions when a government – faced with a difficult, divisive issue on which feelings cross party lines – may wish to reinforce its own stance and improve its negotiating position.
- Referendums are a particularly useful expedient for resolving those matters on which the government seems to be divided. In 1975, Harold Wilson was able to resolve some of the Labour Party's divisions by allowing the issue of membership of the European Community to go to the electorate for its verdict. As a way of getting ministers off the hook or persuading reluctant backbenchers, there is an obvious temptation to consult the people and seek popular support.
- Referendums settle questions in such a way that there is a final solution to an issue which will not go away. The 1979 referendum resolved the devolution issue for several years, as did the European referendum, even if that particular matter has returned to haunt some politicians. Critics of a policy are more likely to accept the result if they know that it is the public view – which is why Labour held its votes on devolution in 1997 before the House of Commons began the legislative process, rather than after. Tony Benn, a leading 'anti', explicitly made this point when talking to the press after the 1975 poll: 'I read the message loud and clear. When the British people speak, everyone – including ourselves – should tremble before their decisions.'

The case against referendums

- Ours is a representative, not a direct democracy. It does not require that people vote on every single item, rather that they elect MPs who, being close to the centre of the argument and able to inform themselves fully on the issue, then vote on our behalf. If we then do not like how they exercise that choice, we can deny them our vote at the next election. If government and Parliament pass the question back to voters for their determination, then they shirk the responsibility which representative government clearly places upon them.
- The referendum can be very complicated for the electorate. Some issues are so complex and require such knowledge and understanding that a worthwhile judgement is difficult for the average voter to make. Making a general assessment of the performance of the government at an election is arguably much easier than deciding on the merits of a single European currency. Sometimes information is very technical and people may lack sufficient information to form a fair and balanced opinion on a topic.
- The result of a referendum can get muddled up with other issues. Thus in 1979 opinion polls suggested that the majority of Scots favoured devolution, but there was a background of governmental unpopularity. It is significant that the Conservatives campaigned for a 'no' vote but argued that this was a vote against the Labour government's plans and not against the principle of devolution; indeed, they promised to bring forward proposals of their own!
- If the principle of giving people a referendum on constitutional issues is conceded, then it is not easy to resist the desire for one on social ones. It is hard to see the logic by which, in a parliamentary system, you can pick and choose your forays into populism and hope to retain respect. Many people would like a vote on capital punishment and, judging by opinion polls, the verdict would be strongly in favour of its return, despite the fact that there is much evidence to show that it has virtually no deterrent effect. Surely ministers and MPs have a duty to give a lead on such issues? They have the chance to hear expert evidence – in this case that of criminologists and that derived from other countries – and can educate the public accordingly. Sometimes a government might quite properly defy public opinion in the long-term interest of society. Political leadership does not consist of slavishly following public opinion, but in shaping it. If Parliament had been the creature of popular prejudice, Catholics would never have been emancipated and pickpockets might still be hanged!
- In addition, there are certain technical problems with a referendum. The wording of the question can be a problem. It has often been said that 'he who frames the question determines the outcome'. In Chile, the notorious General Pinochet gained 75 per cent acquiescence for the proposition: 'In the face of international aggression unleashed against the government of

the fatherland, I support President Pinochet in his defence of the dignity of Chile.' Timing can be another difficulty. For instance, any vote on hanging held in the aftermath of some horrific killing could be unduly swayed by emotional considerations. There is a danger that the circumstances in which it takes place could affect the result. Moreover, the referendum only tells what the public is thinking at a particular time, on a particular day. Logically, further votes are necessary to ensure that ministers are acting in line with the public mood. The status of referendums is also a difficulty. If a referendum is advisory, as in our system it must be (for Parliament makes the law), could one really expect MPs to support reintroduction of the death penalty against their deeply held beliefs? Yet if MPs ignored the popular verdict, the situation would be that people would have been invited to declare their preference and the House of Commons would have exercised its undoubted right to decide differently. This would only damage further people's faith in the parliamentary system.

The case considered

Again, the case is not clear-cut, and many who warm to the idea of referendums on constitutional issues are reluctant to see the public vote on issues such as abortion, capital punishment and gay sex. Much clearly depends on the view taken of legislatures and of the collective wisdom of the electorate to determine difficult issues.

The motives of those who call for a referendum might be doubted. It can be for the wrong reasons; they can become the political refuge of the politician whose purpose may be to dodge a damaging internal party division, and have little to do with the merits of democratic consultation and popular participation. Usually, referendums are advocated by those who think that their side can win. If they are in government then the timing and phrasing of the question is in their hands, allowing them a greater chance to get the outcome they desire.

Lord Jenkins, of whose interest in the rights of voters and politicians we have already made mention, summed up the point about the proper use of referendums when he spoke in the debates on the passage of the Maastricht Bill in 1993. They should be used 'as part of a clearly thought out constitutional scheme and not just as a by-product or a tactical ploy by those who have tried and failed to defeat this Bill in every possible way' *House of Commons Debates*, 1977 (6th series), vol. 2, col. 1257.

Electoral reform versus referendums: some concluding thoughts

We come to see that referendums and electoral reform can form a respectable part of any package of constitutional change. Neither is a pre-condition of democracy, nor is there any reason to fear that change must inevitably lead to any erosion of our freedom. The danger in both cases is that considerations of party advantage play an excessively large part in determining political attitudes than does the better government of the United Kingdom.

Both the referendum and a different electoral system would fulfil the need for popular participation. A revised method of voting would ensure that those elected into legislatures and those who exercise power are representative of a substantial body of popular opinion, whereas a wider use of referendums would ensure that decisions taken are in line with the public mood. If a referendum were to be combined with a right of popular initiative, then there would be an opportunity for even greater responsiveness to the feelings of a substantial portion of the electorate.

Referendums are still viewed with suspicion by some people who dislike the way in which those in authority seem to be appealing over the heads of democratically elected politicians directly to the people in plebiscites in which presentation of the case has been carefully managed. Such fears may have been well grounded in the early continental examples, but there are now so many examples of well-organised votes in Europe and beyond that the fear is greatly overdrawn. However, it remains the case that it is voters who are left to make key decisions, not the people elected to represent them. As such, referendums do not emphasise the importance of Parliament. In contrast, electoral reform exalts the place of legislatures, being likely to produce a more representative assembly.

Of the two devices, the implications of adopting electoral reform are likely to be more wide ranging. Referendums by their nature impact on the fate of particular issues which may or may not be carried through into legislation. A change in the electoral system means more than ensuring that government is in line with popular opinion by occasional consultations on constitutional and possibly social questions. It would almost certainly introduce the idea of regular coalitions into British politics, and change our system from one based on confrontation to one based on co-operation. Paddy Ashdown, the former Liberal Democrat leader whose party stands to gain substantially under a different system, has used the phrase 'partnership politics' to describe a situation in which two or more parties co-operate in coalitions, compromising their partisan beliefs as necessary in order to come to agreed decisions.

In this way, the politics of moderation might triumph over the more familiar adversarial style. As in Germany, a third party (rather larger in the British case) might frequently exercise power in conjunction with a rival which commands more substantial allegiance. As that party is likely to be the Liberal Democrats, there is the real prospect of a twenty-first century of Centre–Left predominance.

To those worried about the degree of Executive dominance said to characterise British politics (Adonis (1993), Ewing and Gearty (1990) and many others), the introduction of electoral reform might strike a hammer-blow at the over-powerful single party. Of course, strong government seems much better to those in power than to those on the Opposition benches, but there might be many politicians, as well as academics and journalists, who feel that under Tony Blair – as under Margaret Thatcher – the more assertive style of leadership and lack of sensitivity to the feelings of the House of Commons are undesirable traits.

To those who fear that the lack of strong single-party government may lead to a lack of effective leadership and result in weak ineffective coalitions, then experience shows that these 'problems' do not necessarily arise. Coalitions can be weak or strong, and if there are many quotable examples of inter-governmental disunity and what the French used to call *immobilisme* at the top, there are other examples of coalitions which have worked effectively.

Referendums or electoral reform?

Electoral reform would ensure that:
- membership of the House of Commons was more in line with the popular will and included representatives of several strands of opinion;
- any government formed would carry greater legitimacy;
- there might exist a new style of politics, based more on co-operation rather than confrontation.

Referendums would:
- enhance democracy, by encouraging popular participation and giving the public a direct say on issues affecting them;
- enable ministers to take decisions, however difficult, in the knowledge that they had public backing for their specific proposal;
- help to resolve issues which cause division within the parties or on which the division of opinion does not fall within the usual party boundaries.

Consider the following:
- both electoral reform and referendums fulfil the need to provide the public with a chance to have a meaningful say in decision making;
- neither is essential nor inimical to democracy; both can be seen as enhancing it;
- party attitudes to both are often decided on the basis of party advantage;
- electoral reform is arguably good for Parliament and the voters, referendums less so for Parliament but arguably beneficial to voters;
- the implications of opting for electoral reform are more far reaching, for the introduction of coalitions might weaken the power of over-mighty governments and produce a new emphasis on 'partnership politics'.

Finally, it is worth pointing out that the two mechanisms are not mutually exclusive. We can have either, neither or both. The early experience of the Blair administration indicates that a change to the established method of voting is in hand in parts of the UK and that referendums are likely to be more common, at least to help resolve constitutional questions. Indeed, ironically, the fate of one issue, electoral reform at Westminster, is likely to be determined by the outcome of using a referendum, probably after the next election.

Reading

Adonis, A. (1993) *Parliament Today*, Manchester University Press.

Butler, D. and Ranney, A. (1994) *Referendums around the World*, Macmillan.

Curtice, J. and Steed, M. (1997) 'The results analysed', in D. Butler and D. Kavanagh (eds), *The British General Election of 1997*, Macmillan.

The Report of the Independent Commission on Voting Systems, October 1998.

Denver, D. (1997) 'The 1997 general election results', *Talking Politics*, 10:1.

Farrell, D. (1997) *Comparing Electoral Systems*, Macmillan.

Ewing, K. and Gearty, C. (1990) *Freedom Under Thatcher*, Clarendon Press.

Magleby, D. (1994) 'Direct legislation in the American states', in D. Butler and A. Ranney (eds), *Referendums around the World*, Macmillan.

Robinson, C. (1998) *Voting Behaviour and Electoral Systems*, Hodder & Stoughton.

13

Should political parties be funded by the state?

Graham P. Thomas

Introduction

Concerns about the financing of political parties started to grow in the 1970s, when fears were expressed that the parties lacked sufficient financial resources to allow them to do their jobs properly. In 1976 the report of the Houghton Committee on financial aid to political parties recommended an increase in state funding. Criticisms of the role played by business and the unions in party funding led the Hansard Society for Parliamentary Government to establish a committee of investigation. Its report, *Paying for Politics*, published in 1981, recommended state aid for 'duly qualified' political parties on the basis of matching contributions. The committee hoped that the proposals would lead the parties to broaden their appeal, to seek new members and to encourage them to seek a large number of individual donors rather than to rely on a small number of large donations.

However, it was during the 1980s and 1990s that the question of party finance became one of the most acute controversies in British politics. There were adverse comments on the secretiveness surrounding the matter, there were allegations that the need to raise large sums of money distorted British politics, and rival allegations of sleaze and corruption were made about the financial affairs of both major parties. The call for reform grew from academic commentators, journalists, think tanks on the Centre and Left, and the Labour and Liberal Democrats. On the other hand, the Conservative government denied that the problem was a real one and refused to countenance the provision of extra money from the public purse, arguing that the essentially 'voluntary' nature of party funding should continue. However, as the Major government became more and more mired in allegations of sleaze against individual ministers and MPs, and as various scandals emerged concerning the financial dealings of the Conservative Party, pressure grew for the matter to be referred to the Nolan Committee, set up by the Prime Minister as the result of widespread concern about the decline of moral standards in public life. Major refused to let Nolan look at party funding, but following Labour's victory in the 1997 general election Tony Blair asked Lord Neill (who had succeeded Nolan) to consider the issue. The report, issued in October 1998, is likely to usher in far-reaching changes to the manner in which parties raise funds.

The controversy

Why party funding is so important

Both major parties rely heavily on institutional sources for much of their finance. The effects of this pattern of fund raising are hotly contested. It is clear that party finance is important in several respects:

- Some commentators believe that the amount of money spent on election campaigns exerts a direct influence on voters. The emphasis on advertising, the use of public relations consultants and the efforts of 'spin doctors' indicate the importance placed by the major parties on this aspect of electioneering.
- Contributions may affect policy making in directions favoured by those who provide the money. Accusations by the Conservatives that Labour was in the pocket of its union 'paymasters' were part of the staple diet of politics in the post-war period, as was the counter-charge that the Conservatives were dominated by big business.
- The internal structure of power within the party may be affected. The Conservatives attacked Labour for the role played by the unions in its internal affairs, while Labour alleged that the secrecy which surrounded the Tories was a cloak for the rich and powerful to manipulate democratic politics in their own interests.
- The cost of politics and of campaigning may affect the pattern of political recruitment, perhaps by deterring those without adequate means from standing for Parliament.
- The disproportionate ability of the Labour and Conservative Parties to raise funds is in sharp distinction to the problems faced by the Liberal Democrats and other parties. There should be something like a 'level playing-field' in this respect.
- Lack of funds has had damaging effects on policy making by the parties. At various times, both the Conservative and Labour Parties have reduced the number of staff involved in policy research and advice for frontbench spokesmen and women, while the Liberal Democrats work on a 'shoe-string' in this area. It has been suggested that this is particularly damaging when parties come into office unprepared for the challenges they will face. It has often led to ill-thought-out legislation being put on the statute book.

Garner and Kelly (1998) argue that the problem of party finance has two interlocking aspects.

- *That the parties have insufficient revenue to carry out their 'essential' tasks*

For a number of reasons the cost of electioneering has grown considerably since the 1970s. The membership of both major parties has declined sharply, a consequence of a dealigned electorate, less involved in party politics. This means that income from subscriptions has fallen, making it likely that the parties will have to rely even more heavily than in the past on a mixture of institutional funding and reliance on a comparatively few wealthy individual donors. Yet a dealigned electorate demands more wooing by the parties; a much greater effort must be made to persuade fickle and changeable voters to 'purchase' the political brand on offer. 'In other words, parties have come to devote more resources to the art of persuasion just as those resources are harder to come by' (Garner and Kelly, 1998, p. 203). Technological change has also increased the costs that parties have to bear. Information technology is extremely costly and the need to keep up to date with technological change means a continuing burden for the parties, only partly offset by the opportunities for fund-raising mailshots to targeted groups of party members or sympathisers. In addition, election campaigns are more frequent. In the past the only national campaigns in which parties were substantially involved were general elections; local government elections were essentially local, with comparatively little involvement (financial or otherwise) of central party organisations. More recently, the role of national parties in local elections has grown and elections for the European Parliament require considerable expenditure. In future, elections for the Scottish Parliament and Welsh Assembly, and for the Mayor and Assembly of London, will make further demands on the fundraising capabilities of the political parties.

Financial pressures have had a number of effects on the parties in recent years. Despite the generally greater ability of the Tories to raise funds, the party has suffered from considerable financial pressures. In the early 1990s there was a considerable deficit, partly caused by the increased costs outlined above and partly by what were allegations of financial mismanagement by Kenneth Baker during his term as party Chairman. Severe retrenchment was ordered by his successor, Norman Fowler, involving the shedding of jobs in Central Office. Particularly significant was the sharp fall in the number of constituency agents, with severe repercussions on the ability of the party to fight elections, especially in marginal seats. There was a marked fall in company donations in the run-up to the 1997 election, sharply curtailing the funds available for advertising. Further redundancies in Central Office followed the disaster of 1997. Labour also suffered financial stringency during the 1980s and early 1990s and was consistently out-spent by the Tories. There were redundancies in Walworth Road and in regional offices, and the number of agents (always significantly fewer than employed by the Tories) fell significantly. The Liberal Democrats have been forced to operate at a much lower level than either of their rivals, with a central income of some £7 million in 1992–93, compared with that of the Conservatives of £26 million. The problem of funding policy research has already been mentioned. Another effect was the growth of sleaze, something discussed in more detail later.

- *That the reliance on institutional funding has grown*

Labour in the past has depended heavily on the affiliated trade unions, which provided some 80–90 per cent of the income of Head Office and over half of the total national income of the party, which included constituency and regional fund-raising activities. In recent years a national membership scheme has been introduced, enabling the party to make direct mail appeals to members, who are increasingly middle class and comparatively affluent. This is one aspect of the drive by New Labour to loosen the links between the party and the unions.

The reliance of Labour on trade union donations is still marked. At the national level affiliation fees and donations (especially at general elections) are vital to the party's viability, while the sponsoring of candidates provides vital finance. In the past, the unions have exerted considerable influence on the party both in government and in Opposition because of the complex organisational structure of the party. The block vote at conference and union representation on the National Executive Committee gave the unions a strong and sometimes dominant voice in party affairs. However, in recent years the Labour Party has introduced further organisational changes aimed at reducing the significance of the union block vote in the party's affairs. There have been several reasons for this move. One was to reduce the political damage of Conservative attacks on influence wielded by what were referred to as Labour's union 'paymasters'. Another factor was the hope that trade union members would also join as individuals, thus boosting the party's finances.

Since the triumph of the modernisers in the party, individuals and businesses have been much more ready to support the Labour Party. In the past, corporate donations were few in number and small in value, while individual donations were not anything like on the scale of those made to the Conservative Party. Recently there has been a change in these trends. An animal welfare group, the Political Animal Lobby donated £1 million, a sum matched by the late Matthew Harding, the Vice-Chairman of Chelsea Football Club. Other businesspeople have made large contributions, including David Sainsbury, former backer of the SDP. Corporate donations to Labour, sometimes from companies formerly associated with the Tories, have also grown. The Industrial Research Trust is reported to have received several large donations from companies and individuals, raising ethical questions similar to those which have so adversely affected the Tories. In the run-up to the 1997 election the

Conservatives attacked Labour over the manner in which the party was financed by the unions and by the use of 'blind trusts' to help fund the Leader and Deputy Leader's offices.

Within months of the election Labour was caught up in allegations of sleaze. During the election campaign the party had promised to take action against the sponsoring of sporting events by tobacco companies. However, once in government it was announced that an exception would be made for motor sport. News leaked out that the party had received a large donation from Bernie Ecclestone, head of the motor racing firm Formula One. In Opposition Labour had argued that large corporate donations were a threat to democracy, which increased the party's embarrassment when the news became public. The Prime Minister had met Ecclestone (a former supporter of the Tory Party) and Max Mosley (another major figure from the world of motor sport and a long-time supporter of Labour), who had lobbied for a change of policy. The news of the meeting, and the existence and size of the donation all had to be extracted with great difficulty. Eventually the matter was referred to the Neill Committee, which recommended that the gift be returned, although it is not clear whether this in fact occurred. Although the reaction of the Conservative Opposition was muted by their own vulnerability in matters of this sort, press condemnation was strong. Blair referred the issue of party funding to the Neill Committee.

The three main sources of Conservative Party funding are constituency associations, corporate donations and individual donations. Although full and accurate information is hard to find, it appears that company donations have usually provided around 60 per cent of the party's central income and approximately 30 per cent overall. Many constituency associations raise often large sums through social events, local appeals, and so on. In addition, the Conservative Party benefits from individual donations, some of large size, both to the party centrally and to local associations. In recent years, the source of these donations, details of which are a closely guarded secret, has caused considerable unease both to outside observers and also to some within the party.

Over the years there have been many accusations about the purchase both of political influence and abuses of the honours system. These go back at least to the time of Lloyd George, who was accused of selling honours in return for contributions to his political fund. All governments have to some extent been attacked for misuse of the system; accusations that honours were given for services to the governing party have been commonplace. However, there were especially fierce criticisms of the connections between the Tory Party and business between 1979 and 1997; the link between honours and company donations was highlighted in particular. Margaret Thatcher was accused of having given peerages and knighthoods in return for substantial donations. It was suggested that industrialists were ten times more likely to receive such awards if their firm gave money to the party. However, it is difficult to establish a causal link, and defenders of the system point out that these were successful men who had been given an honour in recognition of their work for the British economy. Conservatives counter-attacked by pointing out that left-wing critics forgot the honours given in the past to trade union leaders whose unions had made very significant contributions to the Labour Party.

In recent years a number of controversies have drawn attention to the nature of party funding. Investigations by the BBC *Panorama* programme suggested that honours could be obtained in return for donations to the governing party. Then came revelations that the Conservative Party was receiving donations from foreign businessmen, including the Greek ship owner John Latsis, who donated at least £2 million, and various Hong Kong figures. John Major hosted a party for Asian businessmen in No. 10 Downing Street and is reputed to have assured them that no changes would be made to UK tax laws for people who operate businesses in Britain but who are technically resident abroad. The allegations were that the Conservatives were maintaining these tax rules in order to sustain the possibility of donations from wealthy people. 'That these charges may be groundless is almost irrelevant: their very existence sullies the public's faith in the party system' (Garner and Kelly, 1998, p. 205).

Then came the Asil Nadir case. Nadir was making donations to the party, allegedly in the hope of a knighthood, while facing charges of theft and false accounting; these gifts were not revealed in company accounts. Some £440,000 was received by the party, which denied that it had any responsibility to ensure that the Companies Act was being observed. It was later revealed that Nadir had attempted to persuade the then Treasurer of the Conservative Party to get the charges dropped. Although the party accepted that the money should be returned should it be found to have been stolen from shareholders, this was not done.

Several conclusions can be drawn. Conservative politicians, while denying that the party accepted money from foreign governments, stressed that foreign citizens had every right to make donations if they had a commercial interest in the country.

> This is a contentious position. Many of those who make donations from abroad do not possess the vote in this country, yet they are permitted to make donations which indirectly affect the outcome of elections here. By suggesting that such donations are legitimate on the grounds of financial interests, the implication is that economic interests bestow similar rights to those of citizenship. (Fisher, 1997, p. 68)

As part of the reforms to the structure and organisation of the Conservative Party following the 1997 election, William Hague announced that foreign donations would no longer be accepted.

In the run-up to the 1997 general election there was a marked increase in corporate donations to the Tory Party, more than wiping out the party's deficit. There were renewed allegations that Tory fund raisers had linked donations with efforts to obtain honours for donors. The 'sleaze factor' played a significant role in the 1997 general election.

State funding of political parties: the argument

Although pressure for state aid has grown recently, funds have been made available in a number of ways for many years. Since 1918 the cost of registering electors and providing polling stations has been met out of public funds. All parliamentary candidates receive free use of halls for election meetings and free postage for one election address to each voter. In 1987 it was estimated that this subsidy amounted to £13.2 million for the Conservative, Labour and Alliance Parties combined. Since 1947 there have been free party political broadcasts on radio and television for all parties fielding more than fifty candidates. This limits the impact of press advertising and gives some advantage to the less-well-off parties. Free broadcasting and postal services were worth £20 million to the parties in 1997. In addition, subsidies are paid to the Opposition parties in Parliament for research and secretarial costs. Called 'Short' money after Ted Short, the Leader of the House who helped to introduce it, and allocated on the basis of seats not votes, in 1996/7 it provided £1.6 million to the Labour Party, £316,000 to the Liberal Democrats and smaller sums to the other Opposition parties.

The case for state aid

- It would reduce the unfair financial advantage enjoyed by the Conservatives and Labour and decrease their dependence on institutional support. This would prevent privileges being given to certain interests, while others are unfairly disadvantaged.
- It would improve the position of the central party organisations and allow the parties to concentrate on policy making (thus encouraging more coherent and practical policies), recruiting members, and so on, rather than having to emphasise fund raising.
- It would prevent parties such as the Liberal Democrats and other smaller parties being disadvantaged because they cannot command institutional finance. This would give new parties a chance to break into the political system, thus widening choice and allowing groups and interests which are currently unrepresented a place in the political system.
- It would avoid the situation whereby some trade unionists and some company shareholders contribute to causes of which they do not approve. However, Labour supporters point out that trade unionists can 'contract out' of the political levy; shareholders have no such right. Several advantages, it is argued, would be gained from these looser links. It would lead to greater

freedom for the parties to develop their ideas, it would reduce the atmosphere of 'sleaze' 'as fewer doubts would exist over whether policies were shaped by party financial considerations, and it could restore some faith in the honours system' (Garner and Kelly, 1998, p. 211). Some commentators believe it would encourage the move to a modern, classless political system as the parties would no longer be tied to traditional class positions.
• Supporters of state subsidies point to the experience of other countries, especially in Europe, which have introduced similar changes. In most member states of the European Union assistance is given, based on the number of seats held or the number of votes won at the previous general election.

Several reforms have been proposed:

• The state should subsidise party organisations and candidates.
• Public grants should match small individual donations; for every pound raised by a political party the state would provide an equal amount.
• Election spending by the parties should be limited.
• Parties should have to publish their accounts.
• Donations from unions and companies should be banned.
• Contributions by companies should have the same legal restrictions as those imposed on the unions.

The case against state aid

• Perhaps the most compelling argument against the provision of state aid is that it is 'a euphemism for taxpayers' money' (Garner and Kelly, 1998, p. 212). Given that there are so many other demands on the public purse it is difficult to justify giving money to political parties. One of the reasons why the Callaghan government did not proceed with Houghton's recommendations is that there was evidence of voter hostility to what could be seen as a trade-off against hospital beds or other public services. In addition, the public may become cynical at the sight of politicians voting for public money to be channelled to their parties and perhaps to be denied to others.
• Direct state aid would endanger the principle that parties (and other organisations with political aims) exist in a 'voluntary' capacity. There is a danger that governments would attempt to control the political process to their own advantage, leading to constant tinkering with the legal position. Any scheme of public funding would be highly bureaucratic and open to abuse. 'Sleaze' is not confined to the United Kingdom, and countries such as Italy and Germany have had scandals concerning party funding despite having appreciable levels of public provision. The difficulty of trying to regulate the level of institutional funding can be illustrated by reference to the American example. Despite strict federal laws concerning donations by unions and corporations, there are many opportunities to bypass the

system by making donations to Political Action Committees, which then channel the money to candidates of their choice. In practice, this and other loopholes 'can give to well organised Republicans an enormous advantage. In 1984, for example, the Republican National Committee raised $246 million, compared with a mere $66 million raised by the Democrats' (McKay, 1993, p. 138).

- There is a danger that state funding would end the need for parties to seek members in order to raise funds, thus making them remote from their supporters and further alienating the public from the political process. There is no guarantee that public funding would improve the performance of parties, and fund raising acts as a cohesive force in party political activity.
- It can be argued that donations by companies and unions are legitimate expressions of political action, so long as the process is fairly regulated by law and open to public scrutiny. Existing party alignments represent real divisions in society, and rather than distorting the political system, donations by the unions to Labour and business to the Conservatives indicate that legitimate interests are being represented.
- There is great difficulty in deciding who would benefit from state subsidies; issues of who would decide which parties would receive funds, whether independents and 'fringe' candidates would be eligible and whether individual citizens would be forced to contribute to parties not of their choice, and to which they may have rooted or even moral objections, need to be addressed. Minor (perhaps 'extreme') parties may be given an artificial stimulus by the injection of state funds. It is also possible that parties which have lost public support would be given an artificial stimulus. They would continue to exist in some kind of comfortable limbo, simply fulfilling the fantasies of those running them. It is for this reason that the nationalist parties have opposed state funding, fearing that it would bolster the position of their opponents more than it would help them.
- On the other hand, if the distribution of public funds were to be on the basis of 'rewarding' parties for success in winning either seats or votes (or both), as both Houghton and the Hansard Committee envisaged, it is unlikely that minor parties could benefit. Without showing evidence of support among the voters it is difficult to imagine that voters (who are also taxpayers) would be willing to provide the necessary funds.
- Public subsidies could either strengthen central party organisations at the expense of the grass roots, leading to an over-powerful centre, or could have the reverse effect, as in the USA, making the national parties largely redundant. This has opened the way to the phenomenon of candidate-centred campaigns, in which the emphasis is on the individual candidates being responsible for their own fund raising and election campaigns. This has had major consequences for party cohesion and discipline, and for the ability of parties to aggregate and articulate interests across the political spectrum.

The Report of the Commons Home Affairs Select Committee

The issue was examined by the Commons Home Affairs Select Committee, the report of which was released in March 1994. Its terms of reference were

> to examine the case for and against state funding of political parties, excluding their work inside Parliament; the methods by which the parties are at present financed; the adequacy of those funds for the tasks which the parties perform; and the desirability or otherwise of controls over the sources of finance or other statutory requirements being placed upon donors or recipients.

The report was signed by the six Conservative members of the Committee; the five Labour members issued a minority report.

In their evidence the parties were divided. Labour, the Liberal Democrats, the Green Party and the SDLP were in favour; the Conservatives, the Ulster Unionists, the SNP and Plaid Cymru against.

The majority report rejected the idea of a general extension of state funding or any substantial reform of the law on party funding generally. The Conservative majority emphasised the voluntary nature of political activity and argued that reliance should continue to be placed on the honesty and integrity of the political parties. The minority report did not recommend public funding but it did argue that far-reaching reforms were necessary to the whole area of party fund raising. Reference was made to the 'enormous scandal' which surrounded Conservative Party fund raising in the 1980s and early 1990s. The minority report went on to make a number of detailed recommendations for change. Most of these were taken up by the Neill Committee.

The Neill Committee Report

Although the bulk of the recommendations dealt with attempts to end the various scandals connected with the manner in which parties raise money, some of the points did have implications for the provision of public money.

The report recommendation that tax relief on donations to parties should be introduced, capped at £500, was justified on the grounds that it is more democratic that parties should be supported by a large number of small donors than by a small number of large ones. Parties will make greater efforts to attract this type and level of support. It was felt that the present level of 'Short' money was not sufficient to allow the Opposition parties to do their job properly. In the previous year the Tories had received £986,762 and the Liberal Democrats £371,997, with smaller amounts going to the minor parties. Each party should receive three times the current amount, taking the total cost to £4.8 million. There should be extra money to fund the Leader of the Opposition's office and more money for the Opposition parties in the Lords.

The main recommendations of the Neill Report were

- foreign donations to be banned;
- blind trusts to be abolished;
- all national donations of £5,000 and local donations of £1,000 to be made public;
- anonymous donations of £50 or more to be banned;
- £20 million cap on party campaign budgets at general elections;
- tax relief for donations up to £500;
- tripling of state funding to help Opposition parties in Parliament and a new £2 million fund for policy research;
- shareholders to approve company donations and sponsorship;
- new laws for referendums to include equal state funding for 'Yes' and 'No' campaigns;
- the establishment of an Electoral Commission, with powers to police the system, ensure openness and enforce the spending cap.

Conclusion

The report of the Neill Commission highlighted the extent to which the two main parties had become dependent on large donations from wealthy individuals and organisations. This has given rise to a widespread perception that money can buy access, or even influence, and while the report agreed there was no direct evidence that such influence has been bought, there is a widespread and damaging public perception that such is the case. Many critics feel that the present 'market-based' system of party finance distorts representative democracy. It also means that there is an ever-present danger that parties will run into financial problems which will endanger their capacity to perform their various roles. It is clear that in the 1990s there was considerable public cynicism about politicians and the political parties. Protestations of integrity by the politicians themselves will no longer be as acceptable as in the past. The demand for more information about the affairs of the political parties is part of an increasing call for greater openness. The suspicion that politicians are manipulating the political system either to ensure their hold on power or in their individual self interest is corrosive of faith in the democratic system. The demand for 'more light' will grow. On the other hand, whether the Labour government will seek to extend state funding at a time of considerable financial stringency (and given the current horrendous financial problems of the Tories and the comparative affluence of Labour) remains to be seen.

Should political parties be funded by the state?

The case for

- The provision of 'matching funds' by the state would force the parties to broaden their appeal and seek a large number of small donors rather than relying on either institutions, such as companies or unions, or rich individuals.
- It would end, or at least reduce, the distortion in policy making caused by Labour's need to conciliate the unions and the Conservatives' need to woo big business.
- It would reduce the influence that institutions have in the internal affairs of the major parties.
- It would produce more of a 'level playing-field' and allow the Liberal Democrats and other smaller parties to compete on something like equal terms.
- It would help the parties to produce better-thought-out policies, especially in Opposition.
- It would help to combat the prevalence of 'sleaze' in political life.
- It would bring Britain into line with the practice in most comparable liberal democracies.

The case against

- It would make fresh demands on taxpayers when there are almost limitless alternative calls on the public purse.
- The sight of public money going to politicians could *increase* cynicism about the political process.
- Parties are 'voluntary' organisations and the provision of public money could endanger this vital aspect of the democratic process.
- There is a danger that governments could seek to manipulate the process to their own advantage.
- It would increase bureaucracy.
- The provision of public money has done little to reduce the scandals surrounding the political process in the USA, Italy and other democracies.
- State funding could reduce the need for parties to seek members and supporters, thus further alienating them from the people they are supposed to serve.
- Difficult questions of which parties would benefit would be raised; 'extreme' parties might be given an artificial stimulus.
- Taxpayers might be forced into subsidising parties they might not support or to which they might even have moral objections.
- Public funding might result in an over-powerful national party organisation or lead to the weakening of the party, which is a marked feature of the American political system.

Reading

Blackburn, R. (1995) *The Electoral System in Britain*, Macmillan.

Bogdanor, V. (1997) *Power and the People*, Gollancz.

Fisher, J. (1997) 'Donations to political parties', *Parliamentary Affairs*, 50:2, April.

Garner, R. and Kelly, R. (1998) *British Political Parties Today*, Manchester University Press.

Lemieux, S. (1995) 'The future funding of political parties', *Talking Politics*, 7:3, Spring.

McConnell, A. (1994) 'The "Crisis" of Conservative Party funding', *Talking Politics*, 7:1, Autumn.

McKay, D. (1993) *American Politics and Society*, Blackwell.

Norton, P. (1997) *The Conservative Party*, Prentice Hall.

Pinto-Duschinsky, M. (1988) 'Party finance. Funding of political parties since 1945', *Contemporary Record*, 2:4, Winter.

Seyd, P. (1988) 'In praise of party', *Parliamentary Affairs*, 51:2, April.

Thomas, G. P. (1992) *Government and the Economy Today*, Manchester University Press.

Thomas, G. P. (1999) 'Party finance', in B. Jones (ed.), *Political Issues in Britain Today*, Manchester University Press.

IV

Debates on issues

14

Law and order: is toughness the only answer?

Bill Jones

Introduction

Most years the Conservative Party Conference debates crime and the nation is presented with the unedifying spectacle of 'old ladies with blue rinses' calling for the return of capital punishment and the birching of young offenders. Opinion surveys suggest that most people tend to agree with such an approach; hence the electoral emphasis which Conservatives have placed on being 'the party of law and order'. Much of the debate reduces to the question of what human nature is basically like: do humans respond best to love or to fear? Machiavelli believed the latter and others, including Marx and Rousseau, the former. Conservative politicians tend to follow Hobbes, who believed that the prime purpose of government is to provide law and order and that strong government and law enforcement is necessary to deter potential law breakers. Labour has tended to disagree and argue that we are the products of our environments, so that someone born into poverty with few prospects is more likely to break the law as the law provides them with few of the advantages it accords the rich and privileged. However, the electorate has generally preferred to believe the 'tough' message to the 'tender' and New Labour was quick, under Tony Blair, to deflect the Conservatives' accusation of being soft on crime with the slogan 'tough on crime, tough on the causes of crime'. This chapter considers the arguments for and against being tough towards those who break the law.

Background: The crime wave

During the 1980s crime figures leapt upwards, doubling from the 2.5 million indictable offences in 1979 to over five million in 1990. During the 1990s the figures have gradually fallen, hitting a new low for the decade of 4.6 million in 1998 (table 14.1). Criminologists argue about the statistics used and say that such rising figures can often be explained by better police reporting

Table 14.1   *Recorded crime, 1999*
Notifiable offences recorded by the police by offence

Offence group	12 months ending March 1999 (old rules)	Change since March 1998	
		Number	Per cent
Violence against the person	230,756	−25,314	−9.9
Sexual offences	34,915	+764	+2.2
Robbery	66,172	+3,520	+5.6
Total violent crime	331,843	−21,030	−6.0
Burglary	951,878	−36,554	−3.7
Total theft and handling stolen goods	2,126,718	−18,255	−0.9
(of which) Theft of and from vehicles	1,071,828	−24,194	−2.2
Fraud and forgery	173,728	+37,496	+27.5
Criminal damage	834,370	−27,476	−3.2
Total property crime	4,086,694	−44,789	−1.1
Drug offences	21,306	−2,030	−8.7
Other notifiable offences	41,974	+4,329	+11.5
Total all offences	4,481,817	−63,520	−1.4

practices, more insurance claims or the growth of new laws (which tends to increase the rate of offending). Even allowing for statistical exaggeration, however, it is obvious to virtually everyone that crime has been a growing problem in Britain for the past thirty years and that drastic action is necessary to curb the growth of crime, especially among the key offending group: young people aged between fifteen and twenty-four. Many believe the only way to solve the problem is by getting tough with the criminals.

In favour of toughness

Inherent evil

Some argue, in common with the Christian viewpoint, that humans have a propensity towards sin and it is only by being devout Christians that salvation can be achieved. According to this view, 'man is inherently sinful', as Margaret Thatcher maintained, and there is little to be done about it except to follow the precepts of self discipline and obedience inculcated by family, church and those entrusted with civil authority. Otherwise it will be inevitable that life will be anarchic, lawless and perhaps even, as Hobbes warned, 'nasty, solitary, brutish and short'.

Rightwingers fear that these restraining bonds on potentially anarchic behaviour have been fatally weakened in recent years, causing the current crime wave. They point to the 'permissive sixties' (when, by no coincidence, Labour was in power), when young people were enjoined by silly irresponsible people to 'let it all hang out' and challenge all forms of authority. They also argue that such ideas permeated the educational system, thereby sowing the seeds of future crime waves.

Revenge

Rightwingers have no problems with the idea of revenge, which they see as a natural and just emotion. According to them, those who transgress the law 'deserve' everything they get and society has the right to feel duly satisfied with the revenge which has been meted out.

'Common sense'

To some extent this concept is anything its advocates wish to make it but, for those on the Right who cite it, it usually means that, as people are deterred from breaking the law by the threat of legal sanction, so it follows that an increase in the penalty will increase the deterrent. To choose an example: if a sentence of two years' imprisonment does not deter a house burglar, then the sentence must be increased to three or four years. Moreover, if prison itself does not seem to deter a stratum of offenders, then the experience of incarceration must be made more punitive, with privileges limited and comforts removed. It follows too that young offenders, the prime offending age group, should be dealt with rather like unruly children used to be treated in a bygone age: physical punishment. In the Isle of Man birching of young offenders used to be part of the penal system; Conservative Conference-goers were, and still are, closely wedded to the notion that, as such treatment 'cured' Manx offenders – though this was never decisively proven – it should be applied to young criminals in the mainland of the UK.

'Prison works'

This slogan is most closely associated with the Conservative Home Secretary, Michael Howard, who won huge applause by using the 1993 Party Conference to launch it. He had already claimed that prison life was too cushy: 'prisoners enjoy a standard of comfort which taxpayers would find hard to understand'. He now argued that prison was an effective deterrent and that it succeeded, at minimum, in removing dangerous criminals from society while they were locked up. In consequence the Conservatives embarked on a substantial programme of prison building to house the burgeoning number of criminals sentenced to such punishment. Howard told the conference: 'There is a tidal wave of concern about crime in this country. I am not going to

ignore it. I am going to take action. Tough action.' He announced a series of
new measures, including the building of six new prisons. Under the Conservatives prison sentences had increased dramatically; between 1984 and 1987
sentences for serious crimes such as rape, robbery indecent assault and man-
slaughter increased by anything from 12 to 90 per cent. In September 1993 a
new programme of 'privatised' prisons (i.e. run by private companies, not the
state) was announced – twelve contracts to be agreed by 1995 – based upon
allegedly successful practice in the USA.

The death penalty

Geoffrey Dicken, a former Conservative MP, once confided that at his selection
meeting at Littleborough and Saddleworth he boldly announced his support
for Margaret Thatcher and the return of the death penalty and was duly
readopted as the candidate for a reasonably safe seat. Many other Conservative MPs have said and believed similar things about the death penalty, not
to mention their above-named erstwhile leader who supported this point of
view but believed it to be a matter of conscience requiring a free vote. This
approach can be traced to the view of the Babylonian King Hammurabi (1782
BC), whose somewhat bloodthirsty penal code advocated 'an eye for an eye
and a tooth for a tooth'. In other words the taking of a life requires an equal or
'revenge' taking of a life. In Britain the death penalty was abolished in 1965
but surveys show that the majority of the public would like it to be reintro-
duced. In the USA many states have either retained the measure or readopted
it in response to public demand and these positions help fuel the constant
demand for similar action in the UK.

Islamic law

Islamic law is often cited by supporters of the 'tough' approach as evidence of
its success. It is based on the teachings of the Koran and the principle of
retribution: the victim is allowed to exact equal punishment on the law breaker.
Famously, we understand, criminals are punished by lashes in public, ampu-
tations (for thieving) and ultimately beheadings (for serious crimes such as
rape), also in public. We also understand the crime rate in Muslim countries
such as Saudi Arabia to be impressively low, and that a clear causal connection exists between tough punishment and law-abiding behaviour.

The media

The media are blamed for many things but advocates of the tough approach
are usually convinced they encourage lawlessness. It is obvious that television influences behaviour, otherwise businesses would not fork out their
huge advertising budgets. It follows, say opponents of the media, that images

portrayed on film and television influence the behaviour of society in less benign ways than buying one brand of cornflakes rather than another. It is true that there are thousands of murders depicted on the small screen; it is suggested by right-wing 'toughies' that such a media diet causes a desire to emulate in the young and otherwise easily led, to seek some of the glamour with which the media invest gangsters and anti-social behaviour. For example, it was suggested that the film *Natural Born Killers*, which told the story of two psychopathic youngsters engaged on a killing spree across the USA, had caused several 'copycat' killings by other youngsters in the USA and in other countries. Furthermore, the two boys who killed the infant Jamie Bulger were alleged to have been influenced by a particular violent horror film available from video shops.

Arguments against the tough approach

Inherent evil or goodness?

Some philosophers have held to a more optimistic view of human nature than Hobbes and Machiavelli. John Locke, for example, believed that humans living outside the confines of the state would be co-operative and reasonable. Rousseau believed something similar, attributing many human failings to the corrupting effect of human society as it had developed ('man was born free, and everywhere he is in chains'). Karl Marx was more emphatically convinced of this view, arguing that human nature was naturally noble and good and that its faults were the deforming effects of a competitive free market economy which made men enemies of each other and created vast unjustifiable wealth for a small minority of property owners, with vast masses who lived in miserable poverty. It is unsurprising, perhaps, that such a philosophical perspective would appeal to the Left, those who wished to change society. They argue that in one sense the criminal is the consequence, the victim of a system which robs, distorts and destroys. Accordingly the 1960s were a time of joy and liberation to the Left, when old ideas were rudely jettisoned and youth freed itself from the straitjacket thinking of a parental generation still in thrall to the Victorians. It follows from this line of thinking that crime is a result of the divisions in society caused by the economic system and that a more equitable society will be a less crime-ridden one. New Labour however, as already mentioned, chose to toughen its traditional line on crime during the 1980s to reassure the voters of 'middle England'.

Revenge and the Christian approach

The desire for revenge may be a natural and understandable emotion for a victim in the wake of a crime, especially a serious one, but it does not accord with Christian morality which enjoins us to 'turn the other cheek'; nor does it serve to alleviate the problem of crime. For example, longer sentences may make victims feel a little better but there is precious little evidence that they help to deter further offending; rather the reverse as young offenders learn, through imprisonment – the 'university of crime' – to become more socialised into a life of law breaking and to become more skilled at their new profession (see below). Revenge only produces a temporary and arguably unworthy feeling of satisfaction: it solves nothing.

'Common sense'

At the heart of so-called 'common sense' is often an assumption of questionable validity. So it is, according to liberal critics of the tough approach. To assume that ever-increasing punishments of offenders will solve problems of law and order does not bear close examination. First, incarceration is expensive and if it is used too prodigally – for example, for theft – the costs will usually exceed by many multiples the amount originally stolen. Second, prison does not rehabilitate but merely leads to repeat offences. Third, it is not the sentences which deter, according to research, but the chances of getting caught. It seems that criminals do not often apply the dictum 'if you can't do the time, don't do the crime'; rather, they make a hard-headed calculation of their chances of being caught. Finally, too many punishments reduces their effect. In late eighteenth-century Britain it was possible to be hanged for stealing a trivial amount, encouraging criminals to commit greater crimes as the punishment was no different; hence the saying that one 'might as well be hung for a sheep as for a lamb'.

'Prison works'

Some of the arguments against prison have already been touched upon above, but following Howard's 1993 policy shift in favour of imprisonment seven high court judges pronounced his judgement wrong. Lord Ackner said that the causes of crime 'lay deep in society, in the deterioration of personal standards, the family and lack of self discipline'. Lord Justice Farquharson could not understand why more people were imprisoned in the UK than in other countries: 'My general philosophy is that you should never impose a prison sentence when you can avoid it . . . I have never believed prison rehabilitates anyone.' And Lord Bruce Langland added that he felt the deterrent effect of prison diminished with successive spells inside: 'Prison may satisfy public opinion and the victim's understandable feelings, but it has no rehabilitation effect whatsoever . . . a great deal of dishonesty is contributed by politicians.' More criticism was directed at the then government's policy of reducing spending on probation services and prison education. Sir David Ramsbottom, Chief Inspector of Prisons, in November 1996 concluded that Wandsworth was effectively 'warehousing prisoners'. *The Economist* (2 November 1996) added that 'there are more than 500 pieces of international research on prison regimes. Most of them agree that regimes with more education and more rehabilitation work produce prisoners less likely to reoffend.'

Alternatives to prison

Penal reformers point to the fact that the number of inmates in British prisons has increased worryingly over the 1980s and 90s. Richard Tilt, Director of the Prison Service, predicted that the prison population would break 80,000 by 2003 and would require more than two dozen new prisons at a cost in excess of £2 billion; each prisoner costs over £600 per week, more than the cost of a good hotel. As a result of this situation a number of new alternatives have been looked at:

- *Tagging* This approach involves an electronic transmitter locked on to the prisoner's limbs so that he or she can remain outside prison but still be supervised by the authorities.
- *Community service orders* These require offenders to work off their debt to society through useful activity; for example, Eric Cantona's coaching following his conviction for kicking a spectator at a match.
- *Victim restitution* According to this approach victims are brought face to face with those who have offended against them. The pain and contrition involved seem to prevent further offending as well as proving therapeutic for the victim.

Death penalty

The arguments against the death penalty are well rehearsed by its opponents. First, it would be a retrograde step for a civilised society. Most people, even supporters of the death penalty, would agree that the medieval practice of hanging, drawing and quartering offenders – effectively disembowelling them in public – is inappropriate in the present day. Yet bringing back the death penalty would halt this civilising process substantially and in practice reverse it. Second, Britain does not suffer from a major murder problem: under 700 people die this way each year compared with some 20,000 in the USA. Third, there is little evidence that the murder rate has increased since the death penalty was abandoned in 1965. Fourth, it would place extra pressure on judges and juries striving to administer justice. Fifth, it would not be possible to reverse miscarriages of justice – of which there have been many high-profile examples over the past two decades – if the accused has been executed. Finally, to reserve the death penalty for terrorists, as some recommend, would play into their hands by creating martyrs. Interestingly, when Conservative MPs, away from adoption meetings and election campaigns, hear the arguments debated coolly and rationally in the Commons, as regularly occurs, they invariably vote to retain abolition.

Islamic law

Those who cite the Sharia law of Muslim countries do not allow for cultural differences; there is no guarantee that a similar approach would work in modern Western countries. Moreover, such harsh measures as public beheadings, it can be argued, are scarcely the hallmark of a civilised society according to Western standards.

The media

The debate over the role of the media in relation to crime, especially violent crime, is intense and based on a large number of empirical studies, but is still inconclusive. There are so many influences crowding in on members of society – work, friends, family, regional and national sentiments – that it is almost impossible to disentangle the media from them and attribute due importance to them. Some apologists for the media claim it is undemocratic and a violation of free speech to attempt to control the media's output in any way. Other apologists claim that depictions of violence on the screen, far from encouraging imitation, actually release tensions in society – 'cathartically' – by acting such scenes out peacefully through drama.

Crime prevention

Criminologists maintain that it would be more cost effective to spend money on prevention rather than the regular billions on detection, apprehension and punishment:

- *Better protection of property* for such easy targets as cars and credit cards.
- *Neighbourhood Watch schemes*   There are over 40,000 extant in the country and they seem to provide an effective defence against crime as well as a spur to community solidarity.
- *Targeting of known offenders*   The Holme Wood estate in Bradford used this tactic to bring down the rate of joyriding and burglary by over 50 per cent in both cases.
- *Victim contact*   Already mentioned above, this approach, when used by the Thames Valley Force, brought down the reoffending rate from 30 to 4 per cent in 1998.
- *Head Start Programme*   This was begun in the 1960s in the USA whereby children in high crime areas were given two years of nursery education. Research reveals that such children went on to be relatively high achievers and non-offenders. The Home Office will spend £200 million on a similar scheme in the UK.

Is toughness the only answer?

The case for

- Inherent evil: humans are naturally prone to commit crimes.
- Revenge: victims are entitled to have revenge on those who have harmed them.
- Common sense: more punishment increases the deterrence of the law.
- Prison works: it takes criminals off the streets and offers deterrents they cannot ignore.
- Death penalty: the only way to punish and deter murder.
- Islamic law: brutal, perhaps, but it creates a country which is crime free.
- Media: exposure to violence and sex on screen and television creates crime-ridden societies.

The case against

- Inherent evil: just as much evidence and theorising that humans are inherently good.
- Revenge: merely wreaks more harm and does little to solve the problem of crime.
- Prison works: creates more able criminals; costs more than luxury hotels.
- Alternatives to prison: tagging is a promising experiment in the UK and USA; community service orders; good results achieved with victim restitution.
- Death penalty: does not reduce the incidence of murder, not civilised and offers no way out when there are miscarriages of justice.
- Islamic law: not suitable for a Western country.
- Media: unclear what impact the media have on society; could act as a 'catharsis'.
- Common sense: this is a meaningless concept.
- Crime prevention: more cost effective via Neighbourhood Watch, victim contact and the Head Start programme.

Conclusion

Whether one concludes that the tough approach is less effective than the 'tender' is often as much a matter of temperament as rational judgement. Some prefer the moral certainties and satisfactions of the right-wing stance which demonises the offender and sanctifies the victim. Others are so intent on blaming 'society' for its own ills that they offer no practical way out of the crime and punishment conundrum. The problem is to find a blend of analyses which define the dilemma of civilisation versus lawlessness reasonably accurately and prescriptions which work in practice to a degree which is satisfactory. The nature of that blend is the stuff of party politics, discussions at work or in the pub. It is also the focus of detailed research by criminologists across the developed world, struggling to find answers to problems which threaten at times to overwhelm us all.

Reading

Benyon, J. and Bourne, C. (1996) *The Police: Powers and Properties*, Pergamon.
Jones, B. (1999) 'Crime and punishment', in B. Jones (ed.), *Political Issues in Britain Today*, Manchester University Press.
Reiner, R. (1993) *The Politics of the Police*, Wheatsheaf.

15

Is high taxation the price of a civilised society?

Clive Gray

The famous claim of Benjamin Franklin that the only sure things in life are death and taxes raises the question of why are taxes so ubiquitous a feature of everyday life? This chapter will discuss the reasons and arguments surrounding taxation as a political issue and will show why taxes are necessary for any society organised on other than purely anarchist lines.

Background

At its simplest all governments require taxation to pay for the provision of public goods and services. These goods and services range from the basics of law and order and defence from external threats, through to welfare provision of health care, education and social security.

While governments may vary in how much of these goods and services is provided, they all require some means of getting their citizens to pay for them. This payment is undertaken, in the main, through taxation: a legally enforced contribution levied on the members of society. The taxes that are raised can be *direct*, taken from the incomes of citizens (e.g. income tax), or *indirect*, taken from the expenditure of citizens (e.g. VAT), and are collected and spent by governments.

Politically, the usual argument in the post-war period has varied around the issues of *how much* tax should be levied and *which form* of taxation should be used. More recently, the argument has shifted to asking *whether taxation is necessary* anyway. Each of these issues involves slightly different sets of concerns and arguments but are really centred around the key question of *in what sort of society do we wish to live?* To answer this question it is necessary to investigate the arguments surrounding taxation as a political issue, examining the case for taxation and comparing this with the case against.

Why taxation is necessary

The simplest case for taxation is that without it many goods and services would need to be funded directly by consumers through market mechanisms. If markets worked efficiently then this would be unproblematic. Unfortunately, this is not always the case. Market failure, in whatever form, would mean that goods and services would either not be provided at all, their price could be manipulated to unnecessarily high levels, or their supply could be inadequate (both the latter can occur with monopolies).

By means of taxation the state can therefore ensure an adequate supply of goods and services at an acceptable price. Indeed, it is often argued that some goods and services (the 'public goods' of economics) would not be provided anyway by private markets because of their very nature. Such goods and services (e.g. pollution control) are shared by all members of society and cannot be divided up between individuals: either everyone benefits or no one does. In this case state intervention is necessary to ensure that everyone contributes to the benefit that they receive.

Beyond this economic argument, however, there are also political arguments that imply that tax is a necessary element in any well-ordered society. These can be summed up as: redistribution arguments; social justice arguments; citizenship arguments.

- *Redistribution* is concerned with the allocation of the resources of society among its members. In all except completely equalitarian societies there are inequalities between people in terms of how much they earn. By reducing the differences of wealth by redistributing it between people, access to a wider range of goods and services can be made available to the less wealthy members of society.
- *Social justice* ties in with this idea in so far as the justification for redistribution is that there is an inevitable unfairness about limiting access to goods and services as a consequence of differences of wealth. In short, the argument states that society as a whole benefits if its members have access to goods and services that are essential to societal well-being (e.g. law and order services should not be limited to only those who can pay for them but should serve to look after the interests of everyone within society). Through redistribution social justice ensures that basic goods and services are made available to all.
- *Citizenship* is relevant to this argument in so far as the assumption that all members of society have equal rights and responsibilities, as citizens, should also mean that they should have access to core goods and services that underlie these rights and responsibilities. By providing these services for all, every member of society is given a stake in that society that should encourage feelings of support for the system, making it less prone to social unrest.

In sum, the case for taxation rests upon the idea that without some form of redistribution for purposes of social justice society would be in danger of discontent or even revolution.

This rather conservative argument in favour of taxes sees the issue of taxation as being a political one in so far as it assumes that taxation is a consciously made choice about the form of society that is wished for. If politically informed choices about the desirability of redistribution and social justice are not made then society would have to take a very different form for the provision of certain goods and services. These differing forms of society could take the shape of an anarchist, communal form of organisation or, at the other extreme, could rely entirely on market mechanisms. Either of these choices, however, would depend upon a very different system of social organisation than the one that is currently in place.

Deciding upon which form of organisation for society is wished for is a political choice, meaning that taxation itself is inescapably political in nature. This point will be returned to after a consideration of the opposing arguments that see taxation as either unnecessary or even dangerous for society.

Why taxation is unnecessary

The assumption that taxation is not only political but also has positive benefits for social stability has been severely questioned by critics who argue that the positive case is, at best, misleading and, at worst, contains the seeds of acute social problems. The arguments that are proposed to support such views can be summed up as concerning: consumer arguments; the burden of taxation; taxation and special interests.

- *Consumer arguments* basically argue that taxation is nothing more than organised theft by some members of society from others. In this view the only people who can be fully trusted to make decisions about their own welfare are individuals, not states. For this reason anything that limits individuals in their pursuit of their own interests is damaging not only to individuals but also to society as a whole.

  Such a view depends upon the efficiency of market mechanisms as allocators of resources for society. If markets work efficiently and effectively then intervention in their workings must detract from the overall social welfare of society. As markets operate on the basis of the decisions and choices that are made by a myriad of individuals they must, if they are working properly, satisfy the needs and wishes of those individuals. If this is the case then social welfare is maximised.

  Taxation, which takes choice away from individuals and passes it to an anonymous state, is thus an attack on the sovereign individual and will inevitably lead to a misuse of the resources of society, leading, ultimately, to a loss of personal freedom (Hayek, 1944).

- *The burden of taxation* does not start from the view contained in consumer arguments that tax is wrong in the first place. Instead it argues that, while taxation may be necessary to correct market imperfections, the incidence of it is problematic. In this argument either too much tax is being raised or it is being levied in a manner that is 'unfair'. The former of these is concerned with how many goods and services the state actually needs to provide to rectify market shortcomings; the latter is concerned with who is actually paying taxes.

   How much the state needs to provide could be a purely economic argument. For it to work as such, however, depends upon a knowledge of economics that has proved to be beyond the grasp of everyone – including economists. As such this remains a theoretical argument which is incapable of solution at the present time (whether it will ever be solved is another matter).

   The incidence of taxation depends upon political choices. The principles of social justice and redistribution that lie behind the case for taxation form a part of the basis upon which political actors make their decisions in this area. It could be possible to levy the same tax demands on every member of society, whereby everybody contributes the same amount to the provision of state goods and services. Usually, however, it is the case that there is a sliding scale of contribution so that the least well off in society contribute less than the better off. This is justified through appeals to redistribution (the better off should pay more) and social justice (it is only fair that this should be the case).

   Agreement or disagreement with these principles forms the basis of the argument, therefore, as to the incidence of taxation. The fairness, or otherwise, of tax demands is thus, once again, a political argument that can only be resolved by political choice.
- *Taxation and special interests* is an argument derived from *public choice* theories (see Mueller, 1989). It essentially argues that taxation creates both winners and losers: the winners are those who benefit from the provision of public goods and services; the losers are those who pay taxes. It is assumed that the winners in this game are a small group of special interests within society who have a vested concern in seeing the continuation of the provision of goods and services by the state. These winners are more easily mobilised in defence of their interests than are the mass of losers who have no special interests to defend.

   In this case taxation gives rise to the creation of groups which can manipulate politicians in favour of themselves, thus skewing the delivery of goods and services. The mass of taxpayers are at a disadvantage as they are relatively difficult to mobilise and may end up paying more in taxes than is actually necessary as a consequence of the manipulative behaviour of special interests.

The arguments against taxation are largely based around a picture of a society that is made up of free, rational individuals. Left to their own devices it is assumed that public welfare will inevitably follow from the mass of decisions that these individuals make. Such a view is political in itself, being based on an ideology of individualism. It is to ideologies that attention now turns.

Ideology and taxation

The arguments in support of, and opposing, taxation are based in differing ideologies that are concerned with the elements of what makes a decent community of individuals. All of these ideologies are premised upon an acceptance of some form of market system but differ markedly in terms of how they view this market and what, if anything, needs to be done with it by the members of this decent community.

The arguments for taxation can be supported by reference to ideologies that range from socialism, through liberalism to conservatism. The arguments against taxation are largely based in forms of liberalism and conservatism. The overlap that is evident from this statement requires some clarification as it would appear that the same ideologies can both support and attack taxation at the same time.

The factor that has key importance in this is the view of the market that is adopted. Ideologies are not single entities: they are made up of streams of thought that can differ markedly from each other. In the case of taxation this is evident in the splits and tensions that characterise both liberalism and conservatism in terms of whether they accept the market as a neutral mechanism for the allocation of goods and services that operates most effect-ively when left alone, or as something that needs to be controlled for the benefit of all.

Socialism generally has no problems with taxation and accepts that market weaknesses demand correction in the interests of the principles of social justice and redistribution. Likewise, some versions of both liberalism and conservatism accept the necessity of taxation as either a corrective to dangerous potential trends in the operation of free markets, or as a mechan-ism to maintain social cohesion and unity in the face of forces that could lead to revolutionary pressures becoming too great for society to withstand.

Other versions of liberalism and conservatism, however, have a much more positive view of market mechanisms and would argue that societal problems are the result of state interference in the free workings of the market, not of weaknesses in the market system itself. In this case the underlying principles of social justice and redistribution are discounted as being of no relevance. Both of these principles are implicitly seen to exist in markets themselves;

nothing extra is needed to make them a reality than to set markets free from state interference.

The different consequences for society that arise from these views are considerable. The acceptance of the case for redistribution and social justice formed the key elements of the creation of the welfare states of Western Europe after World War II. These states were influenced in this by the ideological predisposition of their governments towards socialism or social liberalism or social conservatism. Taxation thus became a weapon to be used for multiple purposes – not only for redistribution and social justice but also for social cohesion and unity.

No state has entirely escaped the influence of these arguments in the post-World War II period. Even traditionally non-state interventionist systems, such as in the United States, have developed forms of social welfare provision predicated upon taxation as a political tool. However, there have been variations in the extent to which the social welfare consensus has been fully accepted. The 1970s saw a resurgence of more traditional liberal and conservative arguments that were opposed to taxation for redistributive and social purposes, and a consequent reappraisal of the role of taxation within society.

In this reappraisal the role of the market was seen as central to societal well-being. Individuals, the key actors in this ideological line of argument, were expected to undertake a process of rational calculation to safeguard themselves from the potential evils of, for example, unemployment, ill health and old age. Instead of becoming dependent on the state to look after them in such circumstances, the market was argued to be the most effective mechanism for taking care of individuals. For this reason taxation was decried as shifting responsibility from individuals to the state, preventing people from looking after themselves as so much of their income was 'stolen' from them by the state. This heralded a phase of attacks on taxation (at least, on direct taxation: the general result of this process was simply a shift from direct to indirect taxation) aimed at 'freeing' individuals from the dead hand of the state.

Acceptance of tax is heavily influenced by the ideologies that are held by the key political actors. Different ideologies have different views on the value, or lack of it, of taxation, and it is these ideologies that determine the amount of tax that is demanded from citizens and how it is to be paid.

A 'civilised' society?

Franklin Roosevelt, the former American President, said that 'taxes, after all, are the dues that we pay for the privileges of membership in an organized society'. If taxes are a necessary component of an 'organised' society does this mean that they are necessary for a 'civilised' society, or are 'organised' and 'civilised' separate concerns in terms of society?

It is clear that taxation is required if governments are ever to achieve their aims – whatever these may be. Even the most minimal of states, concerned only with the maintenance of internal law and order, requires some mechanism to pay for this. The amount of tax that is required depends upon what it is that governments seek to do; the more active the government, the more policy areas in which it intervenes, the greater will be the tax bill that has to be met.

What governments do, then, is the crucial issue in terms of taxation. Modern governments do more than the simple 'defining' functions of the state, concerned with internal law and order; they are also concerned with the provision of infrastructure and social functions, such as education and health care. The reasons for this scale of involvement vary considerably but a common factor is the belief that the government *should* provide these services.

Providing services implies an element of organisation: staff are needed actually to deliver the goods and services involved, and these staff members must be managed to ensure that they are working effectively in the realisation of the goals of governments. Taxes themselves must be collected and distributed. Thus modern government *is* organised government, involving the full panoply of bureaucratic organisation that is expected and necessary for efficient working.

Is this organised phenomenon of government, however, needed to ensure the creation of a civilised society? This depends upon the view that is held of what governments exist for in the first place. Interventionists would argue that state involvement in the delivery of a wide range of goods and services is necessary for the attainment of a civilised society: governments *should* provide certain things. Non-interventionists and free marketeers, on the other hand, see an active government as a positive danger to the good life: governments *should not* provide things.

The resolution of this clash depends upon whether it is accepted that without state intervention certain goods and services would ever be provided and, if they are, who benefits from their provision. Human rights proponents would claim that provision by itself is only a part of the answer – how widely the benefits of provision are distributed is also of central importance. In this view goods and services that are necessary for individuals to claim their full dignity as members of society must be ensured, even if not actively provided, by the state. Thus social welfare functions, such as education and health care, are necessary for all before any society can be classified as being a decent, if not a civilised, one.

Acceptance of such a view implies that no society can be truly civilised without some form of state intervention. If this intervention is to work the state needs to be organised. For organisation to be effective taxes must be levied on the population. Ultimately a civilised society cannot exist without taxation.

The politics of taxation

Alongside the philosophical issues that are raised by the principle of taxation in the first place, taxation is also an element in everyday practical politics. Decisions about taxation tend, in the main, not to be decided by reference to grand ideas but, instead, by reference to what taxation is used for. In this respect taxation is essentially a matter of political choice, concerned with how the money that is levied from some members of society is to be used for the benefit not only of other members of society but also for the benefit of society as a whole.

This assumes that taxation is necessary but develops arguments about the practicalities of taxation: how much should be levied, from whom should it be levied, what should it be spent on and how should it be spent? All of these are filtered through the ideological spectacles that political rulers wear, leading to the point that taxation, like contact lenses and beauty, lies in the eyes of the beholder.

To this extent taxation is subject to change in terms of the predilections and beliefs of political actors. These will help to determine what is acceptable behaviour for tax-raising bodies to pursue in terms of the everyday realities of taxation. The post-World War II taxation settlement, for example, built around the creation of the welfare state, was heavily influenced by the principles of social justice and redistribution, and these in turn influenced the amounts of tax that were levied and how this was spent. The Thatcherite era reductions of tax demands arose from the acceptance of the beneficial role of the market as opposed to the state as the ideal mechanism for the distribution of goods and services, with consequent effects on management in, and the size of, the public sector.

The case for and against taxation

For: taxation contributes to:

- redistribution;
- social justice;
- the protection of citizenship rights.

Against: taxation works against:

- individual rights;
- equal treatment of individuals;
- the interests of the unorganised masses.

Thus taxation involves a whole range of political choices and decisions. The necessity for taxation to create a 'civilised' society leaves open the question of of what such a society consists. The answer to this is clearly a matter of political choice and belief.

Reading

Hayek, F. (1944) *The Road to Serfdom*, Routledge.
Mueller, D. (1989) *Public Choice*, Cambridge University Press.

16

Globalisation: is it good or bad for Britain?

Barrie Axford

Introduction

These days it is hard to avoid hearing about globalisation. Open almost any newspaper and you will find it the staple fare of leader writers and correspondents. Sample the main evening news on a major TV channel and you are likely to hear the term roll sonorously from the lips of senior politicians and assembled pundits. Such widespread exposure is understandable, because globalisation is very much a *now* term, one that captures the spirit of the times and offers a convenient short-hand for some of the major changes taking place in many walks of life. Primarily these changes flow from the increasing interconnectedness and interpenetration of societies and economies under the impact of economic, technological, political and cultural forces which are global in scope. Governments, businesses, social movements, voluntary associations and individuals are all likely to be affected by the processes of globalisation. But exactly what is globalisation and why does it arouse such interest and concern? In this chapter I want to talk about globalisation as a process which is serving to connect the world. Then I will examine whether the process has any implications for Britain, either good or bad, before concluding with some remarks on the growing significance of globalisation.

Before I begin, a brief health warning. The trouble with any discussion of globalisation is that, much like 'Bigfoot', not everyone believes in its existence, and even those who are convinced tend to offer different assessments of its impact. In a recent and widely discussed book, Paul Hirst and Grahame Thompson (1996) argue that what is often described as a *global* economic system is no more than the build-up of trade and other sorts of economic transaction within *regional* groupings that are largely confined to the so-called 'Triad' economies of Europe, the Americas and parts of South East Asia. They also claim that there was more global trade in the last decades of the nineteenth century than there is now, during a period when powerful nation states and empires dominated world economics and politics. For them, this fact alone demonstrates that globalisation is a myth. Hirst and Thompson go on to argue that, despite widespread rumours of their demise, sovereign nation states such as the United Kingdom continue to play a major role in the management of national economic life and in the regulation of the world economy. Far from dying under the pressures of globalisation, the nation state remains at the heart of world political and economic life, and will do so for the foreseeable future.

This is good knockabout stuff, but supporters of the globalisation thesis believe otherwise, and also insist that the process involves more than economic trends, important as these are. They point to fundamental changes which can be seen in the impact of communications technologies upon the everyday lives of people in different parts of the world, in the growing role of bodies such as the United Nations and the International Monetary Fund in the conduct of world politics, and in the blurring of the boundaries between local, national and global which comes with the easy availability of global products such as MTV, M&Ms and McDonalds. In sharp contrast to the intellectual scepticism of writers such as Hirst and Thompson, the gung-ho sentiments of many economists and management theorists depict globalisation as a recent phenomenon driven entirely by the ideology and the practice of free market liberalism. In their view, this logic now embraces the whole world.

Perhaps the most complete expression of this line of thinking is the work of Kenichi Ohmae, a leading management consultant, who has written about the creation of a 'borderless world' in which mobile or 'footloose capital', as it is called, makes it increasingly difficult for national governments to regulate global financial markets. For Ohmae, globalisation means that traditional nation states, and even the idea of separate national economies, have become irrelevant to the real workings of the global economy. Borders – to taste and imagination as well as to territory and identity – are now either meaningless or just an old-fashioned encumbrance to free markets in capital, goods, people, services and intellectual property. In this thesis only markets matter, or rather only markets, regions and various kinds of economic network, which spill across frontiers and make connections regardless of the nationality of the people and organisations involved.

For the most part Ohmae's vision treats globalisation as an inexorable process which can be manipulated by some big players such as Microsoft or British Airways, but which just 'happens' to most people and to a great many governments. By and large he feels that this should not lead to general wailing and gnashing of teeth, for even if the logic of the global marketplace cannot be resisted, its effects are still likely to be beneficial. In a more recent and less abstract account of the benefits and costs of globalisation, Peter Sutherland, the first Director General of the World Trade Organisation, warned that while globalisation must involve a severe 'shake-out' of inefficiencies in the world economy, it will still benefit some of the weaker areas in the Third and Fourth Worlds because of the opportunities it affords for greater flows of investment capital to poorer countries and more open markets for their goods.

This optimism contrasts sharply with the views of those who see the same economic forces which are applauded by Ohmae and Sutherland as having disastrous consequences. For example, the dramatist and social commentator Jeremy Seabrook is of the opinion that most parts of the world are going to hell in a handcart because of the deleterious effects of market forces. The urban poor in Brazil, Thailand and India all suffer, but so do Third World migrants in the UK and other marginalised Britons – the unemployed, those without the skills to prosper in the job market and those on welfare benefits. The message in his account of globalisation is that the rich go on getting richer and the poor get *Neighbours*, or if they are lucky, *Friends*. All of which goes to show that it is very difficult to divorce judgements about the good or bad effects of globalisation from a particular world view or belief system. It is obvious from these contradictory remarks that globalisation is a complex and ambiguous phenomenon. But exactly what is it about globalisation that causes either tears or rejoicing?

What is globalisation?

Globalisation is a historical process which is re-drawing the economic, political and cultural maps of the world. Hirst and Thompson are right to say that it is not confined to the late twentieth century but, as we shall see, developments in recent decades do suggest a new phase of more intense globalisation. In its most visible and measurable form all that globalisation means is an increase in the volume, intensity and speed of interconnections between different parts of the world. Historically, the rate and scale of interconnection varies, but there is now widespread agreement that in the last three to four decades the world has become more and more interconnected and across much larger distances. For example, in 1960 there were 70 million international tourists; by 1997 there were over 500 million, many of them journeying thousands of miles. At the turn of the century there were only 200 international non-governmental organisations (INGOs, such as Amnesty International and the World Wildlife Fund); by 1990 there were in excess of 5,000. Finally, since 1950 world trade has more than doubled in volume, albeit with some 80 per cent of it taking place between the Western members of the Organisation for Economic Co-operation and Development (OECD).

Many indicators of the increasing pace of globalisation are economic, such as the growth of multinational companies – for example, Nissan and Monsanto – which now account for 29 per cent of world output and 80 per cent of world investment; and the sheer scale of the world's foreign exchange markets, which carry flows to the value of US$1.2 trillion every day. But non-economic indicators also provide a global frame of reference for the activities of a growing number of individuals, groups and governments. Transnational problems, such as refugees, AIDS and global warming, bind us all to a common humanity

and a common future which requires co-operation and the pooling of resources; while the consumption of global commodities such as films and
television soaps wraps everyone into a globalised culture. Of course, national
societies are more-or-less sensitive and vulnerable to these interconnections,
but none can escape exposure altogether. National governments, too, are tied
into an intricate web of global, regional and international organisations and
regimes of governance and regulation, of which the European Union, the
United Nations, the World Trade Organisation, the International Monetary
Fund and the G7 group of leading economies are but a few. Even for ordinary
people, dramatic innovations in information and communications technologies are well on the way to creating a world in which the separating effects of
time and space are irrelevant, save where there is a perceived need for face-to-
face encounters between people. So, these days it is well nigh impossible to
hide from, or even to insulate against, global forces of one kind or another.

All these connections and trends certainly globalise the world because they
promote, intensify and greatly speed up interconnectedness. But the movement of goods, services, capital, people, images and ideas around the world
also has a number of other consequences. First, is a stretching of all sorts of
social and economic relationships across borders. In traditional societies,
relationships were, for the most part, face to face and local, but in a globalised
world relationships are being constituted through loose, transnational networks of people: investment bond dealers, exchange students and, who knows,
fans of the *X-Files*, where there may be little or no physical presence. Second,
the impact of events taking place in one part of the world on other parts is
almost instantaneous, whether we are talking about a crisis of confidence
on Wall Street translating into panic elsewhere, the response of television
viewers to pictures of famine in Sudan, or the impact on British farmers of a
decline in the price for the hides of British sheep caused by the collapse of the
Russian economy and the reduced shopping habits of fashionable Muscovites.
Because of this immediacy, the repercussions of any action or event can be
more or less instantaneous. Third, the compression of time and space spoken
of by geographer David Harvey makes it much more difficult to sustain discrete local and national identities. The boundaries between the local and
the global have become blurred for many people; not just for the jet-setting
businessman, but also for the couch-potato eating a chill-fresh Thai meal in
front of his flat-screen digital television, while watching basketball from the
United States. Obviously a key difference between the two may lie in the awareness of what is going on, and this brings us to the fourth consequence of
globalisation.

Many of these developments are taking place without people being aware
of them, as a backdrop to the everyday business of living. When British shop-
pers buy Danish bacon rather than the domestic variety they are likely to be
influenced by relative prices rather than (what are for them) abstract debates
about the impact of high interest rates or the shutting off of key markets on

production costs in the UK. It is true that they may be swayed by media hype
to 'Buy British', but when they do switch brands they are in fact behaving in
line with the logic of global market forces. On the other hand, some people
may be fully aware of the impact of globalisation and feel alarmed by it. Thus
French, Japanese and Portuguese cultural elites have been fighting a rear-
guard action against what they see as the unwelcome effects of English on the
purity of their own languages, while some people in the United Kingdom have
been outraged by the decision not to include national symbols (such as the
image of the Queen's head or that of Napoleon Bonaparte) on the bank notes
of the new European currency, the 'euro'. The point is that while globalisation
can and does proceed behind the backs of people, redefining their experiences
imperceptibly, it can also provoke strong sentiments and generate profound
opposition.

Even where ordinary people have a limited grasp of the impact of globalisation, there is often a growing consciousness among national elites that the
fate of their country is now utterly tied to the condition of the global economy.
Occasionally, national politicians are enthused by this fact, seeing it more as
opportunity than threat, but more often they adopt a resigned and cautious
stance towards what Tony Blair has called 'the way of the world'. In a speech
to the Labour Party Conference in 1998, Blair described globalisation as
moving so quickly and irrevocably that its operations are outside the control
of individual nation states and even beyond the remit of the current crop of
international regulatory agencies. His advice, both to the Conference and to
fellow world leaders, was to 'manage change' more effectively, exhorting them
all to 'manage ourselves to adapt to changes which we cannot otherwise
control'. Of course, Tony Blair's comments need not be read as a jeremiad, but
they are illustrative of a substantial body of opinion about globalisation. The
sociologist Stuart Hall, writing in a special one-off issue of *Marxism Today* (20
October 1998) says that Blair treats globalisation like the weather – believing
that there is nothing much we can do about it.

Britain and globalisation

For writers such as Kenichi Ohmae, globalisation marks the end of the nation
state. The expansion of the global marketplace and the growth of both international and (in the case of the European Union) proto-supranational bodies
charged with enhancing trade or security, means that nation states have lost
what independence and power they used to have. His argument embraces
all nation states, not just the weakest and most vulnerable, but the more
complex reality is that nation states are affected variably by different aspects
of globalisation. Even if we were to accept Ohmae's thesis, we could still
acknowledge that short-term disadvantage might lead to long-term gain, or
vice versa.

Britain was the first industrial nation and for a time its dominant position in this respect, along with its status as a maritime superpower, meant that it was a driving force in the development of the world trading economy. In addition, Britain's imperial connections gave it unrivalled access to potential and developing markets, as well as opening it to many cultural influences from far-flung parts of the globe. In short, Britain was a global power for a good deal of the formative period of world capitalism, succeeding the declining commercial power of the United Provinces (the Netherlands) as the world's most powerful trading nation, and in turn giving way to the United States of America, which remains the world's only superpower. For most of the twentieth century, Britain has not been either an economic or a military great power, and in the more intense period of globalisation since the end of the 1950s it has rubbed along in the second rank of world states. Relatively weak or fluctuating economic performance for most of this period, combined with a loss of empire and world role and a chronically ambivalent stance towards European integration, all make Britain especially sensitive to some of the major economic, social and political trends of the post-war years. These trends include the following: the creation of multicultural societies through migration from parts of the New Commonwealth; a shift away from a largely manufacturing economy to one increasingly dependent upon the service sector and various forms of banking; the massive growth in foreign direct investment in British regions and localities, usually by foreign multinationals such as Toyota or Philips; an increasing reliance upon trade with our European partners; and the pressure upon successive governments to conform to the dictates of a market economy. All these pressures, and others, are testing the capacity of the UK government to direct or just to manage global pressures in much the same way as Mr Blair has suggested.

In trying to assess the effects of globalisation on Britain, we need to bear in mind our earlier injunction, that some people and countries will benefit from globalisation more than others. In Britain, as elsewhere, skilled workers in the 'knowledge industries' are likely to be winners, while unskilled workers could become part of an employment underclass; the security of middle-class lifestyles may be eroded at the same time as the rewards for possessing marketable skills increase dramatically; some localities have been very successful in attracting 'footloose' foreign capital, others less so. British companies able to take advantage of global markets are likely to prosper, those reliant upon domestic markets which have been insulated from external competition have cause to feel threatened. Nationalists in Scotland and Wales, or those favouring regional devolution in England, may have grounds for optimism because they see greater integration into European and global networks and systems as supporting their independence, thus decreasing reliance on the Westminster government. On the other hand, British nationalists could see globalisation as speeding up the disintegration of the United Kingdom, and construe the products of global entertainment industries as harbingers of doom for

British cultural identity. While it may be possible to quantify some measure of winning and losing, for the most part any such judgement is a matter of perspective and of the level of commitment to the status quo.

The case for globalisation being good for Britain

- From an economic perspective the processes of globalisation entrench Britain at the heart of the interlinked global economy. From this perspective, Britain is well placed to take advantage of the growth of integrated and increasingly competitive regional and world markets. A good example of this process is the benefits that accrue to British industry and other areas of business from being a part of the single internal market in goods, services, capital and people now constituted by the European Union. In addition British firms gain access to other new markets as the doctrines and practice of economic liberalism spread around the world. Russia and the former Soviet satellite states in Central and Eastern Europe, the People's Republic of China and North Vietnam are all now markets of great potential for British goods and expertise. British companies also get easier access to new sources of raw materials and to lower-cost labour forces, particularly for assembly processes that use unskilled labour. There are many examples on offer, but think of running shoes assembled in Malaysia, or footballs in India and Bangladesh. All these activities generate greater profits for British shareholders. In other respects, many economists argue that globalisation helps British firms to diversify their product range and the geographical basis of their operations. A British firm which has operations in a number of countries is likely to find that recessions and booms in the markets where it operates will be out of sync, posing less of a threat to its stability and long-term profitability. Globalisation also helps such firms to take advantage of worldwide financial markets to subvent their investments. If and when Britain embraces the euro and full monetary integration in Europe, the benefits of currency stability in a volatile world financial system, on some accounts, will be considerable.

  Consumers too benefit from economic globalisation. Look how easy it is to buy exotic foods from around the world at any of your local supermarkets. The list of global products now stretches far beyond the consumer icons of Coca-Cola, McDonalds and Levis to include compact discs, digital cameras and Blockbuster videos, as well as fresh fruit and strange fish out of season. As savers too, British citizens now have the ability to diversify their investments more broadly, perhaps buying their house on a loan from a German or a Japanese bank, or taking out a personal pension with a French company.

  In a world of footloose capital, much foreign direct investment is attracted to Britain by the promise of social and political stability, skilled workers and relatively low wages. Inward investment from major European and Far Eastern companies supports the regional policies of the British government and, by creating jobs, both reduces the burden of welfare provision and contributes to the buoyancy of local and regional economies within the UK. While some jobs are lost because the same forces encourage some British companies to shift jobs abroad, foreign firms have set up shop in the UK and hired British workers. It is also argued by some economists that globalisation further contributes to the stability of the British economy because competition from foreign producers has made it difficult for firms producing in the UK to raise prices even where they face heavy demand for their products. Needless to say, many of these claims are contested, and even where they are not in doubt are understood to involve costs as well as benefits.

- Increased exposure to the world economy and to the risks attendant upon such exposure have made it more and more difficult for politicians to avoid the necessary policy changes required to deal with the challenges of globalisation. Some of these changes relate directly to the nation's economic competitiveness and involve, or are likely to involve, significant social costs to sections of the British public, including the dismantling of areas of welfare provision. For some observers such pressures are a further demonstration of the corrosive effects of globalisation upon national life and independence. But for others they are no more than a necessary adjustment to the rigours of an interconnected and interdependent world. The up-side of such pressures is to lock Britain, along with other nation states, much more firmly into collective solutions to global problems. Issues of great concern, such as environmental pollution and AIDS, are now considered capable of solution only through multi-lateral efforts. No single national government, including the United States, believes nowadays that it can or should bear the full costs of its own security, and recognises that global security can only be bought through collective action – in the UN and through bodies such as the Organisation for Security and Co-operation in Europe. The onus on collective solutions is also apparent in the concern over how best to reform the world financial system which surfaced during the crisis in currency markets in the summer of 1998. All these developments point to a mature and comfortable adjustment to global pressures by the United Kingdom. On a different tack, the rapid 'Europeanisation' of domestic policy and law has seen Britain's freedom of action on matters related to corporal punishment in schools curtailed by judgements in the European Court of Human Rights and the EU's own Court of Justice. On some accounts this is a constraint on national decision making and national independence, but understood in the context of prescriptions about world peace, environmental protection and human rights, it might be taken as a boost for universal values and the beginnings of a more humane world society. In this version, globalisation does not so much

destroy or seriously weaken nation states, as require a redefinition of their
role as managers of international affairs and as guarantors of peace, security and prosperity for their citizens.

- Economic and political globalisation often have cultural effects. At the very
least this means that all sorts of cultural goods are now routinely available
to British people. American and Australian 'soaps' are the staple fare of UK
mass television audiences, while British-made programmes sell profitably
to many parts of the world. The rapid developments in electronic communications have made it easier to connect with friends, relatives and business associates abroad, and this, plus the relative speed and cheapness of
international and inter-continental travel, enables family and other social
relationships to be maintained over huge distances. Our awareness of the
world is also enhanced by the speed with which news – of famine, scandal
and impending economic gloom – can be relayed by the print and broadcast media, and our experience of the world has also increased through
tourism and through formal exchanges among colleges and universities
around the world. On these measures, at least, globalisation has contributed to the creation of a more cosmopolitan society in the UK. A globalised world is one which is characteristically hybridised, and Britain has
become more of a multicultural society in the past few decades, building
on (as well as superseding) the legacies of empire. Different cultural traditions have become fused – who now can think of tea as being anything
but British; while football has become a, perhaps *the*, universal game – the
local and the global are intertwined in a fruitful accommodation, one with
the other.

The argument against globalisation, since it is bad for Britain

- The main case against globalisation is that it exposes Britain to risks over
which national government has no real control, and whose effects are
clearly detrimental to economic well-being and national independence.
Much of this concern relates to the ways in which an unregulated free
market global economy is said to contribute to the destruction of jobs and
communities, social solidarity and economic security. In a recent diatribe
against the ravages of global capitalism, the social theorist, John Gray,
who was once committed to the free market ideology of Thatcherism, noted:
'We stand on the brink not of the era of plenty that free-marketeers project,
but tragic epoch, in which anarchic market forces and shrinking natural
resources drag sovereign governments into ever more dangerous rivalries'
(Gray, 1998, p. 66).

This is opposition to globalisation of almost biblical scope and gravity,
but for those who argue that globalisation is inimical to Britain, the
evidence is all around. For example, one of the consequences of having a

global economy is that no part of the world is insulated from the economic consequences of seemingly 'local' problems. The loss of Russian and Far Eastern markets for meat product manufacturers in Denmark and Germany has encouraged them to look for other markets, not least in the UK, where the strong pound makes prices for their products attractive. As a result, British manufacturers suffer and jobs are lost. The collapse of Far Eastern markets for high-tech products, such as the semi-conductors used in computer hardware, has resulted in over-capacity in segments of the consumer-electronics industry as world demand has declined. A number of foreign companies with manufacturing facilities in the UK have closed plants – for example, Halla, the Korean company, with a factory in South Wales, Siemens, on Tyneside, and Fujitsu (the latter with great publicity because it was sited in County Durham, part of the Prime Minister's parliamentary constituency). Some of these organisations blame the anti-inflation policy of the British government – with its preference for high interest rates and a strong pound to combat inflation – for their decision to close, as one of the effects of a strong pound is to make exports from the UK less competitive in global markets. For cynics, this policy too is the result of the government's desire to demonstrate its credibility and prudent management to international regulatory bodies such as the International Monetary Fund and to the financial markets. Overall, say opponents of globalisation, footloose multinational companies will pull investment and manufacturing out of the UK as the need arises, and even where they stay it is only because they see short-term advantages to be gained from being located in a low-wage economy. Some opponents argue that the jobs created by foreign multinationals tend to be those requiring few skills and little education, and that this contributes to a decline in real wages for already marginalised sections of the population.

- On a related issue, one of the engines of globalisation is the dramatic innovations that have taken place in computer and communications technology. In the workplace, new technology not only makes it easier to relocate production, but it also has major effects upon the organisation of work, by redefining traditional jobs and making some skills redundant. Critics believe that more flexibility in the workplace not only creates job losses, as computer-aided production does away with the need for labour-intensive methods, but also de-skills sections of the workforce, casting them adrift from the mainstream of society. The social consequences of these developments are held to be considerable, producing a permanent, unemployable underclass, heavily reliant on the state for the means of subsistence, and even a middle class for whom job security is a thing of the past. With exquisite and unfortunate timing, all this is taking place just at the point where British governments are in the process of dismantling key parts of the welfare apparatus put in place at the end of World War II. For critics of globalisation, short-term job contracts, reforms in health service provision and the privatisation of pensions are all to be understood as the domestic consequences of worldwide changes in economic life and the tribute that national governments must pay to global capital.

In this account of the bad effects of globalisation, national government is in thrall to forces beyond its control. For the most part these are the faceless powers of global financial markets, although for journalist Alan Watkins (*Independent on Sunday*, 16 August 1998) the power of global finance is made flesh in the person of financier George Soros, who speculated against sterling with such dramatic effect in 1992 that the UK was forced to leave the European Exchange Rate Mechanism. Accountable government in the shape of elected Members and loyal officials gives way in key areas of policy making to unaccountable institutions of governance, such as the OECD, the International Monetary Fund and the European Commission. Perceived as worse still is the continuing obeisance to those shadowy and imprecise 'market forces' which owe allegiance to no one.

- For opponents the cultural fall-out from globalisation is far less benign than supporters admit. One of the less well-known facets of the liberalising of world trade is the massive growth in illegal drug trafficking and the increase in drug dependency in all metropolitan countries, including Britain. The same is true of the global traffic in pornography and the relative ease with which it may be accessed through the Internet. With the opening up of borders there has been a significant increase in the volume of illegal migrants, and while it is acknowledged that some of these are admissable for political reasons, many are 'economic' migrants who become part of an employment 'black economy' or else make demands on the state for subsistence.

Where supporters of globalisation applaud the availability of various cultural products, opponents claim that the deregulation of the media and market forces in general are undermining important elements of British culture and identity. It is claimed that the high standards and public service ethos of both the BBC and the ITV network have been eroded by the competitive challenges posed by multinational media conglomerates such as Rupert Murdoch's News International Group. The advent of both terrestrial and satellite digital television, which promise anything up to 500 channels, is taken less as a statement of choice and more as a recipe for 'dumbing down'. In this the spectre of the 'Americanisation' of British culture still looms large, and this extends to anxieties about the ways in which American-style campaigning techniques have permeated British politics, introducing a strong whiff of presidentialism. Resistance to globalisation is also apparent in the objections of some fans of Manchester United Football Club to the abortive takeover by BSkyB, a company in which Rupert Murdoch owns 40 per cent of the shares. Rather than a fruitful meshing of the local and the global, these opponents saw the ownership of the club by a global company as a serious blow to local pride and identity.

Conclusion

Globalisation matters to a great many people in Britain, and it touches everyone. The arguments for and against set out above suggest that it is possible to come to quite different conclusions from the same pieces of evidence, or else to remain profoundly ambivalent. Ambivalence is an understandable response. For example, those in favour of the application of market principles to economic life and business practice often applaud the steps being taken to turn the European Union into a more complete and efficient economic unit. Many supporters of this view see the European internal market as an appropriate response to the pressures and challenges of globalisation. These same people may remain deeply opposed to the strengthening of European institutions of governance, seing them as a dilution of the authority of Britain as an independent nation state.

As we have seen, many arguments start from a committed view of the effects of globalisation and simply use any evidence to endorse their position, ignoring any nuances. This is understandable, even if it is rather blinkered, because some major issues about lifestyle, government and prosperity are posed by globalisation and many commentators and activists have positions to defend. Thus we may be staring into the abyss, as John Gray argues, or be on the brink of a brave new world, as Kenichi Ohmae suggests. The more mundane reality is that globalisation brings both costs and benefits for Britain. In August 1998, a leading Cabinet minister described Britain's economy as being on a knife-edge, faced with the global instability fomented by crises in Japan, Russia, Brazil and elsewhere. Such an observation underlines both the interdependence of the world economy and the uncertainties which follow from that interdependence. In fact, during the financial crisis of 1998, Britain was less exposed to the turmoil in Russia and Asia than many other countries. Whereas German and Austrian banks had $40 billion at risk in Russia, British banks had less than $1 billion. Yet no country can escape the toils of the world economy even if it wants to.

Because of this, Tony Blair may be right to think of globalisation as like the weather, always with us and potentially damaging. The Blairite project, which looks to entrench the rhetoric and the 'mindset' of globalisation at the heart of his government's attempt to modernise Britain, might thus be evaluated as a systematic attempt to come to terms with a complex reality, rather than a craven response to overwhelming forces which could swamp Britain. Taken overall, the effects of globalisation on British society are usefully summed up using the categories offered by political scientist Tony McGrew (1998) in his examination of Finland, another European country having to come to terms with globalisation.

Globalisation affects Britain in a number of ways:

- *Institutionally*, where that refers to the fact that globalisation is now firmly on the agenda of government, businesses, voluntary organisations and also of some individuals.

- In terms of the *distribution of resources*, because who wins and who loses are important issues for the politics of the UK.
- *Structurally*, because of the fast-changing nature of the British economy; the changing role of government; and the recasting of national cultural identities in the media-dominated cultures of the next millennium.

The impacts of globalisation upon all these areas of life require adjustments of one sort or another. For government to maximise or to moderate the effects of globalisation on Britain from both the opportunities and the threats posed requires that political leaders act neither as globalisation groupies nor as dyed-in-the-wool sceptics. The challenges of the 'global age' spoken of by sociologist Martin Albrow (1996) demand no less.

Is globalisation good or bad for Britain?

Globalisation can be seen as good for Britain because

- It brings economic benefits in the form of new markets for British goods; easier availability of investment capital; creation of new jobs; and the accessibility of a much wider range of consumer products.
- It creates greater pressures for collective security and the need to collaborate on common problems, such as environmental pollution, famine and human rights. As a result the world is a safer place.
- It facilitates the distribution of global cultural products, such as films and CDs, and makes it much easier to communicate with other parts of the world, as well as cheaper and quicker to travel to them.

Globalisation can be seen as bad for Britain because

- It poses unacceptable risks to British people and British business because it is very difficult to hide from economic recession and to offset the domestic consequences of events elsewhere.
- It reduces the scope for independent action by the British government. Globalising pressures make it very difficult to carry out competitive devaluations of the national currency, and market principles are forcing government to cut back on forms of social protection.
- It replaces national culture with Americanised global variants, especially through television.

Reading

Albrow, M. (1996) *The Global Age*, Polity.

Gray, J. (1998) *False Dawn: The Delusions of Global Capitalism*, Oxford University Press.

Hall, S. (1998) 'Nowhere man', *Marxism Today*, special issue, 20 October.

Harvey, D. (1989) *The Condition of Postmodernity: An Inquiry into the Conditions of Cultural Change*, Basil Blackwell.

Hirst, P. and Thompson, G. (1996) *Globalization in Question*, Polity.

McGrew, A. (1998) *Making Sense of Globalization: Some Questions and Answers*, EVA lecture.

Ohmae, K. (1995) *The End of the Nation-State*, Free Press.

Seabrook, J. (1993) *Victims of Development: Resistance and Alternative*, Verso.

Watkins, A. (1998) 'Let's face it, it's Chancellor Soros who counts', *The Independent on Sunday*, 16 August.

17

Feminism: political success or economic disaster?

Moyra Grant

Feminism is a yawn – but please read on

Many women today, especially younger women, see 'feminism' as deeply uncool. They see it as an aggressive and outmoded movement of the 1960s and 1970s which was full of hairy man-haters in dungarees and they say, 'I couldn't be a feminist – I like reading glossy magazines/wearing make-up/looking good/men, I like men.' They think that crinkly old feminists who whinge about oppression should get a life. Some even reject 'sexual equality' because they think it means 'the same as men' – clearly neither a possible nor desirable aim. This crude and misleading notion of what feminism means – or used to mean – is partly due to media, and especially tabloid, stereotyping, but is also due to the failures of the post-war feminist movement itself, its 1970s puritanism and political correctness. However, that movement should be given its due: for one thing, it achieved remarkable social changes; for another, it is usually necessary for a cause – any cause – to be pursued with extreme vigour, energy and excess for even limited success to be achieved. Post-war feminism could be likened in this respect to the 'black power' movement in America at around the same time, which had to take the issue of equal rights for blacks to extreme lengths even to win the right to vote in the 1960s.

First- and second-wave feminism

The word 'feminism' is a twentieth-century invention and only became a part of our everyday language in the 1960s, but the feminist movement of the 1960s and 1970s is often called 'second wave' feminism.

The 'first wave' focused on the nineteenth-century fight for the franchise – the right to vote – which British women achieved on equal terms with men in 1928, largely due to the recognition of women's increasing participation in the economy during and after World War I. It soon became obvious, however, that winning the right to vote did not lead automatically to equal rights for women in work, education, law, property, taxation, marriage, divorce, or social or private life – and so began a second series of more radical campaigns, often drawing inspiration from American 'women's lib', as it was quaintly called. The 1960s was a time of economic boom and political and social upheaval throughout America and Western Europe, when women encountered radical political ideas at a time of growing educational opportunities, but still found their role bound by contradictions and limited expectations about women's place being in the home, kitchen and bed. There is a story about the radical black activist Stokely Carmichael being asked what was the position of women in the black power movement? He replied, 'horizontal'. Women began to form their own groups and movements with their own, distinctive aims and demands.

However, 'second wave' feminism took several different forms – mainly liberal, socialist or Marxist, and radical feminism. Whereas liberal feminists sought equal opportunities in education and employment through the ballot box, Marxist feminists argued that gender inequality was a product of the dictates of a capitalist economy – that is, the need for a clear male line of property inheritance and a two-for-the-price-of-one system of male bread-winner and female housewife, with women as the property of their husbands and as a 'reserve army of unemployed' to be brought in on the cheap when there were labour shortages. Thus the only way to remove sexual inequality was by class revolution and the overthrow of capitalism itself. (I wonder if Prince Philip knew to which philosophy he was subscribing when he said in 1988, 'I don't think a prostitute is more moral than a wife, but they are doing the same thing.')

Radical feminists, by contrast, saw the oppression of women as resulting from male domination – patriarchy – in every sphere of life and put the sexual revolution – as opposed to the class revolution – first, arguing that women must act collectively – and usually separately from men – to liberate themselves in both the public (economy and work) and private (home and family) areas of life. Some radical feminists therefore advocated lesbianism; a few even argued that women were innately superior to men, embodying distinctive values of nurture, emotion, pacifism and altruism – a view that the American liberal feminist Betty Friedan (1965) called 'female chauvinism'. The most radical of the radicals have provided the focus or target for the crude tabloid stereotypes which have helped to ridicule and marginalise the very word 'feminism' since the 1980s.

The other main factor which has undermined the concept of feminism itself has been the New Right philosophy of the 1980s and 1990s – and perhaps beyond – which is conspicuously patriarchal and preaches 'traditional family values'. Some present-day feminists suggest that this conservative backlash against their ideas is a backhanded compliment and testament to their successes (Faludi, 1991).

So what, between them, have these diverse movements achieved since the 1960s?

Sure, we've come a long way, baby

For one thing, the label 'feminist' can still be a proud epithet; the novelist Rebecca West said that people called her a feminist whenever she expressed sentiments that differentiated her from a doormat or a prostitute.

More concretely: freedom of choice for women was massively enhanced by the provision of free and legal contraception and abortion in the post-war era; moreover, women's whole lifestyles changed and even their health improved significantly as they bore fewer children, more safely.

Women's legal status has also – on paper, at least – changed radically with the Equal Pay Act 1970, Sex Discrimination Act 1975 and growing equalisation in property, taxation and divorce rights. There were, admittedly, many legal loopholes in these laws – for example, 'equal pay for equal work' meant that for years a woman boss could be paid *less* than her male subordinate because it was not 'equal work' – but these anomalies have gradually been removed. One in five women now earns more than her partner and there are fifty women earning over £1 million per annum in Britain today.

The other big improvement has been in education, where girls now increasingly outperform boys in GCSE and A-level exams, and there are now as many females as males in higher education.

In politics, too, the 1997 general election in Britain saw a record intake of women MPs; we have even had a woman Prime Minister, although Margaret Thatcher herself said, just four years before coming to power, that she could not envisage such a thing in her lifetime. As their lifestyles converge, so do their voting habits: male and female political voting patterns in Britain are now virtually identical whereas, until twenty years ago, there were marked gender differences and women were consistently more likely than men to vote Conservative.

Just consider, for a moment, the image and presentation of women in 1950s' films, TV shows, advertisements and books compared with those of today, and it becomes apparent how far the role and status of women have changed in the second half of the twentieth century.

Young women today can choose to be airline pilots rather than stewardesses, surgeons rather than nurses, bosses rather than secretaries; they can choose to wear virtually anything they like in public, to flat-share with men before marriage, to marry or not – and they do not have to withdraw and leave the men to the port at the end of dinner. All of this and more would have been unthinkable fifty years ago.

These genuinely progressive and sometimes profound changes have led many, usually older and/or conservative women, to say, why waste energy fighting a battle that is already won? 'Feminism is no longer necessary', writes newspaper columnist Anne Applebaum, 'because it has become a victim of its own success' (*New Statesman*, 16 January 1998). She argues that inequality before the law no longer exists (though she admits that reality does not always match the letter of the law); and she argues that further changes – in attitudes and prejudices, for example – cannot be achieved by legislation or activism but only by time. Katie Roiphe in the *Sunday Times* (March 1998) similarly said that 'the old feminism did its job so effectively that it is now becoming obsolete' and that women now have to search desperately for 'trivial definitions of victimhood' such as being complimented on their appearance or having doors opened for them by men.

Some – such as Labour's former Education Minister Stephen Byers – go so far as to argue that men can no longer keep up with women's successes and that a new phenomenon of 'laddish anti-learning culture' has emerged, producing the 'redundant rogue male', unskilled, unwanted and unneeded by women and reduced to scavenging Britain's sink housing estates in a deformed celebration of defunct masculinity.

So is feminism dead?

New Labour, new feminism

The debate about the role and place of feminism under New Labour began in January 1998 with the publication of Natasha Walter's book, *The New Feminism*. She argued that although girls were generally doing better at school than boys, that more women were in paid work than men and increasing numbers of women were striding into the corridors of power, there is still a place and a need for a women's rights movement.

For one thing, many of the changes we now take for granted are, in fact, very recent. As late as 1987, for example, Jacqui Lait wrote about Margaret Thatcher, pointing out the irony that 'the wife who made Britain great again', and who was the leader of the Western world, had to get her husband to sign her tax form.

For another, many things have not changed. Gender inequalities – that is, those shaped by economic, social and cultural factors – remain far greater than mere sexual or biological differences warrant.

Women are still poorer and less powerful than men. The majority of women now work; but the labour market is still very gender divided. Women occupy the great majority of menial and part-time jobs and often need career breaks to have children – some women even still get fired from work when they become pregnant – therefore women still earn 25 per cent less than men, with fewer career opportunities, employment protection and pension rights than men. Thirty-one per cent of working women are paid less than £4 an hour, compared with 11 per cent of men, and 80 per cent of workers officially defined as 'low paid' are women. Even more prevalent in many workplaces is a continuing culture of prejudice – the so-called 'glass ceiling' which forms an apparently invisible barrier to women's promotion in jobs such as engineering, management and the police. Women are still a tiny minority in the power elite of Britain today: they make up just 1 per cent of top judges, civil servants and police officers; 4 in 100 surgeons and company directors; 7 in 100 university professors; and still only 18 per cent of MPs, despite the record 1997 election intake. Britain may have had a female Prime Minister, but Margaret Thatcher was singular in every sense of the word – and how many female Cabinet ministers did she appoint? The phrase 'old boy network' still holds.

Moreover, the divide between 'public man' and 'private woman' has not disappeared. Women still bear the main domestic responsibilities; few employers make any provision for childcare and, until forced to do so by the European Union, Britain refused to allow fathers the legal right to paternity leave. The average full-time working father has 46 hours of free time while the full-time working mother has just 13.5 hours per week. Sixty per cent of women want their partners to take more responsibility in the home and only 23 per cent of husbands do the washing up. 'New man' – caring and sharing – seems still to be barely a speck on the horizon. Modern woman seems to feel exhausted rather than liberated: one survey (*The Times*, 10 February 1998) found that 81 per cent feel 'women are expected to perform too many roles nowadays' and the majority feel overworked and underpaid. Some sociologists even refer to modern women's 'triple shift' of paid employment, domestic labour and 'emotion work' or 'gender asymmetry in emotional behaviour'; that is, the far greater number of expressions and actions of love and affection which women perform, compared with men, to make their partners and children feel good (Hochschild, 1983).

In education, girls still get fewer top A-level grades than boys; indeed, half of all female pupils are still failing to get any basic school-leaving qualification at all. Also – and this is where it gets confusing – more men than women gain first class *and* third class degrees; more men than women commit crime and go to jail – just 12 per cent of convicted criminals are women; more men sink on to the streets and into the gutter – that is, more men succeed *and* fail than women. What women have achieved is arguably not equality but mediocrity.

Natasha Walter is also concerned about the violence and abuse which many women suffer at the hands of men. She cites the well-known statistic that only one in ten of all men accused of rape is convicted, and only one in ten rapes is reported in the first place.

However, routine domestic violence is even more under-reported than rape, yet there are 22,000 reported cases of domestic abuse every year in the West Yorkshire police area alone. These involve not just punches and knives, but iron bars, blow torches, hot irons and chain-saws, and many women suffer repeated attacks over many years.

Imagine, for a moment, the pain, fear and trauma of being mugged in the street. Now imagine living with it in your own home, day in, day out. So why do women stay and suffer? A recent major survey (reported by *Dispatches*, June 1998) found that almost 50 per cent of such women are physical prisoners in their own homes, locked in and sometimes tied to a bed or chair for days on end. Others are, almost literally, paralysed with fear, not only for themselves but for their children. If they go to the police, in 80 per cent of cases no action is taken and the domestic punishment intensifies; in most other cases, the man is locked up for the night to cool off and returns to do worse. If he does go to court the most common sentence is a caution and back he comes . . . Over 50 per cent of the women murdered in the UK each year are the victims of domestic violence. We ask, almost scornfully, so why don't these women just get out and go? Many do, if they get the chance. Seventy thousand women and children each year flee to women's refuge centres and elsewhere. They lose their home, friends, family and financial support; they are on the run and in fear for years. Their most frequent comment is, 'he got away with it – I am the fugitive.'

Meanwhile, in July 1997, a British court sentenced a man to just 200 hours of community service for killing his wife, over an affair, by stabbing her eleven times. Domestic violence against women does not yet seem to be taken seriously enough by the legal system.

On a lighter note, there are also (according to a series of polls culled largely from *The Week* magazine) many interesting differences in the way men and women think and perceive their lives; for example, 54 per cent of women, as opposed to 16 per cent of men, think that they lost their virginity too early; 77 per cent of men said that they and their first partners were 'equally willing' but only 53 per cent of women shared this view; and 11 per cent of men wished that they had had sex sooner (but apparently they did not even ask women). Thirty per cent of men think that women with period pains are 'just laying on the theatricals to get sympathy'. The majority of women believe that men still find ways of undermining them at work. Forty-five per cent of schoolgirls but 21 per cent of schoolboys are anxious about their weight; why are there many more female than male anorexics and bulimics? Ask any psychologist and they'll talk about 'compensation for control deficit' – that is, young women have – or, as importantly, feel they have – less control over their lives than young men, and use self starvation as a sad substitute.

Walter rues the fact that the debate about feminism and sexual inequality today, in so far as it is happening at all, tends to focus more on personal and psychological issues – about the way women dress and look and talk and make love – than on measurable economic, political and social problems. For this she blames, not only the media, but some current female writers who take the view that the 'reiteration of feminist fundamentals is boring . . . a list of residual unfairnesses lacks compelling ethical urgency' (Ros Coward, *Guardian*, 7 July 1998).

Legislation has not eradicated sexism – not least among women – any more than it has eliminated racism. Nor have even the supposedly trendy liberal sections of the media eschewed sexism. The very New Labour *New Statesman* magazine, just two weeks after launching a debate on 'new feminism', headlined an article on ministerial spending 'Of course Cherie should have a new kitchen at No. 10' (*New Statesman*, 30 January 1998). A TV advertisement for the flexibility of the Open University system showed a young woman hoovering, shopping, cleaning and writing an essay beside her (conveniently quiet) baby. An ITV 'pop doc' series in 1998 called *The Truth About Women* was described by its director David Green as 'capturing the new mood of the nation – in Blair's New Britain women feel much more comfortable. They see Parliament packed [*sic.*] with women MPs and a Prime Minister who treats his female colleagues as equals.' An early episode had Melinda Messenger, Denise Van Outen and Lynn Redgrave discussing the size of their thighs.

All of these media trendies might say that they are simply reflecting the ongoing realities of unequal gender roles – women do use the kitchen and the hoover and maybe even discuss the size of their thighs more than men do – but they are certainly doing nothing in the process to challenge those inequalities. 'Post-feminist' triumphalism seems premature, as does boredom about what is a live issue.

What we want – what we really, really want . . .

The nub of the debate is, of course, what is meant by 'feminism'. Some say that the 'girl power' phenomenon of the late 1990s is feminist; others that the culture of the female icon – viz. Diana – is feminist; and yet others that the celebration of childbearing and motherhood is true feminism. Clearly, there is much confusion.

If 'feminism' means a coherent, visible and itemised political movement with some kind of twelve-point plan of action, then writers such as Anne Applebaum and Genevieve Fox (*New Statesman*, 16 January 1998) say it no longer exists, is no longer needed and anyway no one is listening. Others regret that the fragmented nature of feminism 'signals a sclerosis of the movement' (Delmar, 1986). This seems unduly pessimistic; there is no significant political ideology of the last two centuries which has *not* undergone similar fragmentation.

Moreover, feminism was never a cohesive political movement. In the 1970s there were liberal feminists, socialist feminists and radical feminists, all with profoundly differing aims and strategies. There was never a single voice of feminism. Now there are also free market feminists, anarchist feminists, eco-feminists, postmodernist feminists and New Labour feminists (who are actually liberals) – and the radicals and Marxists have not disappeared either.

'Feminism', according to the standard dictionary definition, simply means a belief that women are disadvantaged because of their gender but that this is not a natural and inevitable consequence of biology; and a corresponding advocacy of equal rights for women. As such, it has surely not disappeared. Walter is right when she argues that new feminism is not confined to any kind of ghetto. It is not a clearly defined movement (though she is wrong if she thinks it ever was); it has splintered and fragmented but, as she argues, splinters of it are lodged in the hearts and minds of almost every woman in Britain. Many may not call themselves feminists but – across all classes, ages and races – they largely want and expect nothing less – and nothing more – than equality at home, in education and at work.

Maybe it is precisely because the *principle* of sexual equality is now so widely accepted that the ongoing and patterned realities of such inequality are hard to recognise or confront. Feminists today are now legitimate insiders, not embattled extremists. Maybe feminism today is less an overt political movement than simply a consciousness – an awareness of material realities.

New Labour demonstrated some such awareness (in a move tellingly described in *Daily Mail* language as 'insidious political correctness') by creating a Women's Unit under Harriet Harman at the Department of Social Security to tackle childcare, employment issues and violence against women; but it was resented and sidelined for trying to tread on other departments' policy toes and, of course, Harman was sacked (and replaced by a man) in the 1998 reshuffle. Even under Harman, the 1997 cut in benefits for lone parents – which, in practice, usually means single mothers – was Labour's biggest mistake and provoked the biggest backbench revolt of that year. However, it was noticeable that not one of the new, young, female Labour MPs – commonly and, again, tellingly called the 'Blair babes' – voted against the cuts. New Labour's clear economic and moral preference for the traditional, nuclear family is a Christian and conservative perspective which does not lend itself to radical thinking about progressive change.

The main causes of continuing gender inequality have long been recognised and are still relevant today. Biology remains a primary factor: women as the bearers of children are excluded from paid work and dependent upon men at certain critical times in their life cycle. They are also, therefore, largely expected – by men and women alike – to be the child rearers; this can exclude them from equality with men for most of their productive lives. Economic dependency or, at best, very unequal economic competition in the workplace, follows. These factors are topped by the cultural values of society which define and differentiate women as inferior – the bad drivers, the emotional hysterics, the illogical, the inadequate mothers, the frigid wives, the DIY failures, the nags, the pre-menstruals, the post-menstruals, the gossips, the gigglers, the gullible, the fluff, the featherbrained, the flippertigibbets . . . Over one hundred years ago, the liberal philosopher John Stuart Mill wrote, 'I deny that anyone knows, or can know, the nature of the two sexes . . . What is now called the nature of women is an eminently artificial thing – the result of forced repression' (*On Liberty*, 1859). This is probably still very largely true now, but is almost impossible to separate and test in any scientific way, and the question still attracts a great deal of attention.

The most informed and productive debate about the role and status of women today is taking place among and within the diverse schools of feminism itself. On the one hand, this suggests that feminism is alive and positively kicking. On the other hand, it hardly seems fruitful if feminists are just bickering among themselves between the pages of sterile textbooks. The debate needs to reach out to ordinary women and men, young and old, if further, real progress towards sexual equality is to be made.

This does not mean sameness. Most men are physically stronger than most women; women still bear children and men do not. Technology has modified these basic biological differences but has not eradicated them – at least, not yet. 'Equality' here – just as in the context of race – means genuinely equal rights and opportunities for people of equal worth and diverse merit. Most men would want the same, says Walter – not only out of a sense of fairness and social justice, but because many men would, in *some* respects, value 'the keys to the feminist kingdom'. This, presumably, does not mean that they want the low status of housewives, the low pay of traditional women's occupations or nine months of weary pregnancy; it probably means that they would enjoy helping to look after the kids a bit more, to emote more, to be allowed to cry more, to expect women to make the first move more often instead of risking repeated and ignominious rejection. It follows that new feminism must include men.

Maybe, then, it is not so new. One of the first and most influential feminist books in Britain was Mary Wollstonecraft's *A Vindication of the Rights of Woman* (1792) – a deliberate rejoinder to most eighteenth-century liberal philosophy about 'the rights of *man*', which meant exactly and exclusively that. Wollstonecraft wrote, 'the first object of laudable ambitions is to obtain a character as a human being, regardless of the distinction of sex' – that is, neither women nor men should be identified primarily as sexual beings, but as human beings. Almost two hundred years later, the seminal feminist Simone de Beauvoir (1954) wrote, 'the fact that men and women are human beings is infinitely more important than all the peculiarities that distinguish human beings from one another'.

This perspective, in turn, raises issues of social divisions other than gender. One critic of Walter's thesis writes, 'I despair. The debate surrounding the state of New British Feminism makes me aware that one thing has not changed: new or not, British feminism is still self-confidently all-white' (Mirza, 1998). Mirza describes new feminists as 'white media feminists with their self-indulgent, in-crowd, middle-class perspectives' and says it is small wonder that they are rejected by the mass of both black and white young women. This is a useful reminder that it is dangerous and simplistic to over-generalise.

The experiences of a successful, white, Western, professional woman would be utterly alien to a black, working-class woman battling against racism and poverty as well as sexism.

However, hopefully, at least most women now recognise that you do not have to be a harridan or a frump to be a feminist. You do not have to rip off your bra or refuse to shave under your armpits (although you can if you want). We can contemplate feminism with femininity and glamour (glam-fem?). It can be charismatic, confident and downright sexy. But it still needs to *be*. In answer to the title, 'Feminism: Political Success or Economic Disaster?' the answer is 'No', on both counts – and, therefore, nor is feminism redundant.

Way to go, baby. How? That's up to you. And that includes you, guys.

Conclusion

The concept of 'feminism' is derided but not dead. It is derided because of the excesses of some elements of the post-war 'second wave' feminist movement itself, the hostile media stereotyping of the concept and the New Right conservative backlash against it. It is not dead because, although the principle of equality for women is increasingly accepted, the reality has not yet been achieved. However, although talk of 'post-feminism' may be premature, modern feminists – as ever – are divided about the meaning of feminism and about how to pursue it; and New Labour's attitude is, so far, ambivalent at best. Modern feminism's main challenge is how to reach out to those parts it is not reaching – particularly young, working-class and black people in Britain today – to persuade them that there is both a problem and a solution.

Assessing Feminism

Political success?

For
- Universal suffrage.
- Free and legal contraception and abortion.
- Radical changes in women's legal status in the post-war era.
- Women's advances in education.
- The image and presentation of women in the media today compared with the 1950s.
- Record number of women in central and local Parliaments and in government; a Minister for Women in Cabinet and a new Women's Unit in the Cabinet Office.

- New Labour's policies on the minimum wage, tax credits, national childcare strategy, child benefit and employment will improve women's lives.
- Perceptions that 'the old feminism' is obsolete.

Against
- Continuing educational inequalities.
- The scale of domestic violence against women.
- Only 18 per cent of Westminster MPs are women.
- The self-inflicted failures of the post-war feminist movement itself.
- The hegemony of New Right anti-feminism in the 1980s and 90s.

Economic disaster?

For
- Women still earn 25 per cent less than men.
- 80 per cent of low-paid workers are women.
- The continuing 'glass ceiling' limiting women's promotion prospects.
- Women make up only 1 per cent of top civil servants, judges and police officers; 4 in 100 surgeons and company directors, and 7 in 100 professors.
- The continuing division between 'public man' and 'private woman'.
- Modern women's 'triple shift' of paid employment, domestic labour and 'emotion work'.
- Lack of recognition of continuing economic inequalities, even among women themselves.
- Legislation has not eradicated sexism or continued, patterned realities of inequality.

Against
- Equal Pay Act 1970, Sex Discrimination Act 1975, growing equalisation in property and taxation and divorce rights.
- Growing occupational equality.
- Growing number of female high earners and millionaires.
- Growing perception of the disadvantaged 'redundant rogue male'.

Reading

Bryson, V. (1992) *Feminist Political Theory: An Introduction*, Macmillan.
De Beauvoir, S. (1954) *The Second Sex*, Jonathan Cape.
Delmar, R. (1986), in J. Mitchell and A. Oakley (eds), *What Is Feminism?*, Blackwell.
Elshtain, J. B. (1981) *Public Man, Private Woman*, Princeton University Press.
Faludi, S. (1991) *Backlash: The Undeclared War Against American Women*, Crown.

Firestone, S. (1972) *The Dialectic of Sex*, Basic Books.

Friedan, B. (1965) *The Feminine Mystique*, Penguin.

Friedan, B. (1983) *The Second Stage*, Abacus.

Greer, G. (1970) *The Female Eunuch*, McGraw-Hill.

Greer, G. (1985) *Sex and Destiny*, Harper & Row.

Hochschild, A. (1983) *The Managed Heart*, University of California Press.

Millett, K. (1970) *Sexual Politics*, Doubleday.

Mirza, H. S. (1998) *Black British Feminism*, Routledge.

Mitchell, J. (1971) *Woman's Estate*, Penguin.

Schneir, M. (1995) *The Vintage Book of Feminism: The Essential Writings of the Contemporary Women's Movement*, Vintage.

Walter, N. (1998) *The New Feminism*, Little, Brown.

18

Is politics still class based?

Jonathan Tonge

Introduction

One of the most famous statements ever made concerning British electoral behaviour was Pulzer's 1967 declaration: 'Class is the basis of British party politics: all else is embellishment and detail' (Pulzer, 1967, p. 98). While stridently expressed, the assertion represented political orthodoxy. For the remainder of the century, however, a steady erosion of the central position of class was claimed (Sarlvik and Crewe, 1983). The question posed by this chapter is therefore straightforward. Has social class itself been relegated to mere embellishment and detail in modern British politics?

The old class paradigm

The period from 1945–70 is accurately described as a period of class align-ment (Butler and Stokes, 1969). The overwhelming majority of voters were allied to the Conservative or Labour Party and the main basis of such loyalty was social class. Four-fifths of the middle class regularly voted Conservative, while two-thirds of the working class voted Labour. Partisan alignment, or loyalty to a particular political party, was also greater from 1945–70 than the present day. Higher figures were recorded for the intensity of loyalty (the number of people very strongly identifying with a particular political party). Between 1964 and 1992, the number of such identifiers dwindled from 42 per cent to a mere 19 per cent (Sarlvik and Crewe, 1983).

Underpinning these themes of class and partisan dealignment was the model of political socialisation. There was a very strong likelihood (approximately 75 per cent) that children would vote for the same party as their parents. Socialisation at work was also important. Rigid class divisions characterised Britain's workplace, with a sharp blue collar (manual worker) versus white collar (non-manual) divide. Managers and workers on either side of the divide often worked, lived and voted apart. Trade union activity among manual workers strengthened working-class support for Labour. The consequence of class and partisan loyalty was a two-party system in which the Conservative and Labour Parties dominated. This duopoly was also preserved by the majoritarian voting system discouraging challenge from minor parties.

The decline of class voting?

While the huge strength of the link between class and voting was readily acknowledged in the 1960s, these links were already beginning to fade (Butler and Stokes, 1969). The shift from the class paradigm, accelerating since the early 1970s, has been attributed to a number of factors. First, there has been a decline in the usefulness of the concept of class. A process of 'embourgeoisement' has been said to be taking place, by which an increasingly affluent working class was said to be adopting middle-class lifestyles. Even critics of the embourgeoisement thesis accepted that traditional class rigidity was in decline. Goldthorpe *et al.* (1987) found high levels of inter-generational social mobility. Traditional class divisions were also eroded by the 'proletarianisation' of the bourgeoisie. Some clerical workers had lower incomes than skilled manual workers. As class appeared a less relevant concept, the strength of its association with party choice weakened. By 1983, this decline had gathered pace to the extent that only 44 per cent of the electorate voted for their 'natural' class party (i.e. middle-class people voting Conservative plus working-class people voting Labour). Either there were a great many temporary 'class traitors' in our midst, or the hegemonic position of class as a guide to voting behaviour was dated.

It appeared that voting based upon social structure had declined within both the working class and middle class. From 1979 to 1992, the Conservatives enjoyed electoral dominance, but the class basis of those triumphs altered. Among non-manual workers, the Conservative lead over Labour declined. Among manual workers, Labour's lead over the Conservatives fell slightly but, in terms of the number of voters, this was the bigger blow. In other words, both parties appeared to lose part of their core 'class vote'.

The desertion of Labour by the working class during the 1980s was so marked that Crewe identified two broad categories of working class. The new working class lived in the south, worked in the private sector, owned their home and were not trade union members; the old working class was based in the north and Scotland, lived in council houses, worked in publicly owned industries and were trade union members (Crewe, 1983). Of course, working-class support for the Conservatives was nothing new. There had always been a 'deviant' working-class Conservative vote of one-third of the members of that class. Working-class Toryism was historically attributed to a number of factors, one of the most important being deference (Nordlinger, 1967). What was startling in the 1980s was the scale of working-class defection to the Conservatives and the economic, rather than deferential, basis of this transfer of allegiance. Perceptions that the Conservatives were the party for the aspirant working class persisted during the 1992 election, exemplified by the 'Sierra Man' incident recalled by Tony Blair:

> I can recall vividly the exact moment that I knew the last election was lost. I was canvassing in the Midlands on an ordinary, suburban estate. I met a man polishing his Ford Sierra. He was a self-employed electrician. His dad always voted Labour, he said. He used to vote Labour too. But he'd bought his own house now. He'd set up his own business. He was doing quite nicely. 'So I've become a Tory' he said . . . (*Daily Telegraph*, 2 October 1996)

As a consequence of such statements, Labour continued to change its policies and the basis of its appeal prior to its 1997 election victory. A largely classless 'politics of aspirations' displaced the old politics of class loyalties. True, 'New Labour' opposed what it saw as the rampant individualism of the years of Conservative dominance. However, Labour's reassertion of the value of community embraced all members of society and disavowed class politics (Fielding, 1995). Working-class voters returned to Labour in the 1997 election, but, at 15 per cent, the party's percentage gain among non-manual workers almost doubled the increase of 8 per cent found in its traditional manual base.

The controversy over measuring class voting

The most commonly used categories of social class in Britain are the six offered by the British Market Research Society. Classes A, B and C1 represent professional, managerial and clerical workers and are regarded as the 'middle class'. The working class consists of categories C2, D and E, comprising skilled and unskilled manual workers, plus pensioners and widows. Disputes over how to categorise social classes have contributed to dissent over whether class dealignment has occurred. The alternative argument, that dealignment has *not* taken place, seems counter-intuitive, but it contains important empirical evidence. Ultimately, the debate over the continued relevance of class in electoral behaviour has become a 'technical' one based upon competing forms of measurement (Denver, 1997).

Class dealignment has occurred if one measures absolute 'natural' class voting. This is calculated by adding the number of non-manual workers voting Conservative to the number of manual workers voting Labour, and expressing the sum of both categories as a percentage of total voters. There is an even easier way, using percentages only, as shown in table 18.1.

Take Labour's share among non-manual workers (22) from the Conservative share (62) to obtain a figure of 40. Deduct the Conservative share of the

Table 18.1   *Voting in the 1964 election (%)*

	Voters	
	Non manual (%)	**Manual (%)**
Conservative	62	28
Labour	22	64
Liberal	18	8

manual vote (28) from Labour's (64) to produce the sum of 36. Add this 36 to 40 to produce a total of 76. Using this method of calculation, the absolute voting index in elections can be seen in table 18.2.

The Alford index allows a measure of relative class voting. The index is normally calculated by deducting Labour's percentage share of the vote among non-manual workers from its share among manual workers. Alternatively, Conservative percentage support among manual workers can be deducted from that found among non-manuals. Either score shows the relative strength of a single party in two social classes. Low scores indicate only a small gap between the party's share among manual workers compared with its strength among non-manuals. The declining scores in table 18.3 are thus indicative of weakening class alignments.

The alternative sociological model rejects the idea that class dealignment has occurred. Instead, it suggests that 'trendless fluctuation' has been the norm (Heath *et al.*, 1985; Heath *et al.*, 1991). The relative strengths of the parties among the social classes have remained largely unchanged. This

Table 18.2   *Absolute class voting in British general elections, 1964–97*

Year	Percentage of 'class voters'
1964	76
1966	78
1970	64
1974 (Feb.)	64
1974 (Oct.)	59
1979	52
1983	45
1987	44
1992	47
1997	29

Source: Sanders (1998).

Table 18.3   *Class voting: the Alford index, 1964–97*

Year	Labour	Conservative
1964	42	34
1966	43	35
1970	33	31
1974 (Feb.)	35	29
1974 (Oct.)	32	27
1979	27	25
1983	25	20
1987	25	19
1992	27	20
1997	21	13

Source: 1964–92 figures from Denver (1994), 1997 figure adapted from Denver (1997).

argument was originally based upon use of the odds ratio, calculated by the odds of a middle-class person voting Conservative rather than Labour divided by the corresponding odds for a working-class person. It was claimed that Labour's electoral problems of the 1980s were caused by changes in social structure, not class dealignment. The reduced size of the working class accounted for half of the fall in Labour support.

The different measurements used by the dealignment and the sociological schools have each been criticised. The class dealignment school has not sufficiently considered relative party strengths within the classes. Furthermore, some dealignment could be said to be nothing more than the temporary desertion of huge numbers of Labour Party supporters in the 1980s. The clear unpopularity of parts of Labour's left-wing agenda in the 1980s contributed to two huge electoral defeats in 1983 and 1987, flanked on either side by narrower defeats in 1979 and 1992. In 1983 and 1987, the Party polled only 25 per cent and 27 per cent of the vote, respectively. In response, it was pointed out long before the party's 1997 triumph that class dealignment 'does *not* infer the decline of Labour' (Crewe, 1993, p. 101). Labour has made steady inroads into the Conservative Party's non-manual support.

In rejecting the idea of substantial dealignment, Heath *et al.*'s sociological model 'minoritises' the working class (Rose and McAllister, 1986). It redefines the working class to form a small percentage of the population. Given that this (lowest) section of the working class is unlikely to provide fertile territory for the Conservative Party, the discovery of continued class loyalty to Labour within this group was perhaps unsurprising. The use of the odds ratio was criticised as ignoring the existence of third parties, although this measurement was replaced by more sophisticated log linear analysis.

By the late 1990s, however, both the absolute and relative measurements of class voting appeared to be drawing the same inescapable conclusion: that

Table 18.4　*Relative voting index in general elections, 1964–97*

Year	Relative voting index
1964	6.4
1966	6.4
1970	4.5
1974 (Feb.)	5.7
1979 (Oct.)	4.8
1979	3.7
1983	3.9
1987	3.5
1992	3.3
1997	1.9

Source: Sanders (1998).

class voting was in decline in Britain. Far from 'trendless fluctuation', the 1997 election indicated less class voting even in the type of relative voting index favoured within sociological models. Again using the 1964 figures as an example, the relative voting index is calculated by using the odds of a non-manual worker voting Conservative rather than Labour (62/22) divided by the corresponding odds for a manual worker (28/64), producing an odds ratio of 6.4. The declining figures in table 18.4 indicate reduced differences in the relative strengths of the parties in the classes.

The demise of class alignment in 1997 was most striking in the non-manual sector, once dominated by the Conservatives. Electors divided almost equally between the Labour and Conservative Parties. Labour's support among manual workers was double that enjoyed by the Conservatives. Even at 58 per cent however, in a 'landslide' election, this support was substantially lower than the figure attained by Labour in this category in the 1960s.

Why class dealignment?

Accepting the overwhelming evidence that class dealignment has taken place, the question to be answered is why? Political partisanship has decreased as a result of changes in social class, community values and political beliefs. Nonetheless, partisan dealignment does not necessarily indicate class dealignment. It may instead reflect growing disillusionment with the performance of parties. Class dealignment means that the link between social class and party choice has weakened, irrespective of the changes of size in those social classes. A number of reasons for class dealignment have been offered.

First, there is increased political awareness. Greater coverage of politics in the media has created a more sophisticated electorate. Longer news bulletins and the broadcasting of Parliament are two contributory factors. Second, greater educational possibilities have increased public knowledge. Record numbers entered university during the 1990s. The media and education may undermine partisanship, as they (newspapers excepted) provide even-handed coverage of political events. The decline in trade union membership, from a peak of 12 million in 1979 to 6 million by 1998, has also affected class loyalty to the Labour Party. The perceived failure of parties in office, presiding over relative British economic decline, many have contributed to declining loyalty. Increased mobility may have weakened local political solidarity.

Another important factor has been the development of a multi-party system, with the growth of nationalist parties in Scotland and Wales and the rise of the centre party. This growth was partly a *consequence* of class dealignment. However, the options afforded the electorate by the growth of these parties also contributed to dealignment. The Scottish National Party (SNP) and, in Wales, Plaid Cymru, have taken votes from all political parties, and in Scotland the SNP offers serious rivalry to Labour. The centre, reborn through the growth of the Liberals in the 1970s, the Liberal–SDP Alliance of the 1980s and, finally, the Liberal Democrats in the 1990s, challenged the two-party, class-aligned duopoly.

Issue voting

With class voting in decline, the search has been under way for an alternative model of how Britain votes. The variety of models put forward has led to the accurate observation that 'there is evidently no single correct answer' (Fisher, 1996, p. 178). Broadly however, instrumental models of voting have displaced the class paradigm. These models often offer competing explanations of the precise reasons why electors vote the way they do, but they suggest a rationality to voting. One of the main instrumental models is the consumer voting model, sometimes termed 'issue voting'.

The issue-voting model suggests that party preferences are determined by electors on the basis of party policies. By the 1979 election, it appeared that there was a clear correlation between voter assessment of issues and party choice, a link which strengthened according to the salience of the issue to the voter. Nonetheless, from the outset the model encountered problems when confronted with empirical reality. In each election from 1983–92, Labour suffered resounding defeats despite being favoured by the electorate on two of the three most important issues in the election, as identified by voters. For example, Labour's lead on the 'top three' issues in the 1992 election, the NHS, unemployment and education, proved worthless on election day. The model was also criticised for failing to note how party preferences, rather than objective, rational judgements, shaped views on policies (Heath *et al.*, 1995).

It was, however, the seeming empirical failings which were more troubling. If the issues which electors highlighted as the most salient were not determining electoral outcomes, which issues were?

Economic voting

The most influential response to the problems of the issue-voting model has been that which explains voting in terms of economic rationality. The term 'pocketbook' voting originated in the United States and its influence upon the British electorate appears increasingly pervasive. The economic 'feel-good' factor helped the Conservatives to an overwhelming election victory in 1987. In 1992, however, the growing belief in the paramount importance of economic factors appeared to be sorely tested by the return of a Conservative government in the midst of a recession. Sanders (1992) explained this victory by the series of measures undertaken by the Conservatives in 1990–91 to boost personal economic well-being. The consequence was that the Conservatives performed well in terms of both 'egocentric' and 'sociotropic' voting. The former is conditioned by perceptions of one's personal economic well-being and outlook. The latter is shaped by perceptions of the economy as a whole. The Conservatives performed better on both counts in 1992. Egocentric voters were assisted by the Conservative government in the run-up to the 1992 election. Sociotropic voting was based upon the legacy of previous Conservative booms and the perceived unacceptability of Labour's economic strategy. Accordingly, the Conservatives continued to enjoy a substantial lead on the question of economic competence.

The resounding defeat of the Conservatives in 1997 again apparently called into question the validity of economic factors as electoral determinants. The Conservatives lost despite presiding over a set of economic indicators which on any objective measurement appeared more favourable than those prevalent during the party's election victory five years earlier. Indeed, it was commented afterwards that 'the election result was a defeat for economic determinism' (*Spectator*, 10 May 1997). This argument is decisively rejected elsewhere (see Sanders, 1992; Wickham-Jones, 1997). Economic factors were important, in that the Conservatives paid dearly for losing the confidence of the electorate in their economic competence. This abandonment of faith was a consequence of Britain's enforced exit from the European Exchange Rate Mechanism (ERM) in September 1992. From this point onwards, the Conservatives never regained their lead over Labour on the (sociotropic) question of which party could run the economy most effectively. Tax increases, such as VAT on fuel, which followed the ERM débâcle, ruined Conservative chances of benefiting from egocentric voting. Although a weak feel-good factor had been created by 1997, it was insufficient to save the party. The 'Essex model' of economic voting thus remained intact. Current and predicted economic prosperity are crucial determinants of whether governments are re-elected.

Economic explanations of voting appear more successful as indicators of
voting propensities than most of the linkages described below.

Consumption cleavages

During the 1980s, theories of voting behaviour based upon modes of consumption became fashionable. Voting behaviour is influenced, or instrumentally
aligned, according to whether individuals use public or private provision of
services such as housing, education, health and transport. Using multivariate
analysis, it was possible to determine the modes of consumption which were
significant voting indicators. The consumption cleavage approach held advantages over a class-based analysis as it took account of the influence of changing
lifestyles and patterns of ownership among the classes.

Significant variables for the 1997 election differed across the parties.
Almost three-quarters of the variation in the Conservative vote across
constituencies was accounted for by the five variables of car non-ownership,
professional and managerial occupation, population density, age and housing
tenure (Denver, 1997, p. 16). Of these, only two are consumption variables, and
the presence of occupation, the key 'official' determinant of social structure,
indicates the continued salience of class. Nonetheless, car and home ownership are very important variables. Heath *et al.* (1991, p. 209) calculated
that increased home ownership boosted the Conservative Party's percentage
share of the vote by 4.6 per cent from 1964 to 1987. Strong Conservative
promotion of home ownership possessed a clear ideological basis and was
of practical value in boosting the party's vote.

Aside from the continued importance of class, the consumption cleavage
approach is also weakened in that it remains a largely descriptive rather than
causal account of how people vote (Franklin and Page, 1984). Furthermore,
mass consumption of state 'goods', such as education, means that public–
private consumption distinctions are not particularly useful in analysing overall
voting behaviour. Housing has become a less crucial marker, with council
stock now providing less than one-quarter of the market.

Media influence

Two features characteristic of modern elections are saturation media coverage and a 'presidential' focus upon the party leaders. Newspapers are not
constrained by the requirement placed upon radio and television broadcasters
to offer neutral coverage. Party political broadcasts on television attract sizeable audiences, contrary to popular perception (Powell, 1998). The *Sun* newspaper famously asserted that it was 'the Sun wot won it' for the Conservative
Party in 1992. That newspaper's coverage was scathing of the capabilities of
Labour's leader, Neil Kinnock, as it had been of Kinnock's unsuccessful predecessor, Michael Foot. Yet if newspaper coverage were to determine elections,

Labour would never have held office. The 1997 election was the first in which a majority of newspapers supported the Labour Party.

Coverage of party leaders during election campaigns is considerable. In 1997, Tony Blair, John Major and Paddy Ashdown accounted for almost two-thirds of the BBC and ITV coverage of speakers during the election campaign (Goddard *et al.*, 1998). Despite this, there is some evidence of voter immunity to leadership impact. In the 1992 and 1997 elections, only 7 per cent of electors declared that the party leader was the main influence upon their party choice (Cowling, 1998).

Gender

Women have traditionally favoured the Conservative Party to a greater extent than men in general elections. In contests since 1959, only in 1966 and 1997 did more women vote for Labour than the Conservatives. In contrast, a majority of men have favoured Labour on no fewer than six of the ten elections since 1959. There were strong signs by the 1980s that the gender gap was narrowing, a development seemingly only temporarily reversed by strong female support for the Conservatives in 1992. There was virtually no gender gap in the 1997 election, with hostility to the Conservatives shared equally.

The reasons offered for the gender gap were never entirely convincing. Traditional reasons centred upon female support for the family, a stance most closely associated with the Conservative Party. In the 1980s, many women, like men, appeared to associate greater economic prosperity and fulfilment of aspirations with the Conservative Party.

Age

Successive general elections have indicated a tendency for older people to vote Conservative. The Conservatives were also able to secure more first-time voters than Labour in each of their four general election victories from 1979 to 1992, although on each occasion the margin was by less than that across the total population. The 1997 election provided a striking confirmation of the greater favouring of generational differences in voting, as table 18.5 indicates. These differences are normally linked with greater radicalism in youth, compared with increased conservatism associated with ageing. Older people have also lived through a twentieth century dominated for considerable periods by the Conservative Party.

Religion

Outside Northern Ireland, religion makes little impact upon voting behaviour in the United Kingdom. Catholics of all social classes show a greater propensity to vote Labour than their class position might suggest, particularly in the

Table 18.5   *Voting by age in the 1997 general election*

Age group	Conservative (%)	Labour (%)
18–29	22	57
30–44	26	50
45–64	33	43
65+	44	34

Source: Denver (1997).

west of Scotland. Non-conformist groups such as Methodists have historically been associated with support for the Liberal Party while the Church of England used to be described as the 'Tory party at prayer'. Although these voting connections remain, they appear very dated, as the links between religious groups and party choice are not contingent upon religious affiliation.

Ethnicity

Approximately 5 per cent of Britain's population comes from an ethnic minority group. Labour has persistently enjoyed overwhelming support from black people, as table 18.6 indicates.

Significantly, Labour's lead extends across the social classes. Labour has captured over half of all black voters in each social class in each general election. As one might expect, there remains a class dimension to voting, in that Labour's lead is greatest among semi-skilled and unskilled blue-collar workers. There is evidence of voting difference between Asians and Afro-Caribbeans. The latter overwhelmingly vote Labour, with Conservative support measured in single figures, below the level of Afro-Caribbean support for the Liberal Democrats. Afro-Caribbeans have traditionally associated their aspirations with Labour rather than the Conservative Party, the latter having

Table 18.6   *Support for the Conservative and Labour Parties among ethnic minority voters in general elections, 1979–97*

Year	Labour (%)	Conservative (%)
1979	86	8
1983	83	7
1987	72	18
1992	81	10
1997	78	17

Source: Saggar (1997).

been occasionally associated with anti-immigration rhetoric. One in four Asians supports the Conservative Party. Palpably against the national trend, the party increased its vote share among ethnic minorities in 1997. Voting swings among ethnic minorities have frequently differed from national patterns.

Geography

The importance of territorial politics was emphasised in the 1997 election. Labour, in terms of seats at Westminster at least, is dominant in Scotland and Wales, as table 18.7 shows.

The most striking feature of Labour Party support is the manner in which it has been maintained in certain areas, despite the *erosion* of its class base. In Scotland, for example, the size of the working class fell from 59 per cent of the population in 1981 to 49 per cent by 1991. The politics of national identity have become increasingly important in Scotland, reflected and fostered by the growth of the SNP. The Labour Party and the SNP have both boosted their fortunes by stressing their Scottishness via support for devolution (Labour) or independence (SNP). The stress upon the politics of identity is not to diminish the importance of class or economic factors. Conservative promotion of 'Britishness' failed dramatically in Scotland in 1997, but there was also a residual hostility based around economic factors. Support for the SNP has owed more to the promotion of the prospective economic gains of independence than to the 'selling' of 'Scottishness' (Brand *et al.*, 1994). The importance

Table 18.7   *Party shares of the vote and Westminster seats in Scotland and Wales, 1992–97*

	Party share (%)		Seats	
	1992	1997	1992	1997
Scotland				
Conservative	25.7	17.5	11	0
Labour	39.0	45.6	50	56
Liberal Democrat	13.1	13.0	8	10
SNP	21.3	21.9	3	6
Wales				
Conservative	28.6	19.6	8	0
Labour	41.3	54.7	27	34
Liberal Democrat	12.4	12.4	1	2
Plaid Cymru	9.5	10.6	4	4

Source: Adapted from Denver (1997) and Coxall and Robins (1998).

Table 18.8   *Regional distribution of votes in general elections in England,*
1992–97

	Conservative		Labour	
	1992 (%)	1997 (%)	1992 (%)	1997 (%)
North	33.4	22.2	50.7	60.9
North West	37.4	26.7	44.9	54.2
West Midlands	56.8	47.8	38.8	47.8
East Midlands	47.2	35.5	37.5	47.9
East Anglia	51.0	38.7	28.0	38.3
South West	47.6	36.7	19.2	26.4
South East	54.5	41.4	20.9	32.0
Yorkshire/Humberside	37.6	27.9	44.2	51.8
Greater London	45.3	31.2	36.9	49.4

Source: Adapted from Denver (1997) and Coxall and Robins (1998).

placed by the Labour Party upon capture of the growing middle-class vote in
Scotland has influenced the SNP, which has also diluted much of its left-wing
agenda of the 1980s.

Geographical factors were also important within England during the 1980s.
They remained so in the 1990s, but talk of a North (Labour)–South (Conservative) divide appeared much less relevant following Labour's 1997
victory. The regional distribution of votes is shown in table 18.8.

The geography of voting may not adequately explain electoral behaviour.
The concentration of Labour supporters in the north reflects the fact that a
greater percentage of working-class people live there. It is true, broadly, that
the percentage of Labour supporters increases as one travels north through
England. Nonetheless, the geography of voting has shifted since the 1987
election. In the 1997 election, the swing to Labour was highest in London
and the south-east. Labour's 1997 electoral strategy abandoned the 'one more
heave' approach of the former leader John Smith. Instead, Labour realised the
need to transcend its northern class base and attract southern middle-class
support (Johnson *et al.*, 1994).

Conclusion

None of the main parties pitch their appeal at a single social class in modern
elections. Labour, traditionally seen as a class-based party, had ten campaigning principles in the 1997 election. All these principles concentrated upon

modern voter aspirations not a defined social class. In so far as 'class appeal' exists, the major thrust of all the main parties at elections has been to reassure what might be termed the 'uncertain class'; those hovering between working-class and middle-class status, as society, through an expanding middle class with ever-growing numbers in non-manual occupations, is re-shaped from a pyramid into a diamond.

This argument does not suggest that class is dead. Those who argued that class dealignment was significant were still prepared to concede in the 1990s that class remained the biggest single factor in determining modern behaviour (Crewe, 1993). Class nonetheless remains as the main factor by default. The search has been under way for several decades for a replacement for class-based analyses of voting behaviour. In an increasingly socially mobile, affluent and largely secular society, a coherent and durable alternative explanation of voting behaviour is not easy to locate. Following the revival of the Labour Party in the 1990s, it was again true to say that a majority of working-class people vote Labour. Within an enlarged middle class, it is true in a normal election (1997 might be seen as exceptional) that a slight majority of middle-class people vote Conservative. However, class divisions are less marked than three decades ago. Fewer people vote a certain way because of their class. The consequences have been greater electoral volatility and a different approach to the conduct of elections by the parties.

Is politics still class based?

The case for

- A majority of people still see themselves as belonging to a particular social class.
- Occupation (non-manual or manual) remains a crucial voting variable; only car and home ownership were more important indicators in 1997.
- The relative strengths of the parties in the social classes have not changed dramatically.

The case against

- Over half of the electorate do not vote for their 'natural' class party.
- Class-based models of politics fail to accommodate the rise of centre and nationalist parties.
- Class divisions have faded; as society becomes increasingly middle class, old class issues such as redistribution and public ownership are less important.

Reading

Brand, J., Mitchell, J. and Surridge, P. (1994) 'Social constituency and ideological profile: Scottish nationalism in the 1990s', *Political Studies*, 42, 616–29.

Butler, D. and Stokes, D. (1969) *Political Change in Britain*, Macmillan.

Cowling, D. (1998) 'A landslide without illusions', *New Statesman*, May.

Coxall, B. and Robins, L. (1998) *Contemporary British Politics*, Macmillan.

Crewe, I. (1983) 'The electorate: partisan dealignment ten years on', *West European Politics*, 6, 183–215.

Crewe, I. (1993) 'Voting and the electorate', in P. Dunleavy, A. Gamble, I. Holliday and G. Peele (eds), *Developments in British Politics 4*, Macmillan.

Denver, D. (1994) *Elections and Voting Behaviour in Britain*, Harvester Wheatsheaf.

Denver, D. (1997) 'The 1997 general election results: lessons for teachers', *Talking Politics*, 10:1, 3.

Denver, D. (1997) 'The results: how Britain voted', in A. Geddes and J. Tonge (eds), *Labour's Landslide: The British General Election 1997*, Manchester University Press.

Fielding, S. (1995) *Labour: Decline and Renewal*, Baseline.

Fielding, S. (1997) 'Labour's path to power' in A. Geddes and J. Tonge (eds), *Labour's Landslide: The British General Election 1997*, Manchester University Press.

Fisher, J. (1996) *British Political Parties*, Harvester Wheatsheaf.

Franklin, M. and Page, E. (1984) 'A critique of the consumption cleavage approach to British voting studies', *Political Studies*, 32, 521–36.

Geddes, A. and Tonge, J. (eds) (1997) *Labour's Landslide: The British General Election 1997*, Manchester University Press.

Goddard, P., Scammell, M. and Semetko, H. 'Too much of a good thing? Television in the 1997 election campaign' in I. Crewe, B. Gosschalk and J. Bartle (1998) *Political Communication: Why Labour Won the General Election of 1997*, Frank Cass.

Goldthorpe, J., Llewellyn, C. and Payne, C. (1987) *Social Mobility and Class Structure in Modern Britain*, Clarendon.

Johnson, R., Pattie, C. and Fieldhouse, E. (1994) 'The geography of voting and representation: regions and the declining importance of the cube law', in A. Heath, R. Jowell and J. Curtice (eds), *Labour's Last Chance? The 1992 Election and Beyond*, Dartmouth.

Heath, A., Jowell, R. and Curtice, J. (1985) *How Britain Votes*, Pergamon.

Heath, A., Jowell, R. and Curtice, J. (1987) 'Trendless fluctuation: a reply to Crewe', *Political Studies*, 35, 256–77.

Heath, A., Jowell, R., Curtice, J., Evans, G., Field, J. and Witherspoon, S. (1991) *Understanding Political Change*, Pergamon.

Nordlinger, E. (1967) *The Working-Class Tories*, MacGibbon and Kee.

Powell, C. (1998) 'The role of Labour's advertising in the 1997 general election', in I. Crewe, B. Gosschalk and J. Bartle (eds), *Political Communications: Why Labour Won the General Election of 1997*, Frank Cass.

Pulzer, P. (1967) *Political Representation and Elections in Britain*, Allen & Unwin.

Rose, R. and McAllister, I. (1986) *Voters begin to Choose: From Closed-Class to Open Elections in Britain*, Sage.

Saggar, S. (1997) 'The dog that didn't bark? Immigration, race and the general election', in A. Geddes and J. Tonge (eds), *Labour's Landslide: The British General Election 1997*, Manchester University Press.

Sanders, D. (1992) 'Why the Conservatives won – again', in A. King (ed.), *Britain at the Polls, 1992*, Chatham House.

Sanders, D. (1998) 'The new electoral battleground', in A. King *et al.* (eds), *New Labour Triumphs: Britain at the Polls*, Chatham House.

Sarlvik, B. and Crewe, I. (1983) *Decade of Dealignment*, Cambridge University Press.

Wickham-Jones, M. (1997) 'How the Conservatives lost the economic argument', in A. Geddes and J. Tonge (eds), *Labour's Landslide: The British General Election 1997*, Manchester University Press.

19

Reforming the welfare state: benefit or burden?

Rob Baggott

Background to the debate

Welfare reform is supported by all the major political parties, and has considerable public support. Why then is it so controversial? One reason is that it is not, as is so often depicted, a single issue. For most people, welfare reform means simply altering the levels of, and entitlement to, social security benefits. This, however, is a rather narrow view and fails to take into account the fact that welfare issues are complex and interlinked. In a broader sense, the welfare state has two main aspects. First, systems that regulate and provide income – this includes the payment of social security benefits and the provision of reliefs, subsidies and grants. It also includes taxation and national insurance systems, which not only fund the welfare state but affect levels of disposable income. Second, it includes the financing, provision and regulation of services that are regarded as having important implications for social welfare, such as housing, health and social care, education and training.

The modern welfare state, where government accepts a high level of responsibility for the welfare of its citizens, is a relatively recent creation. During World War II the coalition government deliberated plans for national reconstruction once hostilities had ceased. Out of this process came the Beveridge Report, published in 1942, with its identification of the 'five giants' – want, idleness, squalor, ignorance and disease – and its detailed proposals for tackling these social evils. The post-war welfare state can be regarded as successful in many respects. It certainly simplified the haphazard system of welfare administration and created a more comprehensive and inclusive set of services than had previously existed. By creating national systems, particularly with respect to the NHS and social security, there was great potential for a more rational and fair system. However, this proved difficult to achieve in practice. For example, in the NHS the funding of services continued to reflect historical factors rather than the need for health care and, as a result, the disparities between populations continued to prevail. With regard to social security, some claimants – particularly the elderly – were discouraged by the stigma attached to 'the dole'.

Worries about the administrative efficiency, fairness and quality of welfare services intensified during the 1960s. But in the following decade such considerations were overshadowed by a preoccupation about the cost of welfare services, largely because of the economic and industrial crises of this period which placed a severe strain on public finances. Also in this decade a systematic critique of welfare policies began to emerge which sought to undermine the rationale for state services in health, housing, education and social security. These were in harmony with the neo-liberal ideas gaining currency in academic and increasingly in political circles. The belief that rolling back the welfare state would help to produce both a better society and a healthier economy began to take a much firmer hold.

Even before the Thatcher government arrived on the scene, Labour ministers were extolling the virtues of curbing public expenditure and declaring that 'the party was over'. But the 1980s saw a much more systematic attack on the welfare state than they had envisaged. The Thatcher government envisaged a much leaner and cheaper welfare state acting as a safety net for those in desperate circumstances. The main theme of this policy was to target help on the needy and to encourage others to make provision for themselves. This project succeeded in some respects – there was an expansion of means-tested benefits, for example – but it failed in others. Child benefit was too important to the middle classes to be abolished and the benefit bill began to rise inexorably as long-term unemployment rose. There was an expansion in private provision and funding for education, housing, social care and education. However, with the exception of housing, where privatisation proved an extremely populist measure, the public was clearly committed to state services in these areas and demanded more, rather than less, spending on these services.

The Major government inherited its predecessors' commitment to be tough on welfare spending. But it achieved little, apart from taking forward the Thatcherite agenda in some areas (education, housing) while soft pedalling on others (health, social welfare). On social security the rhetoric of reform was strong but achievements rather limited. Though efforts were made to combat fraud, reduce entitlement to invalidity benefits and to link unemployment benefits more closely to job hunting, overall spending on social security and the numbers claiming mean-tested benefits continued to grow.

The arrival of the Blair government in 1997 heralded another phase of reform. The incoming government declared its commitment to welfare reform and soon after taking office initiated a comprehensive review. At the time of writing it is still consulting on most aspects of its welfare policies. Although political circumstances have changed, the welfare reform debate is much the same. At a very simple level the case for welfare reform rests on three arguments (see Summary box): these are (1) that welfare spending is not sustainable; (2) that the present welfare state is inefficient and ineffective; and (3) that it undermines personal responsibility and honesty and is unfair. The remainder of this chapter examines these arguments, and the corresponding counter-arguments.

Spending on welfare is unsustainable?

One of the most prominent arguments in recent years has been that the welfare state is simply too expensive. The argument rests on evidence that after World War II public spending on social security, health, housing and education was much lower than is the case today. This much is true; in 1951 14 per cent of gross domestic product (GDP) was spent by the state on welfare. By 1970 this had risen to 20 per cent and by 1995 to 27 per cent of GDP. Certain categories of spending have risen faster than others. In 1951 health spending was about 3.5 per cent of GDP; by 1970 it had risen to almost 5 per cent and by 1995 to almost 6 per cent. Meanwhile, the social security budget grew from 5 per cent of GDP in 1951 to almost 8 per cent in 1970 and 14 per cent in 1995.

Within these budgets it is possible to identify particular areas which have seen the largest increases. For example, in recent years benefits for sick and disabled people have rocketed (from 15 per cent to 25 per cent of total welfare spending). There are also more single-parent families claiming benefit today: the number of lone parents on income support rose fourfold between 1970 and 1996. In 1996 lone parents accounted for over 10 per cent of the welfare budget compared with less than 4 per cent fifteen years previously. These specific increases are identified as the seeds of doom which unless tackled will bring down the entire benefit system in the future. In addition, this argument is bolstered by predictions that the social changes underlying these increases in spending are set to continue. Divorce rates, changes in work patterns – notably the end of 'a job for life' and the growth of self employment – and rising numbers of elderly people are long-term trends. Hence it is argued that even if we can afford current levels of spending, this will not be so in the future.

These arguments became very strong in the 1980s and 1990s, becoming a largely unchallenged 'article of faith' among leading politicians in both Labour and the Conservative Party (the Liberals, in contrast, called for a rise in tax rates to fund a specific increase in the education budget and a top-up pension for the elderly). The unsustainability argument was articulated by tabloid papers and quality broadsheets alike. Yet the argument clearly originates from the Right: only in the 1980s and 1990s did it enter the mainstream of political debate. Prior to this neo-liberal thinkers such as Friedman, who advocated a programme of cutting public expenditure in an effort to improve the economy (Friedman, 1962), were regarded as mavericks. But the policies outlined: reduce tax rates, and encourage private expenditure and private enterprise at the expense of the public sector, became the orthodoxy. The growing welfare budget has been seen as a major target for cuts although, for reasons discussed in a moment, efforts to reduce this have often been counter-productive.

The elite political consensus surrounding the unsustainability argument often distracts attention away from the many flaws within it. These are as follows:

- There is no evidence that increases in tax rates to pay for welfare are either economically or politically unsustainable. Some, such as Baumol, argue that productivity improvements in the wider economy will allow modern capitalist societies comfortably to afford the cost of welfare services such as health care. It should also be noted that the UK currently spends less on average than many other comparable countries, including some of the more successful economies such as Germany. Among EU countries during the mid-1990s only the Irish Republic and Greece spent less on welfare as a percentage of GDP. Furthermore, successive opinion polls undertaken for the British Social Attitudes survey indicate that the public is extremely wary of private welfare and a significant majority support more rather than less spending on welfare services, even if tax rates have to increase as a result.

- Gloomy predictions about demographic trends and the associated costs are more pessimistic than the evidence suggests. There will be more elderly people in the future. However, as Hills (1997) has noted, this does not imply an explosion in public expenditure on the scale predicted by some. His analysis suggests that there is no demographic time bomb that will cause an unsustainable growth in welfare costs, and that the net effect of ageing and higher pension entitlements will increase public expenditure by no more than 5 per cent of GDP between 1990 and 2040, no more than the increase in the recession of 1989–92. Even so, other trends – such as the rise in single-parent families and a decline of 'jobs for life' – could, if sustained, add to costs of the social security budget in the future, though the extent of any increased demand is difficult to predict.

- The unsustainability argument fails to address the underlying causes of the growing welfare budget. What, for example, leads to increased single-parent families, increasing claims for invalidity and disability, and increasing demands for income maintenance, health and social care, and so on? By analysing the root causes of these trends it may be possible to reduce some of the demands on the welfare state, and we shall consider this further in the context of the dependency thesis later in the chapter. A further point is that where it is difficult or impossible to limit demands on the welfare state through such intervention, how will these needs be served if services and entitlements are reduced? The usual answer is that the private sector will fill the gap. This brings us neatly on to the second main argument for reform.

Inefficiency, waste and choice

It has been argued that the welfare state is wasteful, inefficient and unrespons-
ive to the needs of its clients. A number of reasons have been advanced as to
why this is so:

- Critics maintain that the institutions which deliver welfare services have
  no incentive to be efficient. In their view large public sector bureaucracies
  are, by their very nature, poorly managed, not only because of their size,
  but because they are insulated from competition. This perspective is closely
  linked to the New Right critique of state bureaucracy associated with writers
  such as Niskanen (1971), and was a key theme of the Conservatives' reform
  of welfare in the 1980s and 1990s. Policies were introduced throughout
  the welfare state to alter management structures and create competition,
  both between the state and private sector and within the public sector
  itself. This resulted, for example, in the 'hiving off' of social security administration to 'Next Steps' agencies and the introduction of the internal
  market in the NHS.
- It is argued that the welfare state has not been effective at recognising the
  preferences of the people who use its services and has been organised
  mainly around the interests of the professionals that work within it. Indeed,
  the welfare state has often in the past been criticised for being inflexible
  and rather paternalistic in its approach to individuals. Such thinking was
  behind some of the welfare reforms of the 1980s and 1990s, such as the
  'opting out' of schools and housing estates from local authority control,
  which gave parents and tenants a vote in decisions about the status of
  these services. Also, the introduction of the Citizen's Charter by the Major
  government represented an albeit limited attempt to emphasise consumer
  choice and service standards within welfare state institutions.
- A further argument is that the welfare state wastes resources by providing help to those who do not really need it. This is not so much a criticism
  of the institutions that provide welfare services, but of policies that seek
  to benefit too many people. Universal benefits – available to all within an
  eligible group without a means test – are seen as particularly wasteful
  because they give help to people who are wealthy. Hence a millionaire who
  is over sixty-five can claim a basic state pension and a millionairess with
  children can claim child benefit. This argument has been used to justify the
  targeting of benefits and more rigorous means testing. During the 1980s
  and 1990s it was reflected in policies to restrict the rise in value of universal benefits (such as child benefit and the basic pension) and to place a
  greater emphasis on means-tested benefits. The same philosophy could have
  been extended to welfare services such as education and health, as well as
  social security. During the early 1980s there was quite a lot of discussion
  about means testing certain NHS services, so that those earning over a

certain amount would have to pay for a visit to their GP, for example. But the public reaction was hostile and plans were dropped. In social care a form of means testing already exists: elderly people with assets over a particular level (currently £10,000) must contribute towards the cost of residential care. Interestingly, the Blair government has considered plans to target resources more closely to need, indicating that child benefit for higher rate taxpayers might be taxed in future. It also introduced legislation imposing student fees for those whose parents earn over a certain amount of income and it is possible that such 'affluence testing' might be extended to other areas of the welfare state in future.

- A fourth argument is that the welfare state is not simply inefficient in its operation and overgenerous in its scope, but that it creates disincentives that are damaging to the wider economy. This is said to work in two ways. First, the provision of benefits leads to the creation of poverty traps. This means that people who are out of work are no better off (and in some cases worse off) financially if they take a low-paid job because of the rate at which their benefits are withdrawn and because of work-related costs such as childcare. Second, the provision of benefits is believed to undermine the incentive for people to make some provision for themselves. For example, 'savings traps' exist where means tests discourage people from building up savings because they will become ineligible for benefits. Although both savings and poverty traps are criticised primarily as causes of inefficiency, some argue that they also have an important moral dimension that will be discussed in a later section.

- Other commentators have been highly critical of the inefficiency thesis. There have been particular doubts about the effectiveness of managerial reforms and the introduction of competition as a means of improving the efficiency of welfare services. As the NHS case clearly illustrates, efficiency is difficult to measure and the impact of the reforms cannot easily be judged (see Baggott, 1997). Moreover, the reforms have added to costs. Again, the NHS provides a classic example. The creation of the new management systems and the internal market cost between £1.2 and £2 billion in start-up costs and £500 million a year in running costs. Competition also has hidden costs, as revealed by experience in both the health care and education sectors: a particularly salient problem was that the rivalry stimulated by competition served to undermine co-operation and made it difficult to plan services. Furthermore, the opening up of competition to the private sector has been problematic, as with the scandal over the mis-selling of private pensions which came to light in the 1990s. The private sector has a mixed record in health care, with private health insurance coming in for a great deal of criticism, prompting an Office of Fair Trading inquiry in 1997. Finally, most observers believe that the scope for private insurance in areas such as unemployment is very limited, with many insurers reluctant to offer cover at realistic prices to those deemed at risk. Indeed, the problem with private insurance against ill health, unemployment and other social risks is that those who are at greater risk – the poor, the sick, the elderly – cannot afford the high premiums charged by commercial insurers.

- What about the argument that competition enhances choice? Certainly reforms such as allowing schools to opt out of local authority control and allowing GPs to hold their own budgets appeared to introduce greater choice for service users. But in practice choice was limited. When local schools are full, choice means pupils having to travel miles to the nearest alternative. This explains partly why complaints about school places rose by 50 per cent between 1994 and 1996. Choice has also meant that some popular schools are over-flowing with pupils while less favoured ones are operating well below capacity, with obvious implications for the efficiency of both. GP fundholding was similarly a mixed blessing. Choice was enhanced because it allowed GPs to select providers that were able to offer a quicker or an enhanced service to their patients and enabled GPs to put pressure on hospitals, making them more responsive to their demands. However, because not all GPs were fundholders it created inequities between patients, the implication being that the speed of referral and the service provided was not directly related to clinical need.

- The shift from universality towards targeting and means testing of benefits has been criticised as counter-productive. One of the advantages of universal benefits is that they have high take-up rates and in this sense are more efficient than means-tested benefits where stigma or intrusive assessment processes can put off potential claimants. Universal benefits are also cheaper to administer than means-tested benefits because they avoid the cost of assessment procedures. Furthermore, they avoid creating the kind of poverty traps associated with means-tested benefits. Child benefit, for example, is not withdrawn as people take on jobs, and pensioners may supplement the basic pensions with other forms of income without incurring a penalty. The use of means testing (or affluence testing, which is the same thing in principle) is also problematic when applied to services. It is argued that if services become free to the poor only, then the better off will be reluctant to pay for these services through taxation. Another possibility is that a two-tier service could emerge, with richer people receiving a better standard of service for their 'premium'. On the other hand, if services are available to all on the same basis, this strengthens the legitimacy of the service and should reduce variations in service standards. However, although many believe this to be the case – reflected in the phrase 'a service for the poor is a poor service' – the evidence is mixed. For example, one study found that although a majority of those with private health insurance supported increased spending on the NHS, the level of support was lower than among the uninsured (see Besley *et al.*, 1996).

- The view that the welfare state is a drain on the wider economy has been challenged. The education and health services make important contributions to national prosperity given that a healthy and well-educated population is a prerequisite for a successful modern economy. In addition, it has been observed that the social security system also plays an important role as a safety net for those taking economic risks: for example, individuals who are embarking on a career change or those considering setting up a business. The absence of such a safety net might discourage such individuals, leading to economic conservatism, lower labour mobility and less entrepreneurialism – all of which are extremely damaging to the economy.

Irresponsibility, unfairness and dishonesty

The third set of arguments in favour of welfare reform are rooted on assumptions about individual responsibility. They apply to some extent to all welfare services but are employed mainly in the critique of social security. These arguments reflect a belief that the welfare state has had an adverse impact on aspects of human behaviour through the creation of certain incentives. It is a view which originated from the political Right, but which has increasingly attracted the attention of politicians of the Centre and Centre-Left.

- The controversial views of Charles Murray and other American commentators have attracted much attention in recent years. Murray argues that in both the USA and Britain the benefits system has created an underclass dependent on welfare benefits (see Institute for Economic Affairs/*Sunday Times*, 1996). This has encouraged the decline of the two-parent family by making single parenthood – subsidised by the state – economically viable and by allowing young males to voluntarily opt out of the labour force and abdicate their parental responsibilities. These social trends are in turn blamed for a range of other social ills – poor parenting, low educational achievement, crime and antisocial behaviour, unemployability, and so on. Because there is no incentive to take a job, individuals are trapped in a cycle of dependency which is not only bad for the economy, but bad for society and for the individuals concerned.

  Although Murray does not advocate the trimming of welfare entitlements (he believes that slashing them would work but would be politically impossible), others have used his thesis to justify cuts in benefit support. Another set of policies justified with reference to Murray's analysis (but again not advocated by him) is the enforcement of family responsibilities and the linking of benefits to participation in training or work schemes. Murray's own solution is far more radical: to remove responsibilities for welfare to local communities, letting them decide what sort of family arrangements should be supported by the benefit system. Others have challenged the underclass thesis on the grounds that it unfairly blames the victims of poverty and argue that there is little evidence to support the arguments that single-parent families and children born out of wedlock are the main cause of social problems (Institute for Economic Affairs/*Sunday Times*, 1996).

The underclass thesis was enthusiastically endorsed by politicians on the Right of the Conservative Party who identified single mothers as a particular source of social problems and called for them to be encouraged to find work and to have certain privileges (such as higher rates of benefit and priority for social housing) removed. Meanwhile, schemes were introduced to force unemployed people to take jobs and accept places on training schemes. The Child Support Agency was established to force fathers to pay towards the maintenance of their children. None of these schemes were particularly successful, and indeed the CSA can be regarded as a policy disaster, its credibility seriously damaged by a combination of a non-compliance protest campaign and mismanagement.

- Interestingly, the Blair government has pursued policies in some respects similar to those of its predecessor. In Opposition the Labour leadership made it clear that it would seek to reform the welfare state. The ground had already been prepared for this by the establishment of a Commission for Social Justice in 1992 by the then Labour leader John Smith, which went on to recommend radical changes in the welfare state. Following Labour's victory at the 1997 general election, this momentum was maintained by the appointment of Frank Field as Minister for Welfare Reform. Field had for many years argued for a revamped welfare state that would be more sensitive to modern needs and would encourage honesty, work and thrift while discouraging fraud and idleness. Although Field eventually resigned his post, arguing that his radical reform programme had been thwarted by others within government, some of his ideas did have an impact on policy.

  Subsequently the Blair government introduced schemes to encourage single mothers into work and to subject disability claims to more stringent assessment procedures. It was announced that benefits for young people would be withdrawn if they did not participate in the government's New Deal programme, a job creation and training scheme for the unemployed. New contributory schemes for pensions and for long-term care were also considered. However, 'carrots' as well as 'sticks' were introduced: a national childcare scheme for working parents and a Working Families Tax Credit were introduced as an incentive for people to take on low-paid work. New measures were introduced to combat fraud, which has been identified as a particular problem in housing benefit and income support. Official estimates put the amount of fraud at around £4 billion a year.

- While accepting that dishonesty, idleness and fraud are important problems facing the welfare state, critics maintain that the policies introduced are tantamount to victim blaming. They argue that the demonisation of particular groups – single mothers, disabled people, young people – is not only wrong but counter-productive, resulting in the further alienation of these groups from the rest of society. Critics point out the chequered history of job creation schemes and argue that the key problem is the availability of work that can generate sufficient income to keep a family. They also note that relative poverty has increased due to widening social inequalities. In 1979 the richest fifth of the population received 36 per cent of income and the poorest fifth just over 9 per cent. By 1995 the richest group had increased its share to 40 per cent; the poorest had fallen to 7.9 per cent. According to this perspective, raising rates of pay for the low paid and reducing inequalities between the rich and poor are more fruitful approaches to the problems of poverty and social exclusion.

• The Blair government stated its commitment to a minimum wage, but this was set at a relatively low level and has not satisfied campaigners. There is no commitment to reversing the widening inequalities of previous decades. Although there is some evidence of redistribution in favour of the poorest families, the Blair government has pledged itself to maintaining basic and top income tax rates, which are key tools of income redistribution. However, the government recognised that poverty and other social problems are not entirely due to individual fecklessness and the welfare system. It established a social exclusion unit to examine the multiple factors that cause certain groups such as the poor to be marginalised. It also introduced action zones to co-ordinate responses and target resources across a range of social problems relating to housing, education and health in areas where social needs are particularly great.

Conclusion

This chapter has shown that the debate over welfare reform is complex. In each of the areas of debate there are arguments for and against the development of a more 'targeted' and limited welfare state. We have seen that some of the counter-arguments – such as the potential role that social security could play in encouraging economic activity – are underplayed while other arguments supporting reform – such as the unsustainability thesis and the underclass thesis – have been challenged by the available evidence. We have also detected some tensions in the inefficiency thesis: for example, a greater emphasis on means testing has adverse implications for economic and administrative efficiency. However, as the Blair government implements its programme of welfare reform, it is not so much the quality of these arguments, or the evidence, that will ultimately determine the outcome. As I have stated elsewhere (Baggott, 1998), a great deal will depend on the political clout of those who articulate these arguments within government, among organised interests and in the media.

Arguments for and against welfare reform

1   *Spending on welfare is unsustainable*

For reform
- Demographic and socio-economic trends imply demands that cannot be met from public funds.

Counter-argument
- Welfare spending has been relatively stable over the last twenty years and present demographic trends do not suggest unsustainable increases in demand.
- Need to examine what is behind these trends and intervene only where necessary.
- The gap between demand and resources will need to be filled somehow.

2   *Welfare is inefficient and ineffective*

For reform
- Some people who do not need benefits get them and receive free or subsidised services for which they can afford to pay, while some of those who need help do not get it. Benefits should therefore be more widely means tested.
- Benefits reduce work incentives and encourage idleness.
- Welfare state institutions are large inefficient bureaucracies.
- State welfare constrains choice whereas competition enhances it.

Counter-argument
- It is important that some services are 'inclusive' and not just for the poor.
- Universal benefits reach those who are eligible.
- Means-tested benefits discourage those who need help.
- Universal benefits cost less to administer than means-tested benefits.
- Means-tested benefits reduce incentives to work and save.
- Competition can in some situations damage services, add to costs, undermine efficiency, reduce choice and make the consumer worse off.
- Welfare services and benefits can strengthen the economy by encouraging labour mobility.

3   *The welfare state undermines personal responsibility and honesty and is unfair*

For reform
- It encourages people to be dishonest and fraudulent.
- Welfare encourages a dependency culture and leads ultimately to the development of an underclass, with grave social consequences.
- Welfare discourages people from making their own provision and is unfair on those who do make such arrangements.

Counter-argument
- There is no real evidence that welfare services and benefits create an underclass or undermine honesty or self reliance.
- The dependency thesis ignores the factors which lead people to become dependent in the first place.
- People do not choose to be benefit claimants and the dependency thesis is a form of victim blaming.

Reading

Baggott, R. (1997) 'Evaluating health care reform: the case of the NHS internal market', *Public Administration*, 75:2, 283–306.

Baggott, R. (1998) 'Reforming welfare', in B. Jones (ed.), *Political Issues in Britain Today*, Manchester University Press.

Baumol, W. (1995) *Health Care as a Handicraft Industry*, Office of Health Economics.

Besley, T., Hall, J. and Preston, I. (1996) *Private Health Insurance and the State of the NHS*, Institute for Fiscal Studies.

Commission for Social Justice (1994) *Social Justice: A Strategy for National Renewal*, Vintage.

Field, F. (1995) *Making Welfare Work: Reconstructing Welfare for the Millennium*, Institute of Community Studies.

Friedman, M. (1962) *Capitalism and Freedom*, University of Chicago Press.

Hills, J. (1997) *The Future of Welfare*, Joseph Rowntree Foundation, revised edition.

Institute of Economic Affairs/Sunday Times (1996) *Charles Murray and the Underclass. The Developing Debate*, Institute of Economic Affairs.

Niskanen, W. A. (1971) *Bureaucracy and Representative Government*, Aldine-Atherton.

Secretary of State for Social Security and Minister for Welfare Reform (1998) *New Ambitions For Our Country: A New Contract for Welfare*, Cm 3805, The Stationery Office.

20

The environment: our world in danger or Green scaremongering?

Geoff Lee

In the West, in the absence of war, civil unrest, starvation or major natural disasters, it is perhaps unsurprising that our attention is captured by reports of suffering wildlife or a despoiled world. This is also a subject for politicians to grasp for approval and the appearance of statesmanship. Very few right-wing, free marketeers will stand up for disease, destruction and exploitation. The evidence does show that concern for environmental issues is being absorbed into public consciousness and mainstream politics.

Despite the emergence of environmentalism, the debate has never determined political direction. Developing countries resent attempts by the rich, polluting West to stop them 'catching up' and elections in the West still revolve around socio-economic issues.

Nor are the issues clear-cut – many of the scientific findings are extrapolations or hypotheses; some are found to be false, many are disputed and there are huge uncertainties about the long-term trends. Some would add that such Malthusian doom is predictable at the end of a millennium.

The case put forward by an ever-growing number of individuals and political groupings is set out below.

'We have irretrievably poisoned our environment'

The issues are presented below in an order dictated by the amount of press coverage given to them over the last twenty years. As we shall see, this may not be the priority accorded by the public at any point in time, as individuals weigh up immediate interests against the legacy for future generations.

Global warming

In 1984 a British scientist, Joseph Farman, found a hole in the ozone layer above Antarctica which represented 40 per cent depletion and by November

1998 it was 27 million square kilometres. It was confirmed that the ozone had been declining for ten years, caused mainly by chlorofluorocarbons (CFCs) in aerosols and refrigerators, allowing ultraviolet rays to get through to Earth and cause skin cancer and cataract blindness. Lethal skin cancers in the UK increased by 82 per cent between 1979 and 1992. Carbon dioxide was responsible for half of the problem.

In 1991 a hole was identified over Northern Europe (Britain had lost one-fifth of its ozone layer) and by March 1997 the ozone layer over the Arctic had thinned to an all-time low – 24 per cent down on 1979–82 levels.

The British Meteorological Office reported in 1997 that the forests could no longer absorb the excess carbon dioxide. By 2080 some 200 million people would be endangered by flooding and the risk of starvation would have increased for 50 million, as the temperature rose between 2.5°C and 3°C over the next century – greater than any period over the last 10,000 years. The UN Inter-governmental Panel on Climate Change (600 scientists from 50 countries) agreed without dissent. The signs were there, with 1997 being the hottest year since 1860, partly due to the El Niño warming of air and sea in the eastern Pacific, which brought flooding and destruction. The industrialised nations were declared responsible, making up 23 per cent of the world's population but producing 70 per cent of emissions. The United States was responsible for one-fifth of emissions, and one-fifth of those came from its motor cars.

Britain committed itself to reducing emissions from 1990 levels by 12.5 per cent over twelve years at the 1997 Kyoto summit, and the Labour government, promising to 'put the environment at the heart of government policy', offered a target of 20 per cent cuts by 2010. Yet by November 1998 the commitment to taxation to get there was only under consideration, with Treasury and CBI resistance deemed to be winning.

Acid rain

Acid rain is a by-product of carbon dioxide, sulphur dioxide, nitrogen dioxide and ozone emissions, and it would cost Britain £17 billion over the next thirty years to repair the damage to buildings done by acid rain. Britain was condemned as the 'dirty man of Europe' for breaking its reduction commitments. In July 1993 a joint UN and EU survey reported that more than 58 per cent of Britain's trees were moderately or severely blighted – making us the worst of thirty-four European and former Soviet countries.

Deforestation

The World Wide Fund for Nature stated in 1997 that two-thirds of the world's original tree cover was gone, and only 2 per cent was protected (the UK had lost 97 per cent). Over the previous fifty years, 45 per cent of Britain's richest woods had been destroyed. The UN extrapolated in October 1992 that half the world's rainforests would be gone in fifty years.

1997 was declared the Year the Earth Caught Fire by the World Wide Fund for Nature. Six hundred fires a day were reported in Brazil on a 10,000 mile front – all caused by the continuing the work of loggers, cattlemen and peasants. Most coverage was given to Indonesia, where the fires ran out of control, burning deep underground peat and, creating smog that covered six other states. Among the consequences were a ferry capsizing, ships colliding and an aircraft crash. At its height the smog covered 1 million square kilometres of land and sea and affected 70 million people, and 16 national parks, killing both tribesmen and animals.

Air pollution

Our 20 million cars have reduced air quality in Britain by 35 per cent in five years according to the Department of the Environment. Summer smogs are formed when nitrogen oxides and hydrocarbons mix in sunlight to form ozone, mainly in rural areas. In cities, car exhausts produce nitrogen dioxide. In the 1990s all major cities exceeded EU guidelines, with Edinburgh the worst.

The Royal Commission on Environmental Pollution estimated the wider environmental costs of air pollution, including accidents and property damage, at £10–18.5 billion a year. The Committee on Medical Effects of Air Pollutants, a government advisory body, reported in January 1998 that just the immediate effect of pollution (mainly traffic fumes) was to hasten the death of between 12,000 and 24,000 vulnerable people a year and to cause 24,000 hospital admissions.

Industry still contributes its share of air pollution, whether the burning of 'dirty' fossil fuels or the incineration of plastics, solvents and paper to produce lethal dioxins – affecting immune systems, and foetuses and inducing cancer.

Polluted seas

Sewage Britain came under pressure from its European partners in 1990 because it continued to dump 6 million tonnes of sewage in the North Sea when they had stopped. In the following year sixty-three beaches lost their blue flag awards for safety because sewage debris was visible. Despite a £3 billion programme to stop the dumping of raw sewage at sea and ensure proper treatment, in November 1997 fifty-one beaches were still below EU standards.

Chemical pollution Pledges to reduce chemical pollution in 1974 and 1990 were not honoured and wildlife continued to die. By 1995 Britain was failing to meet its targets for reducing five out of twenty-three substances. British fishermen called areas of the North Sea fisheries 'The Hospital', as this was where diseased and mutant fish were caught. Chemical companies came under great pressure to stop dumping – after discharges at four ICI plants during 1996–97, the Environment Agency closed its trioxide plant at Hartlepool in June 1997 after a gas cloud emission. Britain at this time licensed the dumping of 5,046 tonnes of toxic waste through 12,000 pipes into rivers that were the main carriers of heavy metal pollutants into the sea.

Oil pollution   In 1989 the worst oil pollution incident to date took place when the *Exxon Valdez* spilled 11 million gallons off the coast of Alaska, costing £1.8 billion to clean up. This was surpassed in the Gulf War, when 70 million barrels of oil soaked into the desert. In 1991 it was reported by the UK Advisory Committee on Pollution of the Sea that there were 791 oil spills per year, with a steady five-year rise, the annual figure having doubled since 1986. The trend continued with the *Braer* oil tanker disaster in January 1993 and the 1996 *Sea Empress* spillage of 72,000 tonnes off Milford Haven, killing thousands of sea birds. In 1996 the government refused to release reports on oil-rig spills, and said it had no records on individual breaches.

Disappearing fish stocks   In 1990 poison algae spread along 200 miles of England's east coast, with mussels found containing 50 times the toxin limit. Pollution, overfishing (even using satellite tracking), and £30 billion subsidies a year to the industry and the 200 million people worldwide that rely on fishing meant that all the main grounds were found to be at risk by the UN in 1995.

Polluted rivers and drinking water

By July 1998 a quarter of Britons did not drink tap water, buying 800 million litres of bottled water a year – four times more than a decade previously.

Privatisation   The *Sunday Times* in 1989, in its 'Britain's Water Rats' coverage, showed that water quality was declining for the first time since 1958. In the run-up to the sell-off of the water industry, the government legalised discharges of sewage into rivers and streams.

Sewage, pesticide and bacterial pollution   In 1992 the Royal Commission on Environment Protection reported that high proportions of rivers and lakes failed to meet EU standards, with the main bacterial pollution coming from seepage of farm slurry, silage and sewage discharges by water companies. Four hundred towns were drinking dirty water, breaching EU rules on the level of nitrate (a potential cause of stomach cancer), and there were also dangerous levels of metals, parasites and a blue-green algae which carried twenty different toxins.

Industrial pollution   There were found to be high levels of lead in old water pipes, which could cause brain damage, affecting 10 million people (1 in 10 infants) – Glasgow was the worst-affected city in Europe. In total 1,350 toxic tips existed, of which one-third had contaminated groundwater. Londoners were told they had the worst water quality, with 80 per cent of it failing to reach the required standard.

Accidents   In addition to slow deterioration, serious accidents occurred. The most publicised was the aluminium sulphate pollution in Camelford, Cornwall in 1988, which killed 50,000 fish and caused illness and fears of brain damage.

Toxic tips   The *Observer*/FOE publication of the location of 4,800 toxic tips after three months of investigation caused a major furore in February 1990, and in August 1998 a three-year, five-nation study linked the existence of 450 tips in Britain to deformities in babies. In 1992 scientists reported that pollution from mines had been seeping into soil for centuries – arsenic and lead levels in residential gardens were very high. More than 1,000 rubbish tips could potentially explode under housing estates (one did so in 1986) – the total needed for clear-up was said to be £200 million.

Nuclear power and radioactive waste

Health risks   A report produced for British Nuclear Fuels in 1992 showed that Sellafield had sometimes vented 200 times the permitted level of plutonium into the atmosphere. In 1990 the acceptable levels of radiation to which workers could be exposed were halved because the danger had been underestimated. In December 1998 it was revealed, from an unpublished report, that £2 billion was to be spent at twenty-two sites in Britain to safeguard the workers and public from contamination.

Nuclear waste   Britain has dumped 75,000 tonnes of nuclear waste in the Atlantic, more than three-quarters of all such material dumped by Western powers. This was banned at the London Dumping Convention in November 1993. Waste had also been held underwater for twice as long as it should have been. Burying was rejected in March 1997, leaving the fate of high-level waste in Cumbria and the 69,507 cubic yards of intermediate-level waste scattered around the country in limbo. Dounreay was exposed as the most dangerous site in 1998 and closed – for 30 years over 1,700 tonnes of waste had been dumped underground, some catching fire – to remove it will cost up to £10 billion.

Nuclear dustbin   Imports of irradiated fuel have risen eighteen-fold since 1989, but in 1996 the THORP reprocessing plant had processed only one tonne of plutonium from spent fuel in two years. In April 1998 the government agreed to take dangerous waste from a politically unstable Georgia – to Dounreay!

Nuclear accidents These have occurred in the UK and to most other producers. As the USSR disintegrated, its poor records and inability to deal with 610 million cubic metres of waste were thought to require $20 billion of funding to rectify. France has admitted it has been living with a one in twenty chance of a nuclear accident. There were no contingency plans in place for such a threat in the English Channel nor for an accident at Sizewell in Suffolk, which would entail 1 million people having to leave the area for 5 years and the likelihood of 100,000 cancer victims. The British public was not told that plutonium was being transported by air or that it was left in train sidings in London suburbs.

The disappearing countryside

During 1983 and again in 1985 there were moves to cut into London's 1–2 million acres of greenbelt land. The Conservative government claimed a policy of deciding planning applications 'on merit' but by the late 1980s there was confusion within its ranks.

The 1990s saw a new kind of opposition – middle-class protesters and direct action by 'eco-warriors', building tree houses and elaborate tunnel systems to stop the clearing of sites for development. The cost of clearing the A30 road-widening scheme in 1997 was £200 a minute – changing the cost–benefit analysis involved. The new Labour government overturned a public inquiry and backed Birmingham's application to develop farmland in 1997. A Countryside March of 300,000 people took place through London in March 1998.

Unsafe food

Mad cow disease/BSE In 1990 there were fears that eating infected beef could pass on brain disorders, particularly Creutzfeld Jacob disease (CJD) to humans. Through 1994–95 the government refused to concede a connection and criticised the European ban. By 1996 it was clear that the evidence had been withheld for ten years, up to 1.5 million 'mad cows' could have been eaten and three out of four people believed that there had been a cover-up (ICM poll, *Guardian* 3 April 1996). Scientists declared the link proven in September 1997 – that there had been transmission of BSE to humans in different strains of CJD. There was evidence of rules being broken, of illegal exports, of the European Commission hushing up the scandal for five years, and the 1998 investigation revealed ministerial buck passing, scientists blundering around in the dark and decisions taken to protect the industry rather than the consumer, twenty-seven of whom died. Some £3.5 billion was spent on the BSE problem between 1996 and 2000.

Salmonella　More than 1 million chickens were killed in a scare that eggs were infected with salmonella. That infection rate was 39 per cent in 1989 and, far from going away with a change in feedstuffs, the salmonella in eggs was back to that rate by mid-1992.

Genetically modified (GM) food　There was anger about the lack of consultation or debate, with international or European law supervening, and about the growing power of Monsanto, which was leading the campaign for GM food. In several polls, up to six out of ten were against GM food, 85 per cent of people wanted it to be separated at source and 95 per cent wanted it clearly labelled in shops (ICM *Guardian* poll, 4 June 1998). A December 1998 report warning of the dangers to hedgerows, birds and crops was kept secret. In May 1999 the British Medical Association advocated a moratorium on commercial GM crops.

Other　There were warnings about the presence of algae in crabs and nerve poison in supermarket salmon, and that poisoning from listeria bacteria (which kill one in three victims) had been rising rapidly in the 1980s. High levels of the pesticide lindane were found in supermarket milk in 1996 and baby food in 1998. Food poisoning reached a record high in 1992, when 62,607 cases were reported. By 1998 this had reached 100,000, but an official report suggested that the real number was 2 million per year. Toxic pesticides were found in 40 per cent of fruit and vegetables sold in British supermarkets (EU study, November 1998), and high levels of tin in canned tomatoes.

Dumping/recycling

Unlike in the USA, the UK Treasury has not given tax credits for such alternatives as solar, geothermal or anti-pollution measures. Similarly, the deregulators at the Department of Trade and Industry opposed intervention to help environmental initiatives, despite lobbying from businesses who were losing out to Germany, Japan and the USA. Britain is in thirteenth place behind our European neighbours in recycling 20 per cent of our glass. According to Friends of the Earth, by 1997 fewer than a third of companies had moved on waste minimisation and two in five had done nothing to cut waste or improve recycling.

Noise pollution

The EU began to set noise limits in cities and in late 1992 environmental health officers reported a 40 per cent rise in noise complaints. Proposals in

December 1996 by the EU to map and reduce noise were immediately rejected by the UK government as likely to cost billions of pounds. Flights will increase from 1.6 to 4 million per by year 2015, with a further million homes disturbed.

'But these problems can be managed like all the rest'

It is argued that all the above problems can be managed by political realism and responsibility in the West, population and resource control in the developing world, scientific progress continuing to enrich our lives, and a sense of proportion about what we cannot control – climate, tides, volcanoes, asteroids.

Is global warming a political priority?

There have been doubts about the extent of the impact of global warming and the need for panicked political measures. Questions began to be asked in 1990:

- Models used to replicate the Earth's climate from first principles are inaccurate, often ignoring contra-indicators such as clouds.
- The Antarctic had increased in size during the global warming period (according to Edinburgh University, 1991). The key was which period one measured. NASA data indicated that over a ten year period there was neither warming nor cooling.
- The averaging of sea levels, measured in harbours, was defective, and there is an uneven distribution of weather stations, mainly in warmer towns.
- There is no proof that more greenhouse gas produces heat, and the radiation effects are complex. Carbon dioxide actually helps plant growth. Every year the oceans give off 90 billion tonnes of carbon dioxide and decaying plants the same, compared with 6 billion tonnes caused by human activity.
- It has been suggested that if the Greenland ice caps melted and shifted the salt deposits around the Faroes south, Europe could enter an ice age instead!
- There is a convenient alliance between the media that wants a big story, politicians who want a cause and scientists who want funds (the same people who told us we were entering the ice age in the 1970s).
- Don't the 'doomsters' seize on any research to attack economic progress, including that of nations trying to catch up with the West's high living standards?
- Is not the Earth a self-regulating system of great complexity, at times subject to violent changes? Do humans make that much of an impact? We don't even know if it was climate or a rogue asteroid that wiped out the dinosaurs. In April 1998 leading climatologist Svensmark claimed that solar cycles caused global warming.

- Flatulent cows and rotting vegetation were known to be problems, but in 1995 the termite was revealed as an enormous producer of methane – twenty times more ozone depleting than carbon dioxide!

The *Sunday Times* picked up these themes in editorials in 1990 on 'Green-mongers' and 'faddism'. It pursued the same line in 1997, condemning 'hobbits' and 'Jeremiahs', and advocating sensible conservation and disposal which had made the West 'the healthiest, wealthiest society on Earth' (*Sunday Times*, 30 November 1997).

In so far as there is a problem, is it not remediable? In December 1995 a meeting of 150 countries in Vienna agreed to ban all CFCs and related gases immediately, with help given to developing nations. Some countries had banned them as early as 1993 and the EU did so a year before the deadline. Ten years before they had been pumping out 750,000 tonnes a year.

World leaders could also be seen as responding – the United States and Britain brought back to 1995 the deadline for phasing out CFCs, and British 1990 levels of carbon dioxide emissions were brought back to a target date of 2010. The costs to consumers and industry were accepted, measurement was agreed with the EU and this was conditional on other countries' action – to put pressure on the Americans. The slow trading progress between 170 countries – oil producers, the developing and the polluting – rolled on to Buenos Aires in November 1998, with the UK still playing a leading, brokering role.

Acid rain

In 1994 the Forestry Commission said that the problems affecting trees had been as much due to drought, storms, pests and a tougher assessment regime as acid rain. The forests were flourishing again and any sustained deterioration from acid rain would have already been detected.

Deforestation

In 1996 the Brazilians (at last) acknowledged the danger of deforestation and placed a two-year moratorium on exporting mahogany and virola. In 1997 the United Nations Food and Agriculture Organisation reported that deforestation had slowed down in the five years to 1995, and in Europe the stock of natural and artificial woodland had been growing since the 1950s.

The argument over how many of Britain's trees were diseased ranged from nearly 60 per cent to less than 17 per cent, with experts and Friends of the Earth accusing each other of misrepresentation. What is in doubt is the ability of devastated areas to bounce back, as they have after natural disasters such as fires and volcanoes: at what point will we have tipped the balance too far against recovery?

Air pollution

Here the issue is one of political will – to closing roads, cutting speed limits, introducing electronic tolls and diverting traffic – given individual preferences.

There has been no corresponding commitment to public transport and rail services – known to have been deteriorating for decades. Subsidies to the railways and London Underground are already running at £1.5 billion and £500 million respectively – will we pay more? There is a 'double standard' revenue issue: £15 billion is raised on fuel and £3 billion on vehicle excise duty each year. Rises in petrol prices, now cloaked in the name of environmentalism, have to be grudgingly accepted, but do not yet deter.

Opinion polls show support for the *idea* of limits on city car usage but Britons use their cars for 80 per cent of journeys, even those of a few hundred yards, double the rate for short trips in the 1970s (RAC, 17 November 1995).

Polluted seas

What was remarkable, but not as thoroughly reported, was the speed of recovery of the polluted areas and, given time, the wildlife – the collapse of the herring catch in 1976, the banning of its fishing and its recovery by the 1980s shows that recovery is possible.

Sewage The reports condemning 51 beaches seldom went on to say that the rest of the 472 were now meeting targets (89.2 per cent) and had been improving year on year since 1992. South West Water was under most pressure, pursued by 23,000 members of Surfers Against Sewage. But it was issuing the highest bills in the country, had eliminated 140 out of 227 sewage discharges and greatly resented not being given credit for reaching EU standards on 94 per cent of the 134 designated bathing waters in 1995. If holiday makers are so concerned about beach quality, why did they leave 18.8 tonnes of rubbish on them in 1997, up from 17.5 tonnes the year before? In 1997 there were just 39 oil tar spillages – more than a fourfold drop from the 139 in 1976.

Polluted rivers and drinking water

Privatisation, plus pressure group activity, drew attention to the situation. The National Rivers Authority produced a report detailing the deterioration of 500 miles of rivers and doubled its prosecutions over a year. The companies, forced to invest millions of pounds, blamed the government for underinvestment. Government ministers had considered passing on the price of cleaning rivers to consumers as a 'green charge' of £3–10 billion over six years. It was more expedient, however, to let the water companies take the blame for prices well above inflation. At least the problem was now out in the open and being tackled.

One can also underestimate the resilience of nature – just as the overall whale population had recovered, by 1995 it was reported that cleaning up the Thames, Clyde, Mersey and Humber meant that all kinds of species had returned to what had been the filthiest rivers: dragonflies, salmon, seals, lamprey, otters and kingfishers.

Drought   Water consumption has risen by 70 per cent over the last 30 years, but some of the problems caused have not been man-made. Four dry winters in succession led to the devastation of wildlife. In 1995 a £27 million water tankering operation was needed in Yorkshire. The situation was compounded greatly because up to 25 per cent of water used is lost by leakage – a factor of previous underinvestment that the new water companies were now prioritising.

Water quality   In 1991 the *Sunday Times* assembled a panel of experts to prove bottled water a 'rip-off': Kent tap water came top of the poll. The government's Drinking Water Inspectorate maintained that tap water passed 99.7 per cent of quality checks in 1996 and that in 1998 most people were satisfied with it. Though sales of bottled water have risen, partly through fashion, the Germans, French and Italians still drink six, eight and ten times more than us, respectively.

Nuclear power and radioactive waste

The Health and Safety Executive suggested a viral cause of the cancers around Sellafield. Four years after the Gardner Report the Medical Research Council abandoned the research into radiation because there was no medical support and the hypothesis was rejected in the courts.

In terms of policy, the Gulf War's burning oilfields and worries over coal-burning emissions gave the nuclear industry a chance to come back and there has even been opposition to the despoiling of the landscape by wind turbines. Science does seem to be finding ways out – in 1993 American scientists produced clean and cheap energy from hydrogen fusion, and an Italian thorium nuclear reactor was designed – eliminating fears of meltdown and weapons production and offering a solution to all waste by burning it. In 1998 several energy companies intended to offer 'green electricity' – made from renewable sources or waste.

The disappearing countryside

The greenbelt was not, in fact, disappearing – in 1990 the Regional Studies Association calculated it had grown since 1979, and was said to have lost London 100,000 jobs over 35 years.

Tory policy had switched to development of derelict sites by 1988 and in the 1997 general election the Conservatives were committed to protecting the greenbelt, having doubled its size in office. Under similar pressure, in

February 1998 the Labour government also changed direction and proposed a 'green tax' on greenbelt development, scrapping its target of 4.4 million new homes by 2016 and looking to use city and derelict land. The central dilemma remains: more homes were still being demanded and more people wanted them in 'green' areas in the South.

Unsafe food and 'green' products

There is no doubt that we have made mistakes in farming practices. Like crime, however, it is also the *reporting* of food poisoning that has increased. We have literally changed our tastes – with the huge increase in takeaway food and concern for 'healthy eating'.

Supermarkets began to develop 'green' products, but Friends of the Earth was soon running a 'Green Con of the Year Award'. In April 1990 the National Consumer Council confirmed that consumers had lost belief in the claims, and by 1993 supermarkets were withdrawing 'green' detergents and other products. Four out of ten people thought that labelling was a device to raise prices and did not care if toiletries had been tested on animals.

By 1996 polls showed that recession had made people less likely to buy 'green', and Bosnia and other tragedies had put into perspective their belief in changing the world. In December 1998, Labour had to reassure the public that its promised Food Standards Agency had only been delayed in December 1998, rather than killed off by the food lobby.

Dumping/recycling

Our attitude seems to be changing; 1994 saw the enactment of the landfill tax, to take effect in 1997 – the first real 'green' tax, not designed to raise revenue. But forcing companies to buy recycling certificates would add 2p to every £10 retail bill – are we concerned enough to pay?

Noise pollution

In 1997 technological innovation moved forward again at Cranfield University with a device to muffle aircraft noise frequencies. Though vital to those directly affected, noise is bottom of the league of concerns (see table 20.1).

Public opinion: a summary of concerns

It is useful to consider how strongly people feel about environmental issues.

MORI annually checks eleven factors of potential public concern, including donations to environmental groups, use of lead-free petrol, purchasing 'green' products and belonging to a pressure group: saying yes to five of these

Table 20.1   *Degree of concern about environmental issues, 1993*

Environmental issue	Very worried	Very and quite worried	Not very worried and not worried at all
Chemicals in rivers and seas	63	92	6
Toxic waste	63	87	10
Radioactive waste	60	83	13
Sewage on beaches	56	89	10
Oil spills	52	87	12
Tropical forest loss	45	80	18
Loss of UK plants and animals	43	82	17
Ozone layer depletion	41	77	19
Traffic fumes/smog	40	81	18
Drinking water quality	38	70	29
Loss of plants and animals abroad	38	77	21
Insecticides/fertilisers	36	75	23
Loss of trees/ hedgerows	36	79	20
Factory fumes	35	75	23
Traffic congestion	35	75	23
Losing greenbelt	35	72	26
Global warming	35	70	24
Acid rain	31	72	23
Fouling by dogs	29	63	37
Litter and rubbish	29	76	24
Using up UK natural resources	27	66	31
Decay of inner cities	26	65	32
Household waste disposal	22	64	35
Need for energy conservation	21	65	31
Not enough recycling	19	57	41
Derelict land and buildings	19	55	43
Noise	16	44	54

Source: Department of the Environment, by NOP on a random sample of 3,200 adults.

Table 20.2   *Degree of concern over environmental issues, England and Wales*

	% very worried		
Environmental issue	1986	1989	1993
Increased concern			
Traffic fumes and smog	23	33	40
Losing greenbelt land	26	27	35
Decay of inner cities	27	22	26
Decreased concern			
Ozone layer depletion	–	56	41
Use of insecticides/fertilisers	39	46	36
Global warming	–	44	35
Acid rain	35	40	31
Litter and rubbish	30	33	29

Source: Department of the Environment, 1995.

classes someone as a 'green activist'. In 1991 31 per cent in Britain were so classified, twice as many as in 1989. An opinion poll in June 1992 by the *Guardian* and ITN indicated that 70 per cent would be willing to pay higher taxes for improving the environment, and the 1993 Department of the Environment survey showed that in response to the proposition 'The polluter pays even if goods and services cost more', agreement had risen from 27 per cent in 1986, to 31 per cent in 1989, to 62 per cent in 1993. But such pledges have been made before, notably about being willing to pay more council tax for local services, and they have not been translated into votes.

Changes in concern have been occurring, as shown in table 20.2.

Conclusion

One senses that increased press coverage and personal experience are at work in increasing concern. In November 1998 the government announced a new 'quality of life' barometer of thirteen measures, including air pollution, road traffic levels and wildlife populations. It would seem that a combination of perceived action and/or remoteness reduces concern. Amid the plethora of statistics and attention-seeking scare stories, it may be all that we can ask that people make up their own minds on the basis of the empirical evidence around them and on the advice of the leaders they trust.

Our world in danger or Green scaremongering?

The case for concern and action – expressed by scientists, Green parties and pressure groups, from the Countryside Commission and World Wide Fund for Nature to the more radical Friends of the Earth and Greenpeace:

- Statistics show us using up the world's supply of natural resources at an increasing and non-sustainable rate.
- Pollution of our air, water and land is now manifesting itself in proven links to disease.
- Artificial, man-made dangers – from nuclear fuels, pesticide drainage, toxic tips and genetically modified foods – are storing up hazards that are unknown and have no solutions.
- The general population is now increasingly knowledgeable about the problems and is expressing its concerns at the ballot box, by direct action and through consumer behaviour.

The case for reassurance and a measured traditional response is put forward by other scientists, government agencies and mainstream political parties:

- Statistics demonstrate wider, counterbalancing forces at work – humans have little long-term impact on them.
- The political systems have adjusted, in the UK and globally, to take account of the real, proven dangers and the correcting process is underway.
- Science is still finding solutions, just as it has advanced our quality of life before.
- There are no easy, quick fixes to the problems because there are powerful self-interests that are unwilling to accept constraints – so political bargaining and incremental change are the way forward.

Reading

North, R. D. (1995) *Life on a Modern Planet: A Manifesto for Progress*, Manchester University Press.

Porritt, J. and Winner, D. (1988) *Costing the Earth: Liberal Democrat Policies for an Environmentally Sustainable Economy* (publisher unknown).

Index